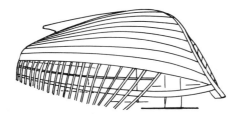

THE BOAT OWNER'S MAINTENANCE MANUAL

The BOAT OWNER'S MAINTENANCE MANUAL

by Jeff Toghill

JOHN DE GRAFF INC.

First published 1970 by A. H. & A. W. Reed
Wellington, New Zealand
First U. S. A. Edition 1971 by John de Graff, Inc.
ISBN   8286-0043-0
© 1970 Jeff Toghill
Reprinted, 1973
Reprinted, 1979

Printed In U.S.A.

Introduction

NOTHING IS maintenance free.

Bring a boat alongside a jetty a bit too hard and she bumps. Whether she is manufactured from fibreglass, aluminium, steel or timber, the result of the bump will be some form of damage. And whether the repair of that damage involves merely rubbing off a dirty mark from a fibreglass hull, knocking out a dent from aluminium or steel, or patching a gouge in timber, the result is still maintenance.

Just leaving a boat idle on her mooring involves maintenance, as marine growth is no respecter of materials and clings equally to timber, fibreglass or metal. Indeed, short of storing the boat in a hermetically-sealed room under hermetically-sealed wraps, there is literally no way of avoiding maintenance problems, and even storage would only preserve the hull and fittings; engines suffer from extended storage.

Obviously then, maintenance is a problem that every boat owner must learn to live with; there is no way of avoiding it. While the actual maintenance work can be avoided by employing marine services to maintain the boat, this merely converts the problem from a practical one to a financial one. Since costs are already a problem for most boat owners, adding labour to the bill is no solution and although there are certain aspects of maintenance which must be done by qualified technicians, there is a great deal that can be done by the boat owner himself.

This book is aimed at just such a boat owner, and is designed to show him how to maintain his boat with the minimum of expense and effort. It shows him how to avoid pitfalls that are not always obvious, but *are*

always expensive. It shows him how to achieve maximum effect with minimum fuss. It shows him how, by giving some thought and planning to his maintenance routine, he can achieve satisfactory results without having to devote hours of time or digging too deeply into his pocket. By revealing many of the technical aspects of the materials, design and building techniques used in his boat it adds another interest to his hobby, and makes the maintenance work absorbing and satisfying.

The book introduces the boat owner to the types of materials used in boat building and describes how they can best be adapted to his own particular problems. It describes the necessary tools for each job and tells how to use them to obtain first class results with minimum effort. It details such maintenance routines as cleaning, patching and painting the principal hull materials in use today. It indicates the problems which are too technical for the average handyman and which must be turned over to an expert if further problems are to be avoided. It describes the types of maintenance materials best suited to each type of boat, and to the pocket.

Sails and engines, since they provide the motive power of a boat, are dealt with in a separate section. Here, maintenance is a considerable problem as much of the work is far too technical for a handyman. However, by following detailed maintenance routines at the correct intervals, the need for costly overhauls and repairs can be reduced to a minimum. This is a case where the proverbial stitch in time often saves far more than nine.

Fitting out the interior of the boat can come within the scope of a boat owner who can usefully handle tools. Likewise minor structural repairs which would otherwise need the services of a shipwright. These are dealt with in detail in a separate section, and although they are not fully comprehensive — many volumes would be required to achieve this — they cover all the most common aspects of fitting out and repair work.

Throughout the entire book, the emphasis is on simplicity. This is no textbook for a professional shipwright or marine engineer. Only maintenance and repair work which is within the scope of the average boat owner is included, and work which requires the skill and the tools of a professional is mentioned, but not detailed.

This book is not only based on my own 25 years of experience in small boats the world over. It includes the thoughts and ideas of hundreds of friends, professional and amateur, who encounter the problems of boat maintenance in the course of their work or play. And perhaps most important of all, it draws on the thousands of problems which, as a marine consultant, I have endeavoured to resolve for my clients.

ACKNOWLEDGMENTS

The author gratefully acknowledges the assistance and co-operation of the following in the preparation of this book:

Perkins Engines Ltd; Outboard Marine Australia Pty Ltd; AWA Limited; Selleys Ltd; Gardner Engines Ltd; Pride Marine Corporation Pty Ltd; International Marine Pty Ltd; Centrifuge Engineering Pty Ltd; Tygan (Australia) Pty Ltd; Stuart Turner Ltd; International Majora Paints Pty Ltd; Kiekhaefer Corporation; Chrysler Marine Corporation; Fibremakers Ltd; British Paints Ltd; Clae Marine Engines; Walton's Boatshed; CYC Australia; Jim Nash, Shipwright; Lucas Toghill, Marine Engineer; Ian Hay, Technical Adviser; Len Rodney, *Power Boat and Yachting* magazine; and many others, too innumerable to detail, whose assistance was equally invaluable, and equally appreciated.

J.E.T.

Contents

SECTION I

Materials and Methods

CHAPTER ONE

Materials

TIMBER

DESPITE THE INCREASING popularity of metals and synthetics for boat building, timber is still the most widely-used material for general purposes, and particularly for repair work. Yet the amateur knows far less about timber and its characteristics than he does about some of the more modern materials. Too often, timber is taken for granted. The wrong type or cut is used for the wrong job. Few would attempt to mix a pot of fibreglass resin without first finding out something about it; yet how many would take any old piece of timber and use it without another thought?

To be able to use timber to advantage in boat construction and repair, it is important to know some of its characteristics; to know, for example, that a piece of timber cut one way will withstand stresses that a similar piece will not withstand if cut another way. Some timbers split easily when worked one way, but not when worked another—useful knowledge when deciding how to cut for thin planks, and how to cut for a solid block.

Wood swells and shrinks when affected by varying factors, principally moisture. Furthermore it swells and shrinks much more across the grain than along the grain: Imagine what an advantage it would be to know this when fitting a tight-fitting section of wood into place. Imagine, also, the effect of using a piece of timber with a crooked grain for the same job.

New timber is usually sawn into planks with the grain running either across the plank or vertically through it. Where the grain runs across the plank end it is said to be *slash sawn;* where the grain runs vertically up and down

the end, it is said to be *rift sawn.* These differences have a marked effect on the behaviour of the plank. Slash sawn planks swell and shrink more than do rift sawn planks.

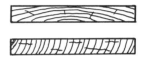

Above: *Slash sawn* Below: *Rift sawn*

The direction of the grain is also important for strength. A square plank will better support a weight at its centre when the grain runs in the direction of the load. The same plank will bend more easily when the grain is horizontal to the load. For this reason a built spar can be designed either for more strength or for easier bending, simply by paying attention to the grain direction.

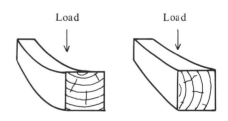

Direction of the grain affects the strength of the timber

Timber must be weathered or seasoned before it can be used, because of the different rate of shrinkage of different sections of the plank. The grain nearest the centre of the tree

15

is harder than on the outer surface and therefore will shrink less when drying out. This tendency causes planks to curve when seasoning, with the convex surface having the closer grain.

Shrinkage during seasoning tends to distort the shape of the plank

There are two basic types of timber used in boat construction: hardwood and softwood. It is a general rule that the hardwoods are those which do not grow too straight and have somewhat crooked grains, and the softwoods are the tall, straight-grained timbers such as pine. Thus, hardwoods are not very suitable for planking and decking, but are quite useable for cut and sawn frames and beams. The softwoods are perfectly suited to long straight planking. The boat builder therefore uses both kinds of woods in the construction of his vessel.

A tree, if grown in an area where it receives the optimum in rainfall, sun and soil conditions, grows very fast and produces a light timber. In poor conditions, the tree is slower to grow and the resultant timber is much heavier.

Weight of timber is a consideration, depending which part of the boat is to be repaired. Gums and teak are heavy, and if used to any great extent, such as for hull planking, make the boat very heavy. Pines are lighter, and this accounts for extensive use of oregon for hull planking. The best all-round timber for boat building then, is long grained, durable, tough wood that can be worked and bent fairly readily. Cross-grained timber is not so suitable.

Timbers vary considerably in their own family. They vary even more from country to country, and indeed a book on the correct timbers to use for building boats would be of use only for the area in which the respective timber was available. For this reason it is not intended to go into any great detail in this volume, but simply to describe the better-known timbers used for boat building, and those which are usually available in most parts of the world.

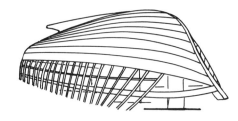

Selection of the right type of timber for each structural part of a boat is of great importance

Spruce

This is the strongest known wood for its light weight, and extremely popular in boatyards across the world. It is particularly suited for masts and spars, but makes good planking and is easy to work for any section of the boat. It is not particularly resistant to rot and requires regular maintenance.

Cedar

Cedar is popular principally because of its natural oil, which has a tendency to resist rot. It is a soft wood and easily worked, and is popular for planking and decking. Its main disadvantage is that it absorbs water very readily and becomes heavy if left immersed for any time. For this reason it is more popular for small boats and dinghies than for large vessels.

Oregon

Probably the most popular of all timbers for general boat-building purposes, particularly for planking and decking. Oregon does not shrink or swell as much as most timbers, and is fairly resistant to rot, although it needs careful maintenance. It is very easy to work.

Many different versions of pine are available on the market, usually all closely related to oregon; indeed many are sold under that description. Oregon has a characteristic light and

16

dark grain, and should not be confused with hemlock, which is sometimes sold in its stead. The grain of oregon is creamy with dark brown winter rings; hemlock is whiter all over, with less contrast in the grain.

Providing they have been properly seasoned, most pines are suitable for boat planking.

Ash

White ash is used fairly extensively in boat building, but more in fitting than in actual construction. It is a beautifully-coloured timber and lends itself ideally to panelling or similar decorative work where its blond colour sets off the darker mahoganies and teaks. It is occasionally used for structural work and is quite well-suited for the task.

Elm

Used principally for structural members, such as beams and knees. It is fairly hard but works quite readily, and has much the appearance of ash, although it is not nearly as strong.

Mahogany

Although mahogany has been used extensively in boatbuilding over the years, and is good for planking or decking, it is used only occasionally these days, chiefly in hull planking where a glossy varnished finish is required. Honduras mahogany mostly is used for this purpose. There are different types of mahogany, of which the Honduras and African are the best known.

Oak

Oak has been the traditional boat-building timber for centuries, and is used to this day for frames and other structural members. Despite its strength, however, it is hard to work and has some disadvantages; oak has gained a bad name for rot in boatbuilding circles. Seasoned timber should be well treated before fitting in place to stave off the possibility of rot setting in. Kerosene liberally painted on is a generally accepted cure. It is known that steamed timbers are resistant to rot, and thus it might be a good idea to steam all oak members before fitting into place.

Tall, straight timber such as these pines, has many uses in boat building

Teak

Teak is, in theory, the perfect timber for boat building, but it has some disadvantages. It is very heavy, and is not as strong as spruce and thus cannot be used where structural strains are considerable. It is very hard to work (although in itself it is not a hard timber) for it dulls the blades of tools very quickly. The reason is not known, although it is suspected that minute specks of silicone ingrained in the timber cause the damage.

Despite its faults, teak has advantages. It is almost completely resistant to rot, and also to toredo worm. It does not weather severely and does not shrink or swell. Indeed, for fittings that are not structural and for planking, teak is ideal. Needless to say, it is also expensive.

Teak does not glue well, and epoxy-based glues should be used. Before application, the surface of the teak should be cleaned with petrol or spirit to remove oily secretions.

17

Lignum Vitae

One of the hardest woods of all, it has only a limited use in boat building. It is very heavy and extremely tough, and although once used extensively in the manufacture of blocks and fittings, has been replaced by the lighter synthetics and alloys. It has a natural oil, and is still used as stern bearings for propeller shafts.

Spotted Gum

The best of the gums for structural use in boat building. It is a hard wood, close-grained and not easy to work, but it steams relatively easily and is popular for all frames and heavy decking. Often it contains sap wood which helps to make it fairly resistant to rot. It is the strongest yet easiest to work of all the gums, and does not break up as many do when dried out.

Maple

Maple is generally a soft-working timber. It is very porous and short-grained and does not bend well, and although easy to plane and saw, is limited by this tendency to splinter under bending stresses. It is particularly suited for cut sections, where the timber can be cut to shape, such as beams, coaming and other coachwork.

Different kinds of maple are available, and not all of them bear the characteristics described above. The best timber for boat work is Queensland Maple which, unfortunately, is becoming very difficult to obtain.

Marenti, or Pacific maple, is a term covering several different maples from the Pacific areas, and these also vary within themselves. Some may be long-grained, some short, depending on the rate of growth, and some may be heavy, some light. In short, care must be taken when choosing maple from the Pacific area for repair work, to ensure that it is a suitable type.

The following list is a guide to the types of timbers used for the various sections of a vessel, both for original building purposes and also for repair. This is not intended to be a firm guide to buying timber for repair work, but it suggests the most suitable timbers that are generally available at moderate cost.

KEEL	Oak or Spotted Gum.
FRAMES, TIMBERS	Oak or Spotted Gum.
PLANKING	Oregon, Honduras Mahogany (varnished hull).
DECKS (LAID)	Beech, Oregon, Teak.
COACHWORK	Maple or Teak.
MASTS & SPARS	Spruce or Oregon.

Buying timber

All timber used in boat building and repair must be of high quality. Timber for planking, stringers, chines, and frames should be selected for straightness of grain, low shrinkage and freedom from defects. There is a very great danger in using timbers which are affected by knots, shakes, sapwood, incipient decay, compression failures and brittle heart, for under the stresses and strains of a boat in a seaway, they may collapse. Purchasing lesser qualities will lead to more and more repair work at a later stage.

Methods of grading timber vary from country to country and the timber dealer should be consulted about his grades. Oregon is generally graded as "Clear Select" and in numbers. No. 1 Clear Select is the best available oregon, and subsequent grades pass down through No. 2 Clear Select and No. 3 Clear Select to "Merch" (short for "Merchantable"), which is the roughest grade of timber.

The controlling factors in the quality of the timber may vary, but the number of knots to a given length will affect its grading. A length of timber with a knot about every six feet or so will probably grade No. 2, whereas closer knots will reduce the timber to grade No. 3.

Bluenose II, the famous Canadian schooner is a fine example of timber boatbuilding. Photo courtesy
Power Boat & Yachting

Dressing timber

At the yard, timber may be in a number of conditions, but two are of particular interest in boat repair work. Timber that is "rough sawn", has not been planed and still has the rough edges of the original milling, and "dressed" timber that has been planed to an exact measurement.

Obviously, the best type of timber to buy has been dressed, thus eliminating the need for further planing. Unfortunately, dressed timber may not always be in sizes suitable for the particular job in hand, therefore rough-sawn timber may have to be bought and planed back to the size required.

This is frequently the case in boat repair work where timbers of awkward sizes are required. Say a section of timber one and a half inches thick is required; this would have to be reduced from the nearest stock-size rough-sawn timber of two inches thickness. If a considerable amount of the one size is wanted, it is often more profitable to ask the timber merchant to plane down a run of it to the size required. Where small sections are to be used, it is usually a case of good old elbow-grease, for the dealer will not want to reset his machines for each individual piece.

Timber can be seasoned naturally by stacking it in the open weather, but artificial seasoning can speed the process considerably

Bought timber may be dressed on two sides or on all sides, and when the dressing has been completed, the timber will be a set size. The sizes vary somewhat across the world, particularly in America and the metric countries. The basic British and Australian measurements are rough-sawn at inch thicknesses and dressed $\frac{3}{32}''$ on each side, which means the final thickness is $1\frac{13}{16}''$.

Anything over an inch thickness rough-sawn is usually dressed $\frac{1}{8}''$ on each side. Thus 3″ timbers would be dressed to a finished thickness of $2\frac{3}{4}''$.

The size ordered from the timber yard must be specified as either finish size or sawn size to be dressed. An order for fifty feet of 2″ x 1″ would be ordered as 2″ x 1″ D.A.R. (Dressed All Round). This would arrive as dressed timber with a size of $1\frac{3}{4}''$ x $1\frac{13}{16}''$.

If the required *final* measurement was 2″ x 1″, then the order would be placed for 2″ x 1″ finished timber and the wood merchant would have to pick out the next size up and reduce it to the finished 2″ x 1″. This would be much more expensive, as his machines would have to be set to plane the required amount to achieve the 2″ x 1″ measurement; plus of course the additional cost of the larger timber.

In short, timber not ordered for the exact size required and specified as *finished* timber, will arrive a fraction of an inch smaller on all

sidcs, as described above. Timber required in the exact sizes of the order must be specified *finished dressed* and will have to be cut from a larger size of timber.

PLYWOOD

Marine grade plywood is made by laminating wood in an uneven number of thin layers. The adjacent layers are so placed that their grains run at right angles to each other. The adhesive is high quality marine waterproof glue of the synthetic resin type, and when correctly used will help to form a sheet of laminated timber that is of high strength, is absolutely waterproof, and will stand immersion for a long period of time.

Since laminated wood is one of the most useful materials for making a hull skin, and since plywood is simple to use, it finds considerable favour among boat builders both amateur and professional. It can be fairly easily bent when in long sheets, and can be joined by scarfing without loss of strength in the main body of the sheet.

The secret of using plywood, whether for interior or exterior use, is to ensure that it is a fully qualified marine grade. There are other grades called exterior and interior plywood and even waterproof plywood, but none of these is suitable for work on a boat, even for interior finishing. Only high-quality marine grade plywood can be used, and this may be used for any task.

Modern techniques have improved the quality and waterproof characteristics of marine plywood, and it can also be impregnated with anti-rot chemicals to assist in combating dry rot in areas which may be difficult to reach later. Indeed, some of the latest processes for impregnating the timber leave only a slight pinkish tint which is quite suitable for subsequent clear finishing. Thus the plywood retains all its characteristics and can be painted or varnished with the added safeguard of the anti-rot impregnation.

Plywood can be bought in a number of

Plywood is used widely in the construction of small boats. It is the ideal material for the amateur because of its ease of working

thicknesses and in different sizes of sheets. Provided it is correct marine grade, the type of timbers used in the lamination and their colours are of no consequence. And providing they have been impregnated, they can be used for construction or repair work almost anywhere in the vessel.

Because of the nature of the laminations, the ends of plywood sheets are somewhat vulnerable, and must always be well protected, or splintering of end-grained layers will result. The ends should be carefully planed and sanded, and sealed before being placed in position, unless they are to be end-glued to

21

another piece of timber. The layers of timber are liable to decay or rot unless some form of protection is used.

FIBREGLASS

Undoubtedly one of the greatest revolutions to hit the boat-building industry has been caused by fibreglass. Developed since World War II it has, despite its high cost, rocketed in popularity among yachtsmen of all types, in every corner of the world. It is estimated that already half the new boats launched are of fibreglass construction, and although it seems impossible to imagine that timber will one day be ousted as a boat-building material, there seems little doubt that fibreglass will make more and more inroads as it is developed to a higher degree.

The popularity of the plastic material lies

Fibreglass has caused a revolution in boat building methods. Giant ocean racing yachts and fast power launches are but a few of the many types of craft moulded in 'glass

in many directions. For the boat owner there is the saving in maintenance costs, although this is often a greatly deceptive factor. Despite what the brochures of the boat-building firms say, fibreglass needs some maintenance, and this increases with the age of the boat. To what extent it will increase cannot be determined at this stage, because the earliest boats have not been in use long enough for the ravages of wind and water to be fully ascertained.

But already there is evidence to shatter the illusion that fibreglass is maintenance-free—notably the deterioration of the outer layer or gel coat after continual exposure to weather. The coat tends to become dulled and—if coloured—faded. This may require only sanding and painting to rectify; but what is sanding and painting if it is not maintenance? Further, once painted, the surface will need the same attention as any other painted surface.

Time will take its toll of any material, and weather will give time that extra nudge. And it is at sea that time and weather act in greatest accord. Maintenance-free materials have yet to be discovered and are at this stage only a key word in the vocabulary of the boat salesman.

Fibreglass, however, *reduces* the need for maintenance, particularly in the early years of its life. Timber (and the paints and varnishes used to protect it) is undoubtedly more vulnerable to the ravages of the weather than are the plastics.

The principal advantage of fibreglass is its resistance to rot and corrosion. It is this aspect of maintenance that is eliminated, rather than the routine day-to-day work. Fibreglass is resistant to heat, rot, rust, corrosion, saltwater, acids—and it can be relatively easily repaired when damaged.

It is not proposed in this volume to deal with the construction of fibreglass boats in any detail, but a few words on the basic methods of laying up the plastic material will assist the would-be shipwright to gain some idea of the

A 53-foot fibreglass yacht, illustrating the high standards now being reached by this fairly modern method of boat building

without the application of heat or pressure. The resin is purchased in the raw state and prepared only minutes before application by the addition of the catalyst. An accelerator is also employed which speeds up the curing, particularly where temperatures are low.

Because of the number of different brands of resin, the choice of catalyst may vary and the manufacturer's instructions should be closely followed to achieve the maximum results when the resin is cured. The curing may be speeded up or slowed by the addition of more catalyst and accelerator, but it is better to stick to the recommended mixtures— according to time and temperature—to achieve the best results.

The correct mixing of the resin, catalyst and accelerator is very important, as also is the control of temperature and humidity at all stages of curing, particularly where large areas are to be cured.

The fibre

The popularity of the glass fibre as a reinforcing material is principally because of its high tensile strength and resistance to biological or chemical attack. It is easily woven into usable material from a strand—not unlike a fine rope strand—which itself is formed by the bundling together of hundreds of fine glass filaments. It is usually available in two forms; Chopped Mat, in which the strands are loosely bound together in a random pattern and then rolled into mat form, and Woven Mat, in which the strands are woven into a material not dissimilar to a loose kind of linen.

Another form of glass fibre—continuous rovings—is used in the industry for spraying the resin and glass fibre through a nozzle. The strands are chopped and sprayed on to the mould simultaneously with the resin. This requires special equipment, however, and for the amateur who is concerned more with small amounts of fibreglass, the chopped strand and the woven mat are more suitable.

Boat construction with fibreglass

In itself fibreglass is not a light material,

material with which he may be working. Although there are numerous forms of fibreglass, and many ways in which it is moulded into boat form, basically all methods conform to a common pattern.

The strength of fibreglass is achieved by encasing a strong fabric in a bonding solution of chemicals which cure to a considerable hardness. In much the same way that reinforced concrete is used to give strength to buildings, so with fibreglass, where tough glass fibres are used for the reinforcing, and polyester or epoxy resin poured around and through them to mould the whole material into a tough, durable skin.

The resin

The polyester resin may be one of several brands, but basically all are the same. A syrupy liquid is changed into a hard solid by the addition of a catalyst which cures the resin

but in a boat it can save weight by the elimination of much of the heavy timber used in
conventional boats for structural members.
When a boat is moulded in fibreglass, only the
principal structural members are included,
although even these are gradually giving way
to "doubled" thicknesses of fibreglass for
strengthening against structural strains.

The boat is built in a female mould, which
itself has been moulded from a cast or model.
The mould is treated to prevent the resin from
sticking, and then the outer or finishing coat
of gel sprayed on. This is given time to harden
before the glass fibre is laid into position—
the number of layers of fibre depending on
the thicknesses of skin wanted—then the resin
is impregnated through the fibre to the thickness required. When curing is completed the
mould is removed and the shell remains.

Usually, large yachts and motor boats are laid
up in one piece up to the deck line. The cabin
and deck structures, if of fibreglass, are
moulded separately and bonded to the hull
later.

Fittings, such as engine mountings, chain
plates, ballast bolts, and so on, are often
moulded into the construction of the hull, and
so designed as to distribute strain and weight
throughout the structure of the fibreglass.

Interior furniture and deck fittings are
usually secured later. If the fitting is fairly
light—to secure interior furnishings, for example—it is possible to avoid drilling holes
in the fibreglass by attaching small pieces of
timber with a special adhesive to the skin of
the boat and screwing the fitting on to these.

ALUMINIUM

Aluminium is, in theory, the best of all boat-
building materials. Light, tough, durable, and
virtually corrosion-resistant, it offers in one

*Fibreglass is easily moulded into any shape, and
withstands enormous pressures, making it the ideal
material for the hulls of fast power boats*

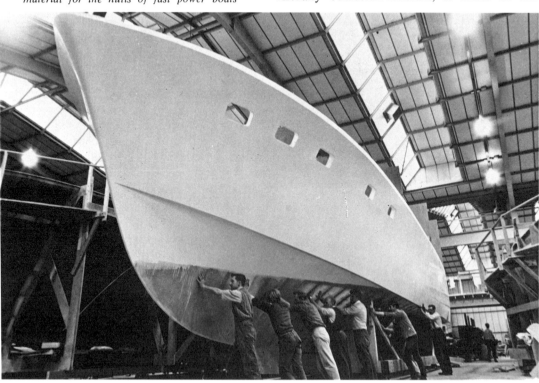

An aluminium yacht under construction. The methods used vary little from those employed in building steel craft

package the answer to ninety per cent of the boat owner's maintenance problems.

Despite this, aluminium has remained principally a material for small boats—although there are some larger aluminium vessels afloat. As a material for manufacturing masts and spars, however, it has found tremendous popularity, among the majority of yacht builders.

Naturally, cost is a big factor. Aluminium is an expensive material for boat building, not only in terms of cost of the material itself, but also in the specialised methods of welding it. But because of its low maintenance properties, aluminium is popular as a small-boat material, since small boats are used principally for hard work running up and down beaches or as tenders out to larger vessels or as "trailerable" boats to pull over all kinds of roads to coastal fishing spots.

Timber would not stand up to this treatment for long, neither would plywood, and steel, although suitable for such hard treatment, would be far too heavy. Fibreglass or aluminium provide the answer in terms of dura-

bility and lightness, but both are higher in cost than timber.

Marine grades of aluminium

Two principal grades of the alloy are recommended by the Aluminium Association as suitable for marine construction; the one mostly in use is graded 5086, although 5083 is a close alternative.

Riveting aluminium

Although welding is used more and more in aluminium construction, riveting is still widely done, particularly in the manufacture of small craft. Rivets are often pre-dipped in an anti-corrosive liquid before use, for once driven home, their inner surfaces are beyond the reach of any anti-corrosive applied to the surfaces.

Aluminium rivets are usually hammered up cold in much the same way as any other type of rivet or the roving of a copper nail. An anvil or other heavy steel object is placed against the head of the rivet and the other end hammered out in a splayed shape to grip firmly and tightly. A more detailed description of riveting aluminium is given later in this chapter.

Most rivets are merely hammered home on a flat surface, but the soft nature of the alloy

Because of its resistance to corrosion, aluminium is a popular material with boat builders. Modern welding techniques are used in preference to riveting, particularly in larger craft

allows a better bond to be made by countersinking the end of the rivet into the metal itself. This requires some practice and skill, but provides an excellent watertight joint when completed.

Welding aluminium

As mentioned earlier, the welding of aluminium calls for specialised equipment and knowledge, and for this reason it is not proposed to deal with the subject in detail.

Aluminium oxidises under intense heat, and special welding guns are required which not only heat the alloy sufficiently to allow a weld to be made, but also keep the surrounding surfaces from oxidising. An inert gas is used to keep air from the aluminium and thus prevent oxidisation.

Aluminium and corrosion

Although resistant to many forms of marine corrosion, aluminium is very susceptible to electrolytic corrosion. Since it is a conductive metal, contact with any other metal of a different electrolytic level in the presence of salt-water will set up an immediate electrical

current, with resultant corrosion. So vulnerable is aluminium to this type of corrosion that even an ingredient of a paint—such as the copper in anti-fouling paint—can set up an electrolytic action.

The fittings used on aluminium hulls—or on masts and spars—must be carefully selected, to avoid this corrosion. Any copper-bearing alloy (brass, bronze, monel) will create immediate and severe problems, and anti-fouling copper paints can be used only after sufficient anti-corrosive, in the form of a zinc chromate paint, has been applied first to the bare aluminium.

Where the use of dissimilar metals cannot be avoided, they must not be allowed to make electrical contact with the aluminium. Mounting pads of timber or—even better—mica, neoprene or some similar electrical insulating material, should be placed between the aluminium and the fitting to break the electrical contact. Zinc plates (sacrificial anodes) should be fitted on aluminium hulls near bronze propellers, as is the case with steel vessels.

Even some forms of stainless steel are not immune from this form of electrolytic action, and since it is the light, vulnerable aluminium that suffers each time, great care must be taken with *any* fitting. Because of its close proximity to copper or brass fastenings and fittings, the mast step of an aluminium mast is very vulnerable. Great care should be taken to check periodically that there is no corrosion progressively eating away at the foot of the mast.

STEEL

Mention the word steel to the average boating man and he will throw up his hands in horror and scream long and loud about rust. Admittedly, looking at some of the red-streaked rust buckets that pass for home-made steel yachts, one could readily forgive him his reaction. But the fact remains that a growing percentage of those lily-white, sleek, shiny-looking craft that slip so easily by are made of steel. The difference lies not with the material, but with the builder.

Steel, certainly, is vulnerable to some form of corrosion, but so is every metal. Aluminium, the so-called maintenance-free metal, is far more vulnerable to its own type of corrosion than is steel to rust. In effect, a metal is only as vulnerable to corrosion as its user permits it to be.

Which boils down to the fact that, correctly used and treated, steel is no more liable to promote maintenance problems than is any other material. Indeed, with modern advances in anti-rust research, correctly treated steel causes almost none of the headaches previously associated with its use in the marine world.

One disadvantage which might never be eliminated, is steel's greater weight. This is only of concern where the boat is to take part in racing; indeed, it can be an asset giving stability in a vessel to be used purely for cruising. Its great durability, strength and long life weigh heavily in its favour when work vessels are under consideration.

When steel is rolled straight from the mills it gathers a "bloom" in the form of the blue sheen familiar to all who have seen a sheet of bare steel. This is known as mill scale which, since it is not an integral part of the

steel, will drop off as the metal ages. It is the mill scale that causes most of the problems of rusting in steel vessels.

Before a single coat of paint can be placed on the new steel, it must be burnished back almost to the bare metal to clear away every trace of mill scale. One of the most satisfactory methods is by sand or grit blasting. Failing this expensive process, the scale must be removed by chipping and wire brushing although,

Steel has long been a favourite material for ships' hulls, but unless correctly maintained brings as many headaches today as it did in the "grand old days".
Photo courtesy Power Boat & Yachting

if time is no object, an equally satisfactory method is to let the steel stand out in the weather until the scale rusts away and then simply clean up the bare steel before painting. This is the method adopted in most big shipyards.

Once *correctly* painted, the steel is invulnerable, and will last indefinitely. Only damage to the paint skin, allowing water to penetrate beneath it, can cause rust to form. This, when it happens, must be treated quickly and effectively if the steel is to be kept rust-free. Detailed descriptions of treatment for steel are given later in this section.

Riveting steel

There are several ways of fastening sheet steel, the most common of which are welding and riveting. A later section deals in detail with welding. Riveting, although still widely used commercially, is rare in the construction of small boats.

A great deal of specialised equipment is required for riveting steel, mostly in the form of a forge to heat the rivets and pneumatic hammers to drive them home, and this tends to make riveting clumsy and difficult for the amateur. Welding has completely superseded riveting for small boats and, indeed, may do so even for large ocean-going vessels because of its convenience and speed.

Welding Steel

The welding equipment in shipbuilding yards is vastly superior to that available for the amateur; but electrical welding equipment is now on sale which can be plugged into normal mains power and used safely and satisfactorily by any amateur who has taken the

trouble to learn a little of the skills of welding. As a result, welded steel is used more frequently for both fittings of boats and the manufacture of the steel hulls themselves, a factor which could well see steel return to favour in the small boat world.

Successful steel welding depends on the technical know-how of the operator. No matter how successful the anti-rust treatment afforded the steel (and no matter how clean it is from mill-scale), poor welding will create difficult corners, cavities, and even cracks into which the demon rust will dive with relish.

It is not sufficient to open the instruction manual with the welding equipment and read the few paragraphs on how to make a good weld. Such cursory details would be better entitled "How to Make a Good Mess".

In this book only a few basic hints are offered to those contemplating using welding equipment. Good basic training from an expert is required before setting out on a mammoth task such as building or repairing a steel hull.

CONCRETE

During the war years, concrete made its debut as a material for boat building. It was at first confined principally to the moulding of pontoons, barges, and harbour sections, but it was gradually developed to the stage where self-propelled vessels constructed of the concrete material became a commercial proposition. Since then there has been a limited but enthusiastic following of concrete as a material for small boats, and in latter years yachts of some size have been laid up in concrete.

The construction of cement vessels (the correct term is "ferro-cement") is based on the same principle as fibreglass, where a reinforcing material is impregnated with a liquid bonding material which later hardens to form a strong, watertight bond. Exactly the same principle can be seen in the construction of buildings where steel netting is laid as the heart of poured concrete to combine the elastic strength of one with the bonding

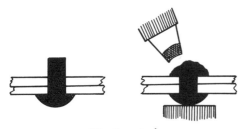

Riveting steel

28

hardness of the other. The endurable product can be moulded to almost any shape.

The reinforcing material used in the concrete is a fine steel mesh, usually chicken wire or similar patent product.

This is laid up on steel frames shaped to contours of the hull and the solid mass of mesh hammered into the exact shape required. Since the finishing coat of concrete is to be very thin, it is important that the mesh does not protrude at any point as it will be difficult to rectify later, and may form a weakness in the skin.

The mesh comprises several layers which when beaten and knitted together becomes a very fine, composite reinforcing. The concrete mixture is then poured or worked through the mesh from the inside to ensure that it permeates all the finer wire and does not leave cavities. From the outside it is finished off with trowel and fairing tool until the required surface is obtained.

When finishing the surface it is necessary to ensure that the wire mesh is completely covered by the concrete mix, or the saltwater will attack it and rust will commence. The result—rust gradually working its way through the mass of wire netting inside the concrete— would be disastrous. Unfortunately galvanised wire cannot be used as an action sets up between the galvanising and the concrete which also results in deterioration of the composite body.

The mix of concrete, sand and other elements can vary considerably, and since this method of boat construction is still in the experimental stages, will no doubt vary even further with research. A basic mix in use in various parts of the world, however, is of sand and Portland cement, in the ratio 2:1 combined with a percentage (usually about 20 per cent) of Pozzolan. This provides a tough, elastic and waterproof coating that is easily laid and easily moulded.

The finished boat is allowed to cure for a minimum of three weeks, after which the finishing touches can be made. Some vessels are moulded up completely as one unit, comprising cabin, hull and deck, without any joins. This has an advantage over the conventional methods of laying the deck and cabin separately in that it prevents leaks and openings between the different surfaces. However, some schools of thought do not accept the moulded deck and cabin, preferring them to be of conventional timber.

The correctly-finished vessel will be strong and light, and will probably require a considerable amount of ballast to float her at her best waterline. Because of the nature of the concrete, it is easy to carry out any further work to the hull at a later date, and the fitting of interior comforts and deck apparatus is no more involved than with fibreglass.

Obviously the mixture of concrete, sand and Pozzolan is of the utmost importance to the finished product, as also is the quality of these materials. Only the best should be used if problems such as shrinkage during the curing period are to be avoided.

Since this is a volume concerning repair work rather than construction, it is not proposed to delve into the intricate details of concrete mixes. A wealth of literature is available to the enthusiast on this subject.

Of all the modern boat building materials, fibreglass is the most popular, particularly for small and medium sized craft

CHAPTER TWO

Tools

A BOOK OF THIS NATURE could not possibly cover the full range of tools for maintenance and repair work on boats. Neither, for that matter, could the pocket of the average boat owner! So comprehensive is the variety of machines and tools in this field that even many professional boatyards cannot afford to equip themselves fully.

For this reason, the tools described in this chapter are restricted to those essential to any boat owner undertaking his own maintenance work, and those which fall within the pocket of most boat-owners. More sophisticated tools are obtainable which make the work much easier and sometimes more "professional", but for the use and handling of these more detailed books of instruction are necessary.

SAWS

There is a variety of saws available for all types of timber work. Although each has an individual purpose and is the best saw for that purpose, the amateur will find it too costly and perhaps unnecessary to buy the full range of saws, particularly for repair work on boats where a little ingenuity can be applied to adapting one type of saw for different jobs.

Power saws are necessary only when a great deal of timber is to be cut, although a band saw is always useful in marine work because of the number of curved cuts that have to be made. This, possibly, would be the most useful all-round power saw for marine work, as it can—with care—be adapted for straight-edge cutting as well as for curved edges.

Hand saws are relatively inexpensive, and here it is advisable to obtain a fairly large range, as the physical work can be made easier

—and the final finish considerably improved —by the use of the correct saw.

The secret of correctly using a saw lies partly in setting up the timber to be cut in a good sawing position and with a firm grip holding it steady, as well as in the method of sawing. A vice or sturdy bench should always be used to reduce movement in the timber to a minimum, and the strokes of the saw should be even and steady, without too much "forcing". Hard, uneven pressure will bend the saw blade and cause jagged strokes which will dig the teeth into the fibres of the timber, making the work much harder than it need be.

Firm, even strokes ensure a steady cut and relieve the pressure on the arm muscles. A good carpenter can saw for a long period with little or no effort on his arm muscles.

Power saws of this calibre make light work of any sawing, but are confined to straight cutting only, Bandsaws are more adaptable to boat work

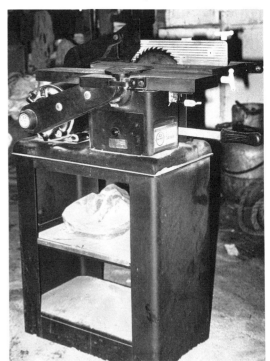

*A vice ensures a firm grip on timber to be sawn —
an important feature if sawing is to be accurate*

Saws should be kept clean and in good condition if they are to perform well. Nothing is more likely to cause trouble than a dirty or rusty saw blade, and nothing will make the work harder. When put away after use, saws should be lightly oiled to prevent rust.

The following is a list of the principal types of saws used in marine work:

CIRCULAR SAW: Power driven, for straight cutting when a large amount of timber is to be sawn. Can be obtained in a variety of sizes.

BAND SAW: Power driven, for curved cutting. Ideal for all forms of marine work. Should be used with the top guide as close as possible to the timber.

PANEL SAW: The traditional hand saw for straight-cutting all types of timber. Usually in two forms: *cross-cut,* for cutting across the grain; and *rip-saw,* for cutting with the grain.

A typical hand saw

TENON SAW: A useful small saw for straight cutting in light timber.

COPING SAW: A light saw for cutting curved work in light timber. The *Fret Saw* is a somewhat larger version of the Coping Saw.

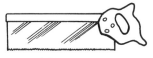

A Tenon saw

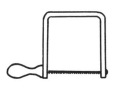

A Coping saw

A Keyhole saw

KEYHOLE SAW: With variations known as *Pruning Saw* and *Compass Saw*. It is used for cutting interior curves. Like the Fret or Coping Saw, these saws, when cutting interior curves, must be started by drilling a hole sufficiently large to insert the blade.

BOW SAW: Used for cutting curves in timber too heavy for a Fret or Coping Saw.

HACKSAW: Somewhat similar in appearance to the Coping Saw, but used exclusively for cutting metal.

SANDERS

Sanding is of great importance in all aspects of boat maintenance, whether it be painting, repair work, or finishing. Furthermore, sanding is applicable to almost every type of material, including steel and the modern synthetic plastics.

The handyman has at his disposal a good range of tools for sanding jobs. Professionals, of course, require more powerful sanders, but even for the amateur, with his limited experience and pocket, there are useful sanding tools to cover most jobs he is likely to meet.

31

Although there are times when hand sanding is a must, generally it is too slow and tedious. Because of the large areas to be covered on boats, particularly large yachts and motor cruisers, power tools are essential if the job is to be done efficiently. Following are details of the principal power sanders of use to amateur shipwrights.

Disc Sanders

These are the most common and cheapest of sanding equipment, comprising a rubber pad to which is attached an abrasive disc, and is fitted into the chuck of a power drill. The pad may be of hard rubber, or of foam plastic —the latter gives a better finish when fine work is the order of the day, or where scoring is to be avoided.

The use of the disc sander requires some experience. It can score the timber badly if the edges of the disc are allowed to touch the surface, and the scoring can be very hard

The orbital sander. The boating handyman's most useful tool, particularly for general maintenance work

Disc sanders must be used carefully to prevent scoring. This one incorporates a foam rubber pad on the disc

to remove. To reduce the danger, the use of foam plastic pads, which do not have a hard edge, or a pad mounted on a ball joint which allows the face of the pad always to lie flat on the timber, is recommended.

These sanders are good for removing paint, or for heavy sanding of timber that can be later finished with finer sanding. No matter what type of disc sander is used, some scoring is unavoidable because of the circular motion of the pad, and finishing with hand or orbital sander is essential before the timber can be painted or varnished.

One of the advantages of using the disc sander is that the drill to which it is attached can also be used with several other accessories useful in boat repair work. Providing it is used with care and only for rough work, the disc sander is a useful and time-saving piece of equipment.

The Orbital Sander

Fittings are available to convert the normal power drill into an orbital sander, but they are not over-successful, and since the orbital sander is a tool that will be used many times over, it is an investment to purchase a professional model. This is the finishing sander, invaluable when fine sanding has to be done, particularly where paint and varnish work has to be sanded back before a final coat is put on.

The orbital sander consists of a large pad on which a fine sandpaper is mounted. This pad is moved by mechanical means in a manner which gives firm, but even, abrasion. The orbital sander will not cut back as hard as a rotary sander, because of the larger area of abrasive in contact with the timber, but the sanding is smooth and without scoring, and is thus very suitable for any finishing work.

Where the surface has to be cut back before finishing, the rotary disc sander can be used first to do the rough work, and the scored surface which will result can be sanded down to a fine finish with the orbital sander. For cutting back between coats of paint, the orbital sander is unsurpassed, and it fits more readily into difficult edges and corners between timber planks, with no chance of scoring or tearing a hole in the timber.

Belt Sanders

Several kinds of belt sanders are available, and an attachment can be purchased to convert the power drill. But once again this is not recommended as, like the disc attachment, the belt sander can score the timber if not used carefully. A properly-constructed belt sander is the only answer for considerable use.

The belt sander cuts more aggressively than the orbital sander and can, if moved onto its edge, score the timber. For this reason it must be held firmly and perfectly flat, when it will provide an efficient and fast means of cutting back evenly all over the surface of the timber.

The belt sander should be used only for heavy cutting back, although by changing the abrasive, a variety of cutting surfaces can be obtained. It is not recommended for small areas, as its size demands a good area on which to work. It is particularly good for cutting down new timber and other heavy surfaces, which would be a long and tedious process if the orbital sander were used.

As with the disc sander, finishing is best done with the orbital sander to eliminate the possibility of scoring. All too often the finer

scratches are not noticed until the varnish or paint has been applied, by which time it is too late to take them out, unless the surface is again cut back.

Heavy Duty Sanders

When a large area, or a very heavy surface has to be tackled, particularly when removing old paint, the smaller home-handyman sanders are not adequate. Then the big industrial sanders come into their own. There is a variety of these sanders available; the best known is the normal heavy-duty floor-sanding machine which, with the appropriate disc in place, will make light work of sanding a boat hull or deck.

Because of their size and relative expense, and also because of the limited number of times sanders of this calibre are required, they are not usually part of the amateur's workshop. However, they can usually be hired at reasonable cost for the occasional job.

The use of the heavy sander depends on the nature of the job on which it is engaged. By and large, however, heavy sanders should be used cautiously, with a careful eye on scoring, because even though the surface may be

There are many areas where power sanders cannot be used without risk of damage to adjacent timber. Hand sanding is the answer in these cases

A small wooden or cork block gives a better grip and abrasive surface for hand sanding

rough, sanders of this size can quickly gouge out a very large chunk of timber; one which may be difficult to cover in subsequent sanding and painting.

Hand Sanding

No matter how many power instruments there may be in the workshop, almost every job will need hand sanding at some stage. Difficult corners and angles make the use of power sanders dangerous, particularly the disc sanders which can so quickly score a timber surface beyound repair. Narrow strips and edges are also beyond the scope of the power sander, and it is here that the old elbow-grease has to be used.

Hand sanding can be done with almost any type of abrasive paper, although there are special papers for special types of work. The correct paper, once selected, should be wrapped around a cork or rubber block to give it shape and something for the hand to grip. There are patent types of hand sanding blocks and these are a useful addition to the workshop.

The sanding should be carried out with an even motion of the hand and arm, running the sandpaper with the grain. Hand sanding

can scratch and score the surfaces as quickly (albeit not as badly) as power sanders unless care is taken to ensure an even rubbing action. Nothing can give quite as fine a finish to varnish or fine paintwork as hand sanding, and usually the real artist will scorn the use of power tools, at least for the final rubdown.

Wet and dry or waterproof sandpaper is good for rubbing back painted and varnished surfaces, and should be used with a slightly soapy solution of warm water. The slurry thus produced must be completely eliminated before painting or varnishing can be begun. A wash down with fresh water and rubbing almost dry with a sponge or absorbent cloth is usually effective.

PLANES

Because of the large sizes of timber used in boat repairs, and also because of the somewhat intricate shaping that is often required, the plane is one of the most useful of all the tools in the workshop. There are several different planes available, but generally speaking the amateur need concern himself with only one—the jack plane, although if very heavy planing is to be done, a German jack plane is very useful.

The jack plane is the maid-of-all-work and can be used for almost any type of planing likely to be encountered in amateur repairs. It usually comes in a number of sizes, of which the 12″-14″ range is best suited for shipwright work. The smaller planes tend to "hobby horse" when used on large surfaces.

The German jack plane is timber-built and is designed for heavy cutting. It has a narrower

A German Jack Plane

blade than the jack plane and this blade is curved, giving it a great cutting ability. The German jack does not have a metal cap-iron as do other planes, but instead has a wooden wedge. It is best for heavy, deep planing, particularly where paint has to be removed.

Other planes, which are not as generally useful to the amateur shipwright, are the smoothing and trying planes, used for fine finishing work. The Surform plane is more like a large file and is used principally for cross-grained work, as it does not tear the grain. It is ideal for rounding off corners and for rough work generally.

The secret of using the plane lies in the adjustment of the cap iron—a fitting adjacent to the blade. The cap iron and the blade must be close together to prevent shavings gathering between them, and the cap iron regulated according to the type of timber to be planed and the finish required.

For normal planing a gap between the leading edge of the cap iron and the blade of about $\frac{3}{32}''$ is suitable. For tougher wood, the gap will have to be reduced to $\frac{1}{16}''$ or even $\frac{1}{32}''$. The cap iron should be fine set for planing with the grain, and reduced to the finer positions for cross-grained or timber inclined to tear.

The planing stroke should be a smooth, easy action, taking the plane along the full length of the timber if possible. Too often trouble is caused if the plane is set too coarse, and this will prevent an even action. A knot or some other hard piece of the timber can

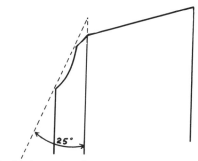

The blade of the plane is ground to about 25 degrees on the bench grinder, and the fine cutting edge finished on the oilstone

quickly take the edge off the blade, which will have to be resharpened. This is far less a chore with the patent sharpener, than doing it by hand.

If the plane does not operate smoothly and the blade has been checked to see that it is not set too coarse, the likely trouble is that the cap iron is not set close enough to the blade, and this should be rectified.

Rounding off corners or edges may need a short, stubby plane known in the trade as a block plane. A Surform will do as well, although the finish will not be quite as neat. To plane across end-pieces, the plane should be brought across the timber from each end, and the stroke finished in the centre. This will avoid the unpleasant breaking away of the end corners which is so common when using brittle timber.

Sharpening the Blade

The easiest and most efficient way of sharpening a blade is to obtain a special sharpening device, available commercially for this purpose. A fine oilstone should be used, with neatsfoot oil in preference to vegetable oil, which is apt to dry out and make the stone sticky with a tendency to clog.

The blade is placed in the sharpener with the angled edge to the stone and briskly moved backwards and forwards across the surface until it achieves the required degree of sharpness. It should then be taken from the holder

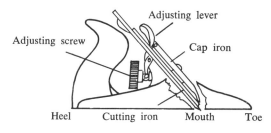

Cross section of plane, showing relation of cap iron to blade

Adjusting lever

Adjusting screw

Cap iron

Heel   Cutting iron   Mouth   Toe

35

and turned over so that the burrs made by the sharpening process can be rubbed off. A few quick strokes should take care of this.

FILES

Files are both inexpensive and handy. An assortment of files is an asset in any workshop and, because of the number and variety, such an assortment will cover work on metals, wood and synthetics. Files vary not only in the type of work they do, but also in shape and size, so that there is rarely a shaping or smoothing problem that cannot be resolved with one file or another.

SQUARE FILES: Tapered on all four sides; used to enlarge rectangular slots and holes.

TRIANGULAR FILE: Tapered on their three sides; used to file cutters and to clear out square corners. Some triangular files are specially designed for filing saw teeth.

ROUND FILES: Used mostly for filing out round holes.

No matter what type of boat or what material in her construction, there are always small jobs and adjustments which need the use of handymans tools

HALF-ROUND FILES: The general-purpose file for a variety of tasks. The flat side is used on flat surfaces and the round side on round surfaces. The round surface to be filed should—as nearly as possible—match the round surface of the file.

MILL FILES: Specialist files, tapered both in width and thickness; used for precision work.

FLAT FILES: Like half-round files, are for general-purpose work; may be either single or double cut, and are tapered both in thickness and in width.

HAND FILES: Similar to flat files, but taper only slightly in thickness, and not in width.

Files are referred to as *single cut* or *double cut,* depending on the way in which the teeth are arranged. Single-cut files have rows of teeth running parallel to one another and set at an angle of about 65 degrees to the centre line. These files are good for tool sharpening, finish filing, and smoothing the edges of sheeting. Double-cut files have criss-crossed teeth which are diamond shaped and fast cutting. These files are best suited to rough work and heavy cutting.

Cross section of files used in boat work

Files are also graded according to the closeness and size of the teeth. Bastard files are very harsh, and smooth files, as their name denotes, relatively smooth. Outside this normal range is the rough file, with extremely coarse teeth, and the dead-smooth file with very fine teeth indeed.

Rasps are files with exaggerated teeth which tear rather than file. They are used mostly on wood but can also be used effectively on softer metals such as lead, aluminium etc, where quick removal of material is required. The curved-tooth file is effective on aluminium and steel and is greatly used where these materials are part of a boat's construction.

Needless to say the smoothness or coarseness of the teeth is influenced by the length of the file; there is a difference between the same type of file in six-inch and twelve-inch lengths.

Filing

There are three basic methods of filing; *straight filing,* which is the most common, and consists of pushing the file in single strokes lengthwise across the work and at right angles, or slightly diagonal to it. Since hand files are designed to cut only on the forward stroke, the file should be lifted off the work when making the back stroke. The strokes should be made along the length of the object and parallel to it.

The second method is known as *draw filing,* and in this case both forward and back strokes are used to file. The hands should be fairly close together if the object being filed is relatively narrow, to prevent breaking the file as pressure must be exerted in working it forwards and backwards. For finishing, the forward stroke should be used more than the back stroke, for the latter tends to bite deeper into the material.

The third method is known as *lathe filing,* and this is the use of a file in conjunction with a lathe. The lathe turns the material and the file is touched against it as required.

Files should be cared for like any other tools if the best is to be expected from them. They tend to get clogged and frequent cleaning is necessary, usually by drawing a light wire brush or stiff nylon bristle along the lines of the teeth. An oily rag will help to prevent rust attacking the teeth, but has a tendency to cause slipping if put on too heavily. Patent spray cleaners are good, they evaporate and do not leave an oily slick on the teeth. Hanging a file is a good way of storing it without likelihood of damage to the teeth.

BENCH GRINDERS

The bench grinder comes in useful in a hundred ways; not only for the workshop, but for the kitchen, garage, and even garden shed. Something always needs sharpening somewhere, and for this reason a relatively low-cost bench grinder is a must. Over and above sharpening tools, this handy gadget can be adapted for several uses by changing the abrasive wheel with wire or felt pads.

As with so many tools, a version of the bench grinder can be achieved by fitting accessories to a standard power drill, but since

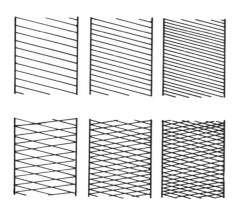

Single and double cut files

it is a relatively cheap piece of equipment, and will come in for such varied use, it is as well to obtain the real machine and not play around with half-hearted adaptations which, in the long run, can be unsatisfactory and even dangerous.

It is the material in the grinding wheel that sharpens the tools, and thus a variety of wheels can be obtained, both in quality and content, and also in shape. Most wheels for tool sharpening are of silicone carbide or aluminium oxide bonded together with shellac. The silicone carbide wheels are for materials of relatively low tensile strength, such as cast iron, brass, copper, aluminium, and so on. Aluminium oxide wheels are used for grinding materials of high tensile strength such as carbon steels, malleable iron, wrought iron, and tungsten.

Grinding wheels are also graded according to softness or hardness. Soft wheels should be operated at slow speeds, and hard or medium-hard wheels at high speeds. Safety markings on the side of the wheel indicate maximum operating speed, and for this reason the wheel recommended by the manufacturer of the machine should be used wherever possible.

Safety first is essential when using a grinding tool for sparks can easily fly around the room. Although they are small and unlikely to start a fire unless they land in gasoline or some other inflammable substance, they can easily blind a person if they fly up into the eye. Many bench grinders have safety shields, but in any case wearing goggles is a wise precaution.

The tool to be sharpened should be held firmly but lightly on the tool rest and moved evenly on to the stone. It should be aligned so that its edge touches the surface of the stone evenly, or an irregular edge on the tool will result, as well as some strain on the axle of the grinder. With round tools such as a punch, the edge to be sharpened should be twirled quickly and evenly on the stone until the right point is achieved.

The stone can become clogged after a while, particularly if the wrong types of metals are sharpened on it. Incorrect speeds can also cause clogging, as can other common substances such as grease. In the average amateur's workshop there is often much grease or dirt around, and these will add to the problems of the grinder unless it is covered and used only for the correct materials. When grinding tempered blades such as that of a plane, the blade should be dipped in water at intervals to prevent it from heating and thus losing the temper in the steel. The most suitable grinding angle for tools of this nature is about 25 degrees. The cutting angle can then be added by means of the oilstone.

DRILLS

The Hand Drill is a tool with which the boat owner will become very familiar if he has not already done so. The more sophisticated electric drills are, of course, more efficient and labour saving, but because few boats have full electrical power by which to operate the drills, there is many an occasion when the old hand drill is dragged out from the toolbox.

The use of the hand drill is simple, and the range of bits much the same as for electric drills. When boring a hole, the drill must be held firmly to prevent "wandering" caused by the turning action of the handle. Other than this it is used in all ways like any other drill.

The Electric Drill allows for more efficient, easier work in half the time, but requires the correct voltage to do so. These drills are available in all shapes and sizes and with variable speeds for different types of drilling. They require little in the way of maintenance other than an occasional touch of oil in the lubricating glands, and, when fitted with one or other of the many attachments, can provide almost a complete portable workshop in the one tool.

Safety first is important in the use of electrical tools, and never does this apply more than when working on board a boat, whether alongside the wharf or marina, or up on the dry of the slipway. Care with electrical connections and leads is of primary importance if serious accidents are to be avoided.

The use of an electric drill needs little in the way of explanation. The correct bit for the screw or bolt should be selected and inserted in the chuck, tightening the latter with a chuck key.

The correct bit is important, not only in terms of size but also in terms of manufacture. Timber bits are not satisfactory for metal work and vice versa. Masonry bits are not suitable for either. The question of matching bits and fastenings is answered in the section on fastenings.

An electric drill, whether held in the hand or in a press, should be used with gentle but firm pressure. A steady hand is required to make the hole neat and accurate as it is very easy, particularly under difficult conditions, to allow the bit to wander. Too much wavering will cause the hole to enlarge beyond the scope of the screw and a larger screw will have to be used in order to get it to "bite".

For drilling metal, a drill press is almost

Although hand drills are necessary under many circumstances (see background), the electric power drill eliminates much of the hard work in drilling

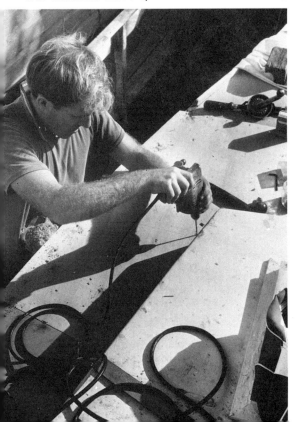

essential to prevent the hole being enlarged —or the drill broken—because of wandering. A punch should be used to "start" the bit and prevent wandering when drilling begins.

Among the minimum requirements of a well-equipped workshop are the following tools. Their use is well known to most handymen and a detailed description is not necessary here.

Screwdrivers

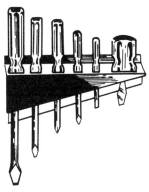

The use of the correct screwdriver for every job ensures easy and accurate fastening

The secret of easy and accurate screwing is to fit the correct screwdriver to the correct screw. Screwdriver blades which are too narrow or thin tend to break away the edges of the screws, particularly those made of softer alloys. Those which are too thick or rounded off so that they do not fit into the screw snugly make the job of driving the screw very difficult and also damage the head of the screw. The diagram illustrates correct and incorrect fitting of screwdriver to screw.

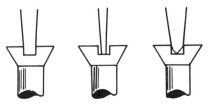

The blade of the screwdriver must fit the slot in the screw head (left). Difficult and irregular screwing will result from too fine a screwdriver (centre) or too thick a blade (right)

39

Chisels

There are several different sizes and varieties of chisels; the main difference is in the width and thickness of the blade. Two basic forms of chisel are of use in marine work and these are the *firmer* or flat blade, and the *scriber gouge,* whose blade is of concave section to allow grooving of timber. The correct maintenance of chisels revolves mostly around the sharpness of the blade, and this should be sharpened carefully on either a grinder—if the edge is pitted or scored—or an oilstone if the edge is blunt. The use of a bench grinder is dealt with in an earlier part of this section.

Cross sections of Firmer chisel (left) and Scriber gouge (right)

Oilstones

Invaluable to any workshop where tools need to be sharpened, the oilstone comes in a number of shapes and sizes. The most common is the flat stone, which is of a convenient size to be portable. Sharpening the tool is done by placing the cutting edge at an angle about five degrees greater than that used for grinding.

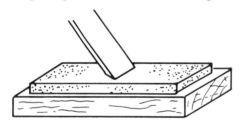

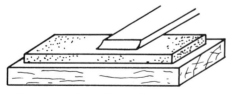

The blade must be held at the correct angle and stroked easily across the oilstone (top). The burr is removed by turning the blade flat on its other side (below)

Neatsfoot oil is used as a lubricant during the sharpening of the tool. The "roughage", "burr" or "wire edge" formed as a result of sharpening can be removed by turning over the blade and rubbing it flat on the stone.

To prevent wear of the stone in one spot it should be used over its entire surface and any accumulation of dirt or grease cleaned off at regular intervals with kerosene.

Hammers and Mallets

No workshop should be without hammers—at least two types—and wooden mallets. A ball hammer and a Warrington hammer are basic requirements, and a claw hammer is handy. Hammers are for driving nails and other metal work. Mallets, with their wooden heads, are for driving chisels.

A rubber mallet has many uses in the workshop, particularly where aluminium is concerned

Hammer and mallet heads tend to become loose with work, and a small wedge driven home into a split in the top of the handle should tighten them.

Brace and Bit

Where larger holes have to be drilled, such as through large baulks of timber, a brace and bit is the correct tool. A set of bits will give a useful range in sizes.

Pincers, Pliers, etc.

So widely used are these items that little can be said about them other than that they are absolutely essential. For cutting wire strands, drawing nails (with support pad

40

underneath) closing split pins—the use of these tools is too wide to cover in a basic volume such as this.

G-Clamps

These clamps are essential in every marine workshop where work of any size is to be undertaken. Even for small gluing jobs, G-clamps have their uses, but they are indispensable when it comes to bending timber, fitting frames, etc. G-clamps come in a range of sizes according to the work they are required to do.

G-clamps are essential for holding together timber sections to be glued or screwed

Spokeshave

This is a kind of plane used for curved surfaces. There are two basic forms: flat-faced, for finishing external curves; and round-faced, for internal curves. Spokeshaves should always be used with the grain. Curves that are too acute or too small to be worked with a spokeshave should be treated with a file, chisel, or gouge, and finished with sandpaper.

Abrasives

A multitude of abrasives is available for finishing work, and the choice of any particular grade or surface depends on the work to be done. Basically there are two forms of abrasive—"dry" and "wet and dry".

"Dry" abrasive paper may be of many surfaces including glass, emery, garnet, etc. "Wet and dry" paper is bonded on a material which can be used in water. This abrasive is ideal for many types of work in the marine field, and is used widely in finishing paint and varnish work, rubbing off anti-fouling, and so on.

"Dry" abrasive is used mainly on raw timber. An extra finish can often be obtained on some timbers by damping the wood to raise the grain before using the abrasive paper.

Of the dry abrasives, emery paper is used principally on metal and glass paper on timber. Garnet paper is similar to glass paper, but has less tendency to blunt with use and thus has a much longer life.

CHAPTER THREE

Fastenings

BECAUSE OF THE CONDITIONS under which they operate, boats are subject to many forms of deterioration. For this reason both the materials used in construction of the vessel and the fastenings holding these materials together must be carefully chosen.

Chapter 1 described the types of materials used and the forms of deterioration to which they are subject. The question of using the correct fastenings is of equal importance since deterioration of the fastenings results in deterioration of the vessel as a whole.

The principal fastenings are of metal and as such are particularly vulnerable to corrosion. Careful choice of the right metal is necessary when fastening sections of a boat together if the repaired section is not to fall apart after a few trips to sea. The metals in general use, their characteristics and methods of use, are described in this chapter.

BRONZE AND BRASS

Because of their resistance to rust, bronze and brass are very popular for boat fastenings. They are both made of the same components —copper, tin and zinc. The quantities of these components vary in each case; bronze has a very small amount of zinc. Phosphor bronze, the most popular of all alloys for fastenings, has a small percentage of phosphorus, and a combination of copper and tin. Brass, at the other end of the scale, has little or no tin, but is a fusion of copper and zinc in the ratio of roughly 7:3.

Between these two widely-used alloys are other alloys which combine the three basic components in different ratios to provide different strengths and machinability. In addition, the alloys may be combined with other components to provide a further range of materials —an important instance is manganese bronze, which is very popular for heavy castings.

Phosphor bronze is the most suitable for marine work. Brass is also suitable, but tends to become brittle and deteriorate through galvanic action, particularly when in contact with saltwater. For this reason it should be used in conjunction with glues if fastening any section of the vessel which will bear structural strength.

COPPER

Copper is very soft, and is usually combined with other metals which harden. Bronze and brass, mentioned earlier, are typical examples. However, copper has its uses as a fastener in the form of copper nails which for years have been the small-boat method of fastening planking either by roving or clinching the nail. This is a good method where two planks must be drawn together, as in clinker planking, although the lasting qualities and the tensile strength of the metal is not good, and severe strain on any one fastening can cause it to weaken.

MONEL

Monel is perhaps the ideal fastening medium for boats. Unfortunately it is also very expensive. It is without peer as a fastening screw in underwater or exposed areas where other metals are liable to eletrolytic action and corrosion and is an attractive and corrosion-resistant fastening for interior fittings where countersinking or stopping is not practicable.

Monel nails are often made in the patent

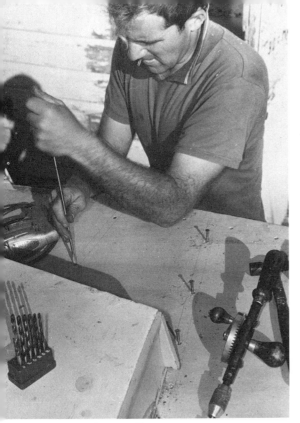

Use of matching drills and fastenings ensures an accurate and neat join

the ravages of saltwater, but they are always suspect. There are few places where, over a period of time, the saltwater will not penetrate, even through epoxy coverings and anti-corrosive treatment.

STAINLESS STEEL

Like monel, stainless steel comes close to the perfect form of fastening for marine work because of its high resistance to corrosion. Although there are many forms of stainless steel, and the correct type must be chosen for marine work, basically stainless steel is an alloy of steel containing chromium and nickel.

Its popularity in the marine field increases daily. It is used widely as fastenings, and also as fittings of all shapes and sizes. Because of its resistance to corrosion it need not be painted and retains its brightness even in contact with saltwater.

The popular forms of stainless steel fastenings are bolts and screws. Keel bolts are frequently made of stainless steel since they are somewhat vulnerable in their position beneath the waterline. Stainless steel fastenings are good for use in any location, particularly where the presence of saltwater or air prevents the use of brass fastenings.

Large vessels require large fastenings, such as this bolt for use in a 12 metre yacht. Photo courtesy Power Boat & Yachting

"anchor" form, in which a series of serrations on the shank of the nail give it an extra grip on the timber. These are good for small work where screwing is not practicable, as they can be driven home with a hammer, yet have the holding power of a screw.

GALVANISED IRON

The strength and versatility of galvanised iron makes it an ideal fastening material for boats. Unfortunately its tendency to rust heavily in the presence of saltwater somewhat nullifies this usefulness. Galvanising prevents rusting, but the zinc coating of the galvanising process is apt to be easily damaged when driving a screw or bolt into position. For this reason galvanised fastenings are confined to areas where saltwater cannot attack them. Since this is almost an impossibility on a sea-going vessel, the use of galvanised fastenings is diminishing.

Galvanised iron screws, when countersunk and covered with an epoxy filler, may escape

Stainless steel has only one weakness; it can become work hardened and brittle if subjected to fatigue strains. However, in the form of fastenings, the metal is rarely subjected to such strains to the extent that failure may occur. Although expensive, stainless steel fastenings more than repay their initial cost.

NAILS AND NAILING

Nails are not used very extensively in marine work other than in the way described for copper nails. However, some interior work requires nailing, particularly in furniture and associated work.

There are different forms of nails for this work, and they are made of different metals. Each metal is designed for a specific use, as also is the shape of the nail.

Basically the design varies mainly in the shape of the head. Although the shank may be round, oval, hexagonal, or "barbed", the shape of the head has more effect on its use. The principal types of nails are:

JOLT HEAD: The common or garden wire nail, used in marine work when galvanised.

FLAT HEAD: May be in copper, monel, stainless or galvanised steel. This nail is the most widely used for marine work.

ROUND HEAD: Usually small nails with decorative rounded heads used for beading or similar interior work.

SPRING HEAD: Rarely seen in marine work. It is used more for house construction.

Nails can be fastened in four ways. The correct method is important if the most satisfactory result is to be obtained.

PARALLEL NAILING: Where the nails are driven in parallel to one another and vertical to the surface of the timber.

STAGGERED NAILING: Where the nails are driven alternatively in parallel rows: the main purpose is to prevent splitting.

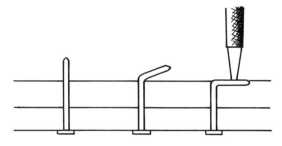

Clenched nailing. A punch is used to drive the clenched nail flush with the wood surface

CLENCHED NAILING: The nail is driven through the timber and the point turned over by means of an anvil or nail punch, and driven back into the timber. This is a popular method for boat building.

ROVE NAILING: Where the point of the nail is "capped" on the other side of the timber with a washer, or rove, and then the nail hammered back over the rove to form a rivet. This is also used widely in boat building (see later in this chapter), particularly for lap strake or clinker work. Copper nails and roves are used almost exclusively.

Nails should be driven home firmly with the square face of the hammer, after starting them with a few light taps.

Countersinking can be achieved either by using the ball point of the hammer (but with care to prevent marking of surrounding timber), or—preferably—with a nail punch to drive the head into the timber.

Splitting can be prevented in some cases by blunting the point of the nail before driving it home. In other cases a hole of the same size as the shank of the nail can be made with a drill or a bradawl.

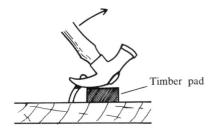

A small block of waste wood gives better leverage for drawing the nail and prevents damage to the timber surface

Extracting nails with either a claw hammer or pincers requires the use of a "pad" if damage to the timber is to be avoided. Any piece of scrap timber of the right thickness can be used for this job.

Roving Copper Nails (Rivets)

This is the best method of fastening with copper nails and its only disadvantage, in relation to clenching, is the time taken and the need for two workmen. But in all other respects it is superior to clenching, particularly where planking is concerned. The procedure for roving copper nails is as follows:

The hole is bored out slightly smaller than the square width of the nail, to avoid any likelihood of splitting the timber. The holes are staggered so that they do not coincide in the same grain, for the same reason. A split along the grain is the bane of a boat-builder's existence.

Roving copper nails: The rove is driven over the nail which is then cut off and riveted back over the rove

The nails are driven in from the outside of the hull and an assistant is stationed to hold a hammer against the head once it is driven home. The copper rove is fitted over the nail on the inside and driven down its length by using a special punch. The concave side of the rove buries itself in the timber and gives an additional grip to the fastening.

At this point the nail is cut off to within about one-eighth inch of the rove and then hammered with a ball head hammer, using light tapping strokes, until the nail spreads outwards and down on to the rove. To finish it off a few severe strokes with a flat hammer will ensure a good fastening and a firm grip and will draw the fastening tight. All this is done with the assistant holding his hammer against the head of the nail. This form of fastening is known as riveting.

SCREWS AND SCREWING

As with nails, the variety of screws—apart from the metal in their construction—depends principally on the shape of the head. Screws, in fact, are used in much the same way as nails, with the added strength and gripping power that comes from the thread on the shank.

COUNTERSUNK: The head is tapered on the shank side and flat on the top, allowing it to be recessed into the timber to make a flush surface, or completely sunk into the timber and covered with a dowel plug or stopper. This type of screw is used for almost all forms of marine work.

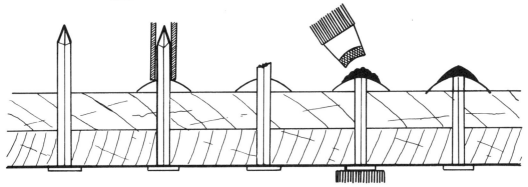

ROUNDHEAD: In this type the head is convex and sticks up above the surface of the timber when the screw has been driven home. Used principally for ornamental work and securing metal strips to timber where countersinking is not practicable.

COACH SCREWS: The head of this screw is hexagonal and a spanner is used to drive it home instead of the usual screwdriver. Usually made only in large "bolt" sizes, and usually of black steel, these screws are confined in marine work to securing large baulks of timber where through bolting is not practical.

The secret of successful screw fastening is the use of the correct bit for the screw. A bit too large will make a hole in which the screw cannot grip, whereas a bit too small will make the work of the screw hard and either split the wood or break the screw if it is of soft metal. Bits are marketed in sizes to suit the grades of screws, and a set of matched bits is good insurance against a lot of wasted time and labour when a big screwing job is on hand.

Countersinking is done with a special countersinking bit, after the hole for the screw has been drilled. The countersinking may merely hollow the surface to flush the head of the screw with the timber, or may be driven down the drill hole in order to countersink the head of the screw beneath the level of the timber. The resultant hole can then be plugged with a stopper, or a wood dowel if the best finish is required. The dowel should be glued into place and flushed off with a plane and sandpaper. The stopper is simply pressed flush with a knife and then sanded down to a good finish.

Joining two pieces of timber with screws is best achieved by drilling out the first piece to the gauge of the screw as described earlier. The second piece of timber should be drilled with a much smaller bit to give the tip of the screw a better "bite". If the second piece of timber is softwood, only a small hole is necessary (even a bradawl can be used), but if hardwood, a bit only a little smaller than the size of the screw should be used.

Metals used in the manufacture of screws vary widely. In marine work, galvanised steel, brass, stainless steel and monel are the most

Drilling procedure in softwood (top) and hardwood (bottom.) The bit matching the fastening is used in the top piece of timber (left), countersunk (centre), and a smaller bit used to "start" the screw in the second timber

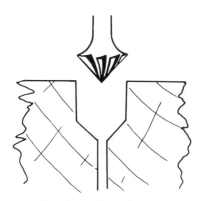

A countersinking bit widens the original drill hole to allow the head of the screw to be sunk below the surface of the timber and covered with a dowel or putty

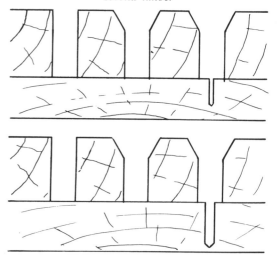

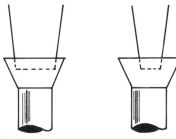

Screwdriver blades which do not fit the full width of the screw head (left) will tend to burr the slot and make screwing difficult

widely used. Brass screws may not be used below the waterline because of their tendency to disintegrate owing to electrolytic corrosion. Indeed, in using screws to fasten any part of a boat, and particularly in securing fittings in place, due thought must be given to the type of metal in both screws and fittings, and the possible effects of corrosion and rust.

BOLTS

Bolts for fastening sections of a boat together are normally used on the heavier parts, such as the major structural members and the keel. They may be of different metals; probably the most popular are bronze and stainless steel.

Monel, nylon and iron are also used in the manufacture of bolts for boat building,

A typical range of fastenings used in boat work: (From left) washer, countersunk bolt, anchor nail, screw, roundhead bolt, copper tack, copper nail, copper rove

although these have some drawbacks, either in terms of strength, corrosion or cost. Whatever the material used, however, it is important to bear in mind that different metals will react electrolytically, and as far as possible only one metal fastening should be used, particularly where it may be in contact with salt water.

When driven through the keel, or any other external member, the question of water tightness arises. The bolt hole should be drilled slightly smaller than the bolt, although not too small or the timber may split. The bolt should be set in white lead or some similar caulking material and driven home firmly. A washer should be fitted beneath the nut, and a felt or leather washer placed against the timber if there is any possibility of leaking. The bolt must be screwed up very tightly.

ALUMINIUM RIVETS AND RIVETING

The joining of aluminium plates is usually done by cold riveting. Welding can also be employed, but aluminium welding requires different techniques and equipment from the usual steel welding, and this is somewhat outside the scope of amateur work.

Where the riveting is required to be watertight—and this is usually the case in marine repair work—some care must be taken in preparing the two surfaces to be joined. The holes must be drilled for exactly the right size of rivet, and where there is any irregularity or looseness, the larger size of rivet should be employed. The holes after drilling should be

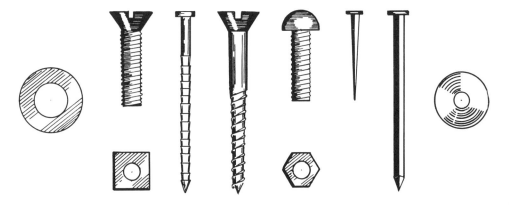

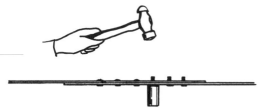

Riveting aluminium sheets is done with normal ball-head hammer, and cold rivets

checked for roughness of edges and filed out where necessary.

To assist in making the rivet watertight, the point should be turned back into a countersunk hole; thus the holes will have to be slightly recessed on the inside to allow for this countersinking. The holes should be not less than two diameters from the edge of the plates, and the holes themselves should be spaced at about three diameters. The diameter of rivets should be as thick as, or thicker than, the thickest point to be joined.

The rivets should be dipped in zinc chromate before they are inserted into the hole, and a layer of epoxy resin or similar filler placed between the plates to ensure a good seal. A flat anvil head is then placed against the head of the rivet and the rivet closed up with a hand hammer so that it is turned back and countersunk in the concave surrounds of the rivet hole. Some practice will be required before a tight, smooth riveting job can be achieved.

GLUES AND GLUING

"Marine glue" is probably one of the most confusing terms used in boat building and repair work. It is confusing mainly because it covers a multitude of materials, from waterproof adhesives to the pitch-like substance used for paving caulked decks. For this section, however, the term will refer to the adhesive glues used for bonding together two different sections of timber.

The term "adhesives" has different meanings, for glues, like so many boat-building materials,

have been developed as the boat-building techniques have advanced. The adhesives used for most marine work these days fall into two main categories: the synthetic resin compounds such as urea formaldehyde, resorcinol formaldehyde and phenol formaldehyde; and the epoxy group of compounds.

The formaldehyde group seems to be gaining more popularity with the marine industry, and of these urea formaldehyde is the most commonly used. The resorcinol and phenol resins are reputed to be stronger, but are more expensive, therefore the amount of glue to be used may have a bearing on the final choice.

These glues are good for all boat-building work, and in particular for plywood construction or repair, and for lamination. Because of the many brands on the market, it is not possible to list each and every one and their uses. However, all manufacturers issue detailed instructions with their products, it is important to study and follow the instructions thoroughly when using the glue.

Generally speaking, glues of good quality are designed to create a bond stronger than the material it bonds. This is a somewhat sweeping claim, but it is sufficient to know that providing they are used properly and according to instructions, most modern glues will provide a more than adequate bond. Although "gluing and screwing" is a popular method in marine work, quite often the purpose of the screws is more to hold the parts together until the glue sets than to add a great deal of strength to the bond.

Some glues are cured by heat, or at least the curing process can be speeded by heat. This is quite in order although care must be taken with any method used to speed gluing that the process does not damage or warp the timber to be bonded. This is particularly the case where a laminated section is to be made up.

Many modern glues have the added advantage of gap-filling. This is obviously useful in repair work where fitting of a new piece or joining of new timber to old may make a watertight join difficult. With the glue filling the cracks, any small errors of fitting can be overcome quite easily and leaks and uneven cracks avoided.

Most of the synthetic resin glues are supplied in two-part packs. The resin is in liquid form and the hardener may be either powder or liquid. The two must be mixed carefully, particularly if the whole pack is not used in the one mixing. To divide the products requires careful weighing (in the case of powder) or measuring (in the case of liquid) as the effectiveness of the glue depends on the correct balance between the two components. Details of the proportion of hardener to resin will be included with the pack.

Once mixed, the glue must be used immediately, hence the need sometimes to divide the quantities and not mix the whole pack. Reducing the temperature can slow the curing process, so the glues will keep longer if placed in a refrigerator. However, the maximum pot-life of a mixed resin glue is usually only about twelve hours, even when kept under reduced temperature.

Conversely, the curing of the glue can be speeded by heat, and although this may be an advantage, particularly where gluing is done under cool or cold conditions, it is a distinct disadvantage when the work is undertaken in the tropics or some similar high-temperature areas. A temperature of 90 degrees F can cut the pot-life of the glue down to as little as half an hour; thus the work will have to be speeded up considerably, or the glue kept in the refrigerator between applications. This makes for difficult working conditions either way.

The application of the glue will vary according to manufacture, but in general the following instructions apply:

The surfaces must be free from all dirt, grease, oil or dust. Petrol or trichloroethylene should be used to clean the faces of the timber, particularly if it is of an oily nature, such as teak. The moisture content of the timber should be between 10 per cent and 12 per

A thin, even layer of glue can be achieved on large surface areas by use of a squeegee

cent, or as near to that zine as possible, and the surfaces should not be too smooth, for the glue requires some roughage on which to obtain a key.

Both faces of timber should be coated with the glue and a short period of time allowed to elapse before they are brought together. This lets the glue penetrate the timber and make for a better bond, before pressure

Gluing is used extensively in timber boats where its strength and waterproof qualities are often tested to the full

squeezes it out. The clamps or screws should then be put into place, and the glued section tightened up under pressure so that the two faces are bonded with as little gap as possible. The curing time will depend on the individual glue and the temperature. Generally speaking, it is not advisable to use resin glues at temperatures below 60 degrees F.

Both the amount of pressure and the temperature of curing should be moderate. If too much pressure is applied, the glue will be squeezed out and will not make a good bond. If an extreme of temperature is used the best bonding effect will not be obtained from the glue. Most glues are designed to cure at room temperature, although a higher temperature is always preferable to a lower.

To ensure a first class bond, the timbers should be left clamped even after the prescribed curing time. Where strain is liable to come on the timber, such as when laminating, the clamps or moulds should not be removed for some days, even a week, in order to hold the timber faces in close contact without strain until the glue reaches its maximum strength.

Although, as mentioned at the beginning of this section, there is a variety of glues available for marine work, care must be taken in selecting a glue of good quality. The type of glue required for marine repair work must be resistant to rot, water (both hot, cold and salt), weather and solvents. Unless it fulfils these requirements, the chances are it will not stand up to the stresses placed upon it when the boat is working in a seaway.

SOLDERING

One of the simplest and probably one of the most used methods of joining metals is soldering. Although restricted to the joining of relatively small pieces of metal, soldering is so simple and requires so few tools that most handymen find a use for it when fitting out.

For the boat owner it is a boon, since there are a hundred and one small jobs on board a

Maintenance of yachts of this calibre require a good working knowledge of tools, materials and their uses

boat which require the use of solder—electrical wiring, fuel lines, tanks are but a few. Although of less use in major jobs, this useful technique is so simple that few well-fitted workshops would not be equipped without soldering gear.

A soldering iron and the solder itself are basically all that is needed. The iron may be of the standard copperhead type which is heated over a gas or spirit flame, or, if mains power is available, electrically heated. The latter is preferable, as the work need not be constantly interrupted to re-heat the iron.

These are the basic requirements, but in order to do the job well, a few extra items are required. These, as a rule, are part of any well-fitted workshop and need not be kept solely for soldering.

Other tools are: a coarse, flat file, abrasive paper, soldering flux and a piece of metal for "tinning". If the iron is not of the electric type, a means of heating will be necessary, and this can range from a simple spirit lamp to a gas jet, blowlamp or fire. In fact, almost any means of heating the iron quickly are adequate.

Before use, a new iron must be "tinned".

Indeed, it is a wise procedure to tin the iron before each use if the best results are to be achieved. Tinning is the process of covering the point of the iron with a thin layer of solder. This has the two-fold effect of preventing oxidisation of the copper, which would interfere with the transference of heat from iron to solder, and also of giving a good surface on the iron to which new solder can take.

The iron should be heated to a moderate heat. Excessive heat will spoil all soldering work and any sign of the iron getting red hot will mean allowing it to cool, and re-tinning. Once heated, the iron should be placed in a vice and the tip of the copper bit filed back to smooth bright metal. Initially this should be done with a file, but for later tinning rubbing the tip on a coarse abrasive may be sufficient.

With the iron still hot, the tip should be dipped or rolled in a special soldering flux, and then covered with solder from a coil or block of the material. Some solders are made with a core of flux, others are pure solder and the use of flux from a tin is necessary.

While the solder is still runny, the bit of the iron is rubbed up and down on a piece of metal to spread the solder all around the tip and ensure a good, even coverage. A wipe off with a rag will complete the job, by which time the tip of the bit should have a shiny, even coat of solder. It is now ready for use.

The use of flux in soldering will depend to a great extent on the type of metal to be soldered. Flux assists in the "taking" of the solder to the metals, and cleans the surfaces at the same time. Although flux can be made by dissolving zinc in muriatic acid, this is a smelly and dangerous job and it is far better to purchase the flux under one of the proprietary brand names.

As with many forms of work, the secret of successful soldering lies in the preparatory work before the iron is even heated. Thorough cleaning of both surfaces to be joined is essential if a good join is to be made. Any skimping at this stage, particularly regarding grease or dirt which may be embedded in the metal, will result in the soldered joint falling apart.

A piece of abrasive (emery) cloth must be used to produce a bright, clean surface. Flux is applied immediately to this surface, and the metal is ready for soldering. The iron should be heated and then wiped quickly on a rag to remove any surface dirt.

With the tip of the hot iron and the solder applied together to the metal, a run of solder on to the surfaces will be achieved. When sufficient solder has been placed on the join, the solder stick can be removed and the iron worked back and forth across the surface. This has the double effect of spreading the solder over the surfaces to be joined and also heating

Tinning the soldering iron

1. Iron heated in intense flame.

2. Point filed back to clean metal.

3. Point rolled in flux and solder.

the metal to condition it for the solder. When the join appears to be well set, the iron can be taken away and the join left to cool. In a matter of seconds, the solder will set, but the join should be left clamped for a few minutes to allow the metal to cool completely.

Needless to say, holding the join firmly in position during the operation is important. A vice is best although not always practical where soldering is done on location, such as with wiring or plumbing jobs. But to obtain a firm join, both sides of the soldered area must be firmly gripped until the job has been completed and the solder set.

If the finished job looks a little rough it can be easily filed or sanded back. It is better to overload the join with solder and file off the surplus than skimp the solder in an effort to produce a neat finish with the iron. At the same time the iron must be kept at a constant heat or, as it cools, it will tend to ruffle up the solder and weaken the joint.

There are many adaptations of the soldered join, and imagination is all that is required when any particular job is approached. Where clamping is difficult, the two ends to be joined can be pre-coated with solder and then brought together and heated with a blowlamp or soldering iron, when they will fuse together. Two ends of wire, cleaned and treated with flux, can be dipped into a pot of molten solder to join them together, although the join may need some trimming later.

As a means of making small joins solder is without equal, but, as with all handyman work, care and good preparation are essential if the finished job is to be a success.

ARC WELDING

Since it is the most common in marine work, arc welding will be dealt with here. Other methods, using gas, are equally successful but require more sophisticated equipment.

The electrode should be of the same composition as the metal to be welded. A "general use" electrode should be chosen which can be used in many different positions, rather than one which requires a special welding angle.

The size of the electrode is controlled by the thickness of the sheet to be welded; the table given in the instruction book should be followed when ordering electrodes.

The current used for welding can be set on the welder itself, and is controlled by the size of electrode used. Excessive current will cause overheating and spattering of the weld. Too little current will make the welding difficult as the arc will be hard to strike and hold and the weld will tend to "bead". The correct current for the electrode in use will be listed in the book of instructions.

The arc is started—once the electrode has been fitted into the handle—by tapping at the surface of the metal with a slight scratching action. The scratching clears away any dirt and makes a suitable contact point for the arc,

A high degree of skill is required to weld up intricate structural work like this aluminium hull framework

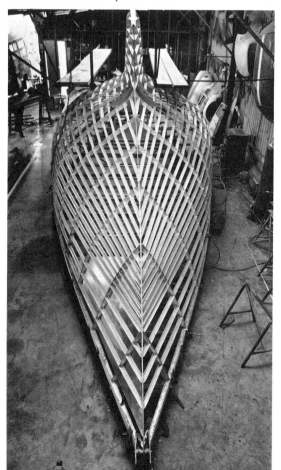

and the tapping action prevents the electrode from sticking to the weld immediately the arc fires.

The metal to be welded must be cleaned off with a wire brush if a suitable contact is to be made. Although paint and similar surfaces do not interfere too badly with the welding once it is well under way, starting the arc on a painted surface may be impossible. The bare metal must be brought to the surface at the point of contact.

The shield must always be used in welding. Indeed, all normal safety precautions should be taken when using electrical equipment; in addition, the shield protects the eyes from the high concentration of infra-red rays, as well as from the intense light. Protection is also given to face and eyes in the event of a splutter causing splattering of the molten particles of the weld.

The weld should be made as evenly as possible with the flow of the electrode metal forming an even, level surface wherever possible. Only practice can achieve good results in welding as even the use of a strange welder

Common weld joints

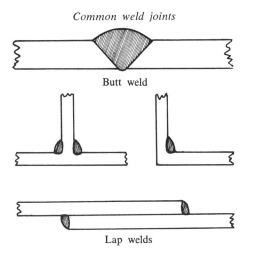

Butt weld

Lap welds

can upset the performance of a normally good workman.

Types of Weld Joints

1. *The Butt Weld*

In this type the ends of two plates or beams are joined literally end-to-end by means of a single "seam" weld between them. There are two systems used; the square butt end and the "vee" butt end.

The square butt end uses the plates in their original condition, where a gap of approximately half the width of the plates is left, and the weld used to fill this gap. The weld must be done on both sides, or a backing piece used and left in position after the weld is finished. This type is successful with plates up to about one-quarter inch thick.

Over this thickness, the vee-butt join is used, where the edges of the plates are tapered inwards to a gap between them at the rear edges somewhere around one-twelfth inch wide. The weld fills the tapering seam between the edges of the plates to achieve much the same effect as splining with timber seams.

2. *Lap Joint Welds*

The welding of overlapping plates or joints similar to lap joints in timber joinery (see Section IV) require more of a bonding joint than a filling joint.

3. *Fillet Welds*

This is a filling or corner weld such as might be used for joining the edges of two plates at right angles to each other. Apart from careful cleaning, alignment and securing of the plates during welding, the actual system does not differ from the butt joint system mentioned earlier. Several layers of weld may be used to strengthen the join.

CHAPTER FOUR

Paints and Painting

GENERAL TIPS ON PAINTING

AS A GENERAL RULE, if something goes wrong with paintwork it is the fault of the painter rather than the paint. Providing the paint is of good quality and not some superseded grade that has spent a few summers on a shelf somewhere, and providing it is mixed correctly with the right thinners, there should be no problem with the paint itself. However, the application is so fraught with hazards that often even a high quality paint suddenly flakes or crazes only a few days later. Somewhere between the preparation of the surface, the opening of the can, and the drying of the newly applied coat, something has been done incorrectly. The disheartening results cannot be brought on to the head of the paint manufacturer.

The art of painting does not start with the opening of the can. It starts when the first scraper or sandpaper is taken out of the box and the preparatory work begun. In fact, by the time the paintbrush comes into operation, much of the secret of a good (or bad) paint finish has already been decided. The basic groundwork of preparation of the surface before application of the paint can make or mar the final finish.

For this reason, a great deal of attention is paid in this section to the preparation of surfaces to be painted. No matter what the material—timber, steel or fibreglass—the final finish will depend on how much thought and care is put into this preparation.

The section on varnishing new timber is a good example of this. Here is a long and arduous rubbing down of the timber surface; the varnish is thinned considerably for the early coats to ensure that it seeps right into the timber; and then, as the coats are painstakingly built up, the thinning is reduced gradually until the final coats are of pure varnish. Only after this time and trouble has been taken will varnished work come up with the beautiful, warm mirror-surface that so enhances the topsides, the coachwork, or the interior of a boat.

Each section of this chapter deals with the individual preparation of the surface for painting, depending on the base material in use. At this point it is worth taking a look at some of the general rules that apply to painting marine work; rules which the painter should have firmly in mind before starting any sort of a paint job.

CAUSES OF FAULTY PAINTWORK

It is as well to be able to spot areas where the present paintwork indicates a bad surface and treat these before approaching the job as a whole. In some cases no special attention is necessary and the general surface preparation will take care of individual spots, but sometimes special treatment is required and this must be done in advance, before the surface is prepared as a whole.

Blistering

There are several causes of blistering, but basically, they all are the result of some surface trouble beneath the skin of paint. A blister is the result of something pushing outwards through the base and building up pressure on the underside of the paint. Almost invariably it is a result of poor surface preparation when originally painted and it must be given correct treatment before any attempt is made to repaint the area.

Timber can give rise to blistering as a result of seepage of water under the paint skin, and this is perhaps the most common cause. Damp timber may allow the paint to seal over initially, but warmth or further dampness will build up a layer of water and cause separation of the paint skin from the timber. As pressure builds up this will form a blister, either full of water, if there is sufficient, or of moist air. Either has the effect of separating the paint skin from the timber.

Resin or gum oozing from the wood can have the same effect, as also can grease, dirt, or any other substance which prevents the paint skin getting a good grip on the timber. Once this separation occurs, almost anything can cause the loose paint skin to buckle or rise into a blister. Heat, too, can raise blisters on paint, although the heat of the sun is rarely enough to buckle the paint skin of its own accord and more often merely evaporates the damp timber under the paint, causing it to separate and bubble as the vapour expands.

Blistering does not always affect all coats of paint; it is not uncommon to find the blisters under the top coats only. This may be because either moisture was trapped between the layers of paint (i.e., the surface preparation

between coats was not good), or the bubble actually formed beneath the undercoats but gradually seeped through them until the tougher, more elastic top coat held it and formed a blister. Whatever the cause, the cure is relatively easy; the timber must be scraped back to bare wood and given time to dry out. If necessary a heater or blowlamp may be used to dry out the saturated fibres, but care must be taken to see that the flame does not lick any remaining paintwork and cause further blistering.

Once the wood has been scraped bare and thoroughly dried out the preparation as for new timber (see later in this section) can be begun. Now even more care will be required to ensure that the affected areas cannot again absorb any moisture, grease or dirt which may blister the new coats of paint.

Steel often gives rise to blisters when moisture is not completely removed from the plates before priming. Steel plates tend to "sweat", and unless they are thoroughly dried out before painting, the moisture trapped beneath the skins of paint will not only cause similar blistering to that described above for timber, but will also set up rust pockets, and this will bring even greater headaches (see section on rust and its treatment). Again, poor preparation is to blame, for the waterproof paints used on steel are designed to keep dampness from getting to the steel from the outside. They can do little to prevent rust if the water is already inside the skin.

Aluminium does not rust, although corrosion

(Top) Cross section of paint skin showing blistering due to moisture trapped between paint and surface. (Below) Water on the surface at the time of painting creates pockets where paint skin will not adhere

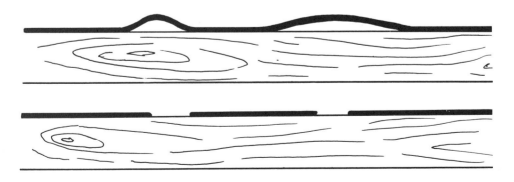

A first-class paint job is the result of hours of care and patience in preparing the surfaces both before painting and between successive coats. Photo courtesy Power Boat & Yachting

can set in and this can blister paintwork above it. Likewise, any moisture trapped beneath the layers of paint can evaporate and form a vapour bubble. However, very often the cause of blistering of paint on aluminium is the poor application of the self-etch primer on the aluminium itself. This primer is a basic adherent which gives the paint a surface to grip on the very smooth alloy. If it is not used, or is incorrectly used, then the paint will not adhere properly and blistering will result. In this case the paint will have to be stripped off and new self-etch primer used to touch up the areas giving trouble.

There are many other causes of blistering, some inherent to one type of vessel or one type of material. Those mentioned here are the more usual ones. However, it is worth remembering that all blistering problems have one common factor: invariably, they are the result of bad surface preparation, and the only cure lies in stripping back the affected areas and building them up again with due attention to the pre-

paration of the surface both before painting and between successive coats.

Peeling

Peeling can sometimes be blamed on the paint itself; it is a wise precaution when choosing marine paints to always buy a reputable brand from a dealer who will ensure that the stock is fresh. A few cents extra here can make many dollars' worth of difference, not only to the appearance of the boat, but to subsequent maintenance.

Peeling can also occur where conditions of dampness, dirt or grease exist, in much the same way as blistering. In fact, blistering is virtually peeling in small areas. Once again the old maxim of proper surface preparation holds good, particularly when the painting is to be done on the mooring, as the salt-laden air can very quickly lay an invisible but insidious film of salt moisture across a surface. There is nothing more guaranteed to cause peeling than salt moisture.

Peeling can also occur when the paint is applied to a surface with a high sheen. The paint is unable to get a firm grip on glossy surfaces unless they are rubbed back to a

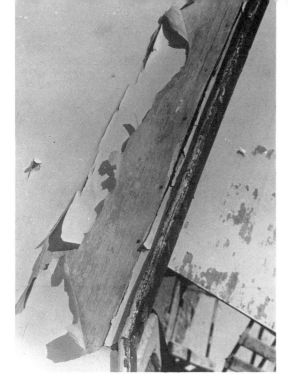

Peeling paintwork usually indicates bad surface preparation

Flaking is often the result of deteriorated paint either as a result of age or poor paint composition

matt—even with slight sandpaper scoring—to give a good "key" for the new paint to grip. This again comes under the heading of surface preparation, although it applies equally when a single touch-up coat is being applied, and not solely for work which is being built up with undercoats and primers. All paintwork to be repainted should be rubbed back with wet and dry sandpaper and thoroughly cleaned off before the new coat is applied.

Flaking

Flaking is usually the result of paint which has aged and become brittle. Blistering and peeling are conditions existing under the paint, whereas flaking is the falling away of the paint. Only one cure is successful for flaking, and that is a complete strip-down to bare timber. If the paintwork is maintained correctly, flaking should never occur, or if it does, then only after many many coats of paint have built up on the surface. It is a common problem, however, when refitting old or neglected boats, and as a rule, although the flaking may be confined to certain areas, the paint has aged

and the entire surface should be cleaned off. A patch-up job here will only mean another patch-up later in another area. Like everything else paint has its life span, and when that is reached, only a complete renewal will be satisfactory.

Often the paint is so loose that a scraper is all that is needed to remove it, and this is the best method if it can be used. Providing the blade of the scraper is kept sharp, the paint should fall away easily, leaving the primer-impregnated timber beneath. The surfaces must be sanded back to a good finish, cleaned and dried thoroughly and then rebuilt as for new timber. The final result will be so superior to a patch-up job that the time and trouble will be more than justified.

Wrinkling

Paint is a fairly elastic skin that can move quite easily, particularly before it ages and becomes brittle. Thus any movement of the surface beneath it can cause wrinkling or "puckering" of the paint surface. Usually the cause is the application of the paint on some soft or pliable material, or on another coat of paint that had not dried properly. The under-surface moves and the paint skin, which is flexible, follows suit, but since it is unlikely that the elasticity of the two will be similar, the paint tends to pucker or wrinkle.

Unless the wrinkling is severe and causing the top surface to crack, it can usually be treated by rubbing back with wet and dry sandpaper and applying a new top coat. But the wrinkling can occur again, and if this is likely, the source of the trouble must be found and treated. If the trouble has resulted from two improperly-dried or uneven coats of paint, however, the rubbing back will take care of it.

Cracking and crazing

Both cracking and crazing can be caused by the paint aging, as with flaking. However, such cracking is usually small and uneven. Large, well-defined cracks, or crazing all over a painted plywood surface, are caused by move-ment beneath the paint.

Another cause of cracking may be the work-ing of seams which have been painted over. This is very common in boats which work in a seaway. It is also common, strangely enough, in boats which are not continuously used, particularly in warm climates. The sun dries out the topsides, causing the timber to shrink and the seams to open. The paint is not suffi-ciently elastic to cover such movement and cracks appear along the length of the seam. In hot climates this effect can be seen on many of the vessels lying to moorings, and the only cure is to take the boats to sea so that the timber swells, closing the seams.

In passing, it is not a good idea to hose down the timber as fresh water can penetrate the open seams and set up dry rot. Neither is it satisfactory to caulk the seams heavily when they are opened, for the timber will swell when it gets wet again and force the caulking out (this is called spewing), which has the same disastrous effect on the paintwork.

Cracking of the paint also occurs when

Cracking and crazing: The crazing is probably due to old paint deteriorating, the deck and hatch seams have cracked due to movement of the timber beneath the paint

timber splits or the grain opens. This is often caused by use of incorrect timber, or insuffi-cient seasoning before use. Crazing or cracking is quite common on cheaper brands of marine plywood where the top veneer opens or "crazes" and begins to separate from the layer beneath. When this happens little can be done, as the paint is only as good as the surface beneath it. Depending on how far the deteriora-tion of the timber has gone, it can either be treated with some kind of filler, or fibreglassed over, or removed and replaced with new timber.

The transoms of motor cruisers and the masts of yachts are common places to find paint cracking. This is usually along the seams and is due to the stress put on these areas, in the first case by the vibration of the propeller, and in the case of a yacht's mast, by the strain of full sails and incorrectly-tuned rigging. The stress may be such that glues may part and caulking may be spewed. The necessary treatment is dealt with in this volume in each respective section.

Pock-marks

Pock marks or, as is sometimes known, "cissing", is the formation of small crater-like patterns across the surface of the paint. If it is apparent the day after painting has been carried out it is almost certainly the result of raindrops or dew on improperly-dried paint. Even though dew may not have been falling at the time, the paint has little chance to dry once the heat goes out of the day. During the night its surface becomes covered with small drops of moisture.

If the patterns appear later, when the paint is well dried, the cause is probably an unclean surface when the paint was applied. Grease will always cause uneven marks, and dampness or dirt will cause definite pock marks when the paint dries. The cure, again, lies in the cleaning of the surface before painting.

Loss of appearance

Needless to say, almost everything from weather to accidental damage can cause the finish of a painted surface to deteriorate. However, there are prominent factors which will affect the finish of the paintwork, even after a long time. Everyone has seen the effect of industrial grime on sandstone buildings; not only causing a drab appearance, but also eating away the very stone. This grime can also affect the paintwork on boats, for smog includes many chemicals which are harmful to paintwork. Thus a vessel moored close to a city can expect her paintwork to deteriorate more rapidly than one moored in a quiet fishing harbour.

The effect of industrial smog can be the loss of gloss as well as some deterioration in the colour and surface of the paint. White paint takes on a yellowish appearance after a while and a matt surface can deteriorate to almost a pock-marked state if not treated. It is important to note that when repainting is about to begin, considerable attention must be paid to rubbing back and cleaning paintwork affected in this way, as some of the chemicals from the grime may be infused into the surface of the old paint and will attack the new paint as soon as it is put on.

Weather plays a big part where paintwork is concerned, and nowhere is this more evident than with varnishwork. The sun plays havoc with unprotected varnish, causing fading and flaking as well as a general deterioration of the surface. Thus, in countries with tropical

Loss of appearance due to scratching, fading, and some chemical action at the waterline — probably oil or floating chemicals

or sub-tropical climate, it is not uncommon to see vessels with highly-varnished topsides or cabinwork completely covered from stem to stern by canvas boat covers.

Wind and rain also take their toll. Dust blown on board and subsequently washed off by rain gradually wears away the surface like a mild wet and dry sandpaper. Salt water, too, adds its part to the gradual deterioration of paintwork, and if there happens to be oil or other chemicals floating around in the water, they attack the boat around her topsides and boot-topping. Indeed, with so much to withstand from the elements, both man-made and natural, it is a tribute to the paint manufacturers that the fine finishes achieved on some vessels last as long as they do.

The right conditions for painting

Next to the surface preparation, emphasised so strongly in this section, the most important part of painting concerns the conditions under which the paint is applied. In order to achieve the maximum result from the effort put into painting, some thought must be given to the conditions at the time. The very best high gloss

paint will not prove itself under damp, sticky conditions because it, like all paints and varnishes, is designed to be applied in dry, warm weather.

First, the area should be dry and dust-free. This is not always easy to obtain, particularly if sanding or similar repair work has been done, and even more so if the boat is inside a shed. Sawdust or the dust from sanding should be gathered up with a vacuum cleaner, since one small flurry of dust can ruin a whole day's painting.

Here is the reason for giving the paint job a miss on a windy day. No matter how thorough the cleaning job, a windy day will bring dust around and new paintwork will have to be rubbed right back again. Even out on the water, assuming the wind is dust-free, there is no let-up. The wind will either catch drips from the brush and send them flying all over the new work, or fiendishly pick up a little spray on the water and send it spattering all over still-tacky paint. The results of painting down a mast on a windy day can often be seen right across the bay on the topsides of other craft!

Cold and damp affect painting. Any form of dampness or condensation will have the effect described under the section on dew

Wind, weather and the sea all play a part in causing deterioration of surfaces no matter what material is involved. Photo courtesy Coronet Boats

A great deal of painting is done on slipways, and these should be suitably located and sheltered to make for good painting conditions. Note: *wall at left designed as wind break*

Pock-marks or unevenness of the surface is bound to result from paint applied when the temperature is low or the air moist. A similar effect can be expected from the sogginess of heat and high humidity. Again, the high content of moisture in the air affects the paint and makes it hard to dry and liable to pock.

The best conditions for painting and varnishing are calm, warm and dry. If the painting is to be done inside, some thought must be given to ventilation, or the paint will not dry properly. However, ventilation is one thing and a howling current of air another. The answer lies in a gentle breeze, sufficient to remove vapours from the paint without stirring up dust in the vicinity.

PAINTING WITH BRUSHES

Despite the fact that using a brush is not always the fastest means of applying a coat of paint —nor does it necessarily mean the best finish —it is undoubtedly the most convenient overall method. Spray painting has advantages particularly regarding finish, but requires a great deal of preparation in terms of masking and thinning the paint as well as the use of expensive equipment. And the roller, which is probably the fastest method of application, can, because of its size and shape, be used only where large, relatively flat areas are to be painted.

The brush is convenient, inexpensive, provides a good finish if used properly, and can be used for almost any type of painting. In addition, it is a better medium for applying certain types of paint than the other two as it works the paint into the surface, giving better adherence and protection.

Perhaps the ideal means of painting is to have each of these methods of application available when their particular use demands it, but this involves expense and a rather cumbersome toolbox, and the average boat owner finds it more practical to settle for one or the other.

The paintbrush is a much maltreated tool. It can, if correctly used and well looked after, provide a good, reliable means of painting almost any surface. Yet more often than not it is used the wrong way, cleaned in the wrong liquid, and very often not cleaned properly at all. Small wonder that the fine high gloss surfaces which can be achieved with the cor-

61

rect use of a good brush are so rarely found, and small wonder, too, that so many painters throw away in disgust what could have been a perfectly good paintbrush had it been treated properly.

The way in which a brush is held in the hand varies according to the type of surface being painted. This is the "pen" grip

The way a brush is held in the hand does not matter greatly providing it is held firmly, so that the bristles force the paint into the surface, and not just skim it around, leaving only a faint skin of paint. The best grip for a large area where the brush can be moved freely is obtained by closing all four fingers around the handle and wrapping the thumb round the opposite side pointing down the handle towards the bristles, in the manner of a golf club grip. This holds the brush very firmly and by even, sweeping wrist actions the paint can be applied with a hard, smooth action which forces it into any recesses or cracks.

A good firm grip for large surface areas

The brush should be dipped into the paint for only an inch or so of its bristle length, and then stroked briefly on the side of the can to take off surplus paint. The brush should then be worked firmly across a small area of the surface in an up and down, round about way, with no heed to brush strokes or direction. When the paint has been spread over an area and worked in so that there is no possibility of a run or missed spot, the pressure can be taken off the brush and the finishing strokes made with light, delicate wrist action in one direction only. This will eliminate the brush strokes and smooth the paint to a fine finish.

For finishing strokes this grip offers a smooth easy action

Some care is needed to see that marks are not made at the points where the brush starts and ends the stroke, and it may be necessary to overlap these points when the next section is being painted and so merge all the strokes into one and eliminate any unevenness. For this operation it is essential that the paint be thin (but not runny), as thick paint will tend to drag the brush and spoil the finishing strokes. Usually the consistency of a newly-opened can is about right, but it may tend to thicken on use, and suitable thinners must be added. Good stirring is essential and the paint should be stirred at regular intervals during the job.

1. Heavy strokes backwards and forwards to lay even coat of paint

2. Irregular hard strokes to work paint into surface

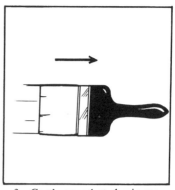

3. Gentle, smooth strokes in one direction to give fine finish

The three basic actions of painting

Where fine work has to be done, such as cutting in or signwriting, the method described above for holding the brush is not really satisfactory. A smaller, thinner brush will be used and this will make the previous grip difficult to operate, and also the wrist actions for finer work need to be more delicate and easier to control. Added to this is the fact that fine edges and other fine work does not require the paint to be worked in as with a larger surface.

The "pen" grip, for fine work

The "pen" grip is best suited for this work. The brush is held firmly but lightly in the manner of a pen and the wrist action is varied to suit the area to be painted.

TYPES AND SIZES OF BRUSHES

A paint job is worth doing well, and this can only be the case when good paint and good tools are used. The right paintbrush for the job is important; to use a six-inch brush to cut in a waterline would be like using a camel to cross the ocean. Six-inch brushes have their uses, but one of them is not fine work where a neat, straight edge is required.

Large brushes are fine for big surface areas where high finish is not so necessary. The anti-fouling paint on the bottom is an ideal case for the big brush. The finish tends to be a little uneven with this size of brush, and it is not recommended even for large surface areas where a good gloss finish is required. In these cases a smaller brush—in the three to four-inch bracket—is more suitable. This gives sufficient bristle to enable the paint to flow on smoothly without the congestion of the larger brushes and is also easier to wield, and thus is less strain on the wrist; an important consideration when the surface to be covered is very large.

For cutting in waterlines, most varnishwork and small objects or surfaces, a one-inch brush is best, although if there is a lot of work to be done, a two-inch brush will not be amiss and will speed up the paint application without too much loss of fine work. However, as the surface area becomes smaller or the work more critical, smaller brushes will have to be used, even down to artist's brushes for decorative work and signwriting.

63

Cutting in a waterline is tricky at the best of times. Using the right type of brush helps obtain a good result

The quality of the paintbrush is important. Cheap brushes will plague the painter by failing to give perfection in the finish, scoring the new paintwork with brush marks, and dropping bristles at maddeningly frequent intervals. Good quality brushes are not cheap and must be cared for when not in use; but they will repay many times over the additional cost.

CARE OF BRUSHES

Good quality brushes are made of fine bristle (synthetic or natural) set in rubber or similar compounds which are not affected by the chemicals in the paint or by the various proprietary cleaning solutions. Providing they are

The right brush for the job is important at all times, even when painting the less visible underwater areas

well cared for, the brushes should last a long time, giving clean, unclogged paint strokes when used. If they are not cared for, the bristles stick together or harden with old paint and lose the flexibility so necessary to ensure that the paint flows on smoothly.

All brushes must be cleaned immediately after use. They should be washed out in turpentine or one of the available brush-cleaning solutions and then examined to see that no paint is still clogging the bristles. If so, it may be necessary to scrape the paint off with a scraper.

The brushes should then be returned to a clean solution of the cleaner and worked with the fingers so that all paint is removed from the inner bristles high up in the brush. When it is quite certain that all paint has been removed, the brushes should be thoroughly scoured in warm soapy water. They may then be put out to dry. If they are to be put away for some time the bristles should be greased and the brushes, wrapped in paper, stored in a dry spot.

If the brushes are in fairly constant use, it is not necessary to clean them other than in the cleaner or turpentine. They may then be stored in a similar solution, so that the air cannot get to and harden the bristles. It is important to note that the brushes must not be stood in this solution on their bristles. If so, the bristles will gradually fold and lose their shape and also become contaminated with sludge or other sediment in the bottom of the container. If they are stored in individual tins (by far the best method), a tin with a diameter much the size of the brush should be used and a good-sized nail driven through the lower part of the handle. In this way the brush can be lowered into the tin until it rests on the nail, thus keeping the bristles suspended in the solution without touching the bottom. Alternatively, a number of brushes can be threaded, by means of a small hole drilled in the handle of each brush, on to a wire support which holds them suspended in a large tin of the solution.

Turpentine or water may be used to store the brushes providing they are not varnish brushes which react with water and harden. A mixture of turpentine and linseed oil is best for varnish brushes.

Whatever the solution used, it must be changed periodically to avoid build-up of sediment, but it is emphasised that this method of storage is temporary and should only be used when it is not convenient to clean the brushes properly as described above.

brush cleaner, or if that is not available, a paint-stripping solution. The brushes should be soaked until the bristles become pliable; then the bristles massaged with the fingers, taking care—particularly with paint stripper—not to get the chemical near eyes or clothes or into cuts on the hand.

When the paint on the bristles is soft, the brushes should be laid on a bench and scraped hard with a paint scraper. If the bristles come out during the process, the brush is too far

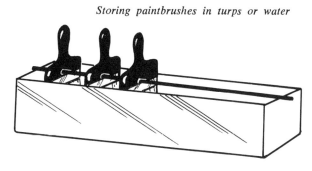

Storing paintbrushes in turps or water

A temporary storage container for single brush

Brushes used for synthetic resin paints must be cleaned and suspended in their own special thinner, as some may react with either water or turpentine and harden.

Before using a new brush, it is best to break it in by soaking in water or a similar liquid that loosens up the bristles and makes them pliable. In all cases, whether a new brush or one that has been stored, a quick, hard rub on a piece of timber or paper will make the bristles flexible and remove any loose ones.

CLEANING A PAINT-HARDENED BRUSH

Old brushes, and brushes hardened with paint, can usually be reconditioned successfully providing the bristle is of good quality and not too worn. They should be fitted up to hang in a solution as described in the previous section, and then suspended in either a patent gone for recovery; but providing the scraper

does not cut the bristles, much of the thick clogging paint can be removed, usually without damage to the brush.

A hot soapy water bath is next on the list, used in conjunction with a scrubbing- or wash-board or similar corrugated surface to massage the bristles firmly with the hot water. Constant treatment like this will bring back the flexibility of the brushes and remove any remaining flakes of paint. It may be necessary to manipulate the brush from side to side and press hard down to massage right to the roots of the bristles, but unless this is done, small flecks of paint will remain rooted high up in the brush.

After the wash-board treatment the brush should be combed out with a wire comb and the whole process repeated until all the flecks of paint have been removed. The brush can then be washed in fresh water and dried. Once dry it should be lubricated with linseed oil and stored in this condition until used.

CUTTING-IN AND SIGNWRITING

Cutting-in—the painting of a sharp dividing line between two different colours—can undoubtedly make or mar a paint job. How many boats have an attractive colour scheme and a well-finished gloss coat, but because of irregular cutting-in lines, look as though junior got at the boat when Dad wasn't looking? Similarly with signwriting, or any other small paint work. What looks worse than a nicely finished hull with an uneven, shaky name daubed on the bow?

Because it is only a small job, and because it is the finishing "fiddly" piece, the small paint job should never be lightly passed over. A clean, straight line between the anti-fouling and the topsides can smarten up even a poor paint job, and can do wonders for a nicely-finished boat. Attention to detail at this stage can "pick-up" the boat and make her stand out against others, for nothing looks more amateurish than a shaky cutting-in line, and nothing looks more professional than a clean, straight sweep.

Apart from the necessary choice of brushes —which are invariably high quality brushes, small enough to suit the particular job, and drawn to either a wedge (in the case of a flat brush) or a fine paint (artist's brush), with no loose or outstanding bristles—the only other piece of equipment required is a mahl stick. This is a stick on which to rest shaky hands,

Cutting in fine edges needs a steady hand and a good eye. Note the way in which the bristles have been "fined" to give a narrow "cutting" edge

and is available from any artist's supply stores or can be made up easily.

Often a long cutting-in line—such as boot-topping—is better done free-hand, without the mahl stick. Careful use of a flat brush—and obtaining as firm a foothold as the slipway will allow—and a steady hand will ensure a line that, although to the painter's eye some inches away may not seem the straightest, will pass muster when viewed from a few feet. Who goes round examining a ship's boot-topping at a distance of a few inches anyway?

It is important to ensure that the line is straight in the first place. And, if starting from

Moulding different coloured fibreglass sections eliminates the need for cutting in and careful paintwork

scratch, ensure that it is not only straight, but suits the sheer of the boat or the surface that is to be cut in. Masking tape can help here, but painting over masking tape can result in an inferior line to one drawn free-hand, and this type of cutting-in is best left for spray painting, where it is essential. Usually most vessels have a groove marked in the hull by the builders to indicate where the boot-topping should end. This is known as a scribing cut and makes the cutting-in of the waterline very easy. If this has been painted out, however, or if the area to be painted has no cutting-in marks at all, the following process can be used:

A piece of string is tacked lightly to one end of the surface to be marked off, and run along the surface to the other end. When it has been adjusted to suit the line required, the far end is also tacked on. The line is then chalked by running a piece of chalk lightly along its inner surfaces. By taking hold of one end and drawing it tight, then plucking firmly on the string, a white chalk mark will be left

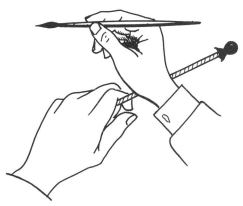

Using the mahl stick

along the surface on which the cutting-in can be done. If the area is very large, or has severe curves, the marking will have to be done in sections, and where a waterline is concerned, great care must be taken to see that these sections run together without unevenness, and also that both sides of the ship are marked identically.

When signwriting, or working on the fine decorative lines that some vessels have painted around bow or stern are to be done, the mahl

Good cutting in at the waterline, the gunwale and along the decorative strip can improve the appearance of a boat one hundred fold

stick is essential. By placing it near the letter to be painted, and resting the painting hand gently on it, much of the shakiness will be taken out of the painting. The hand should be rested somewhere around the wrist, but comfort will dictate the best position for each individual.

The actual lettering is outside the scope of this book, except to mention briefly. Practice is the only possible thing if a neat, professional finish is to be achieved, and the would-be signwriter should practise for many long hours on a piece of board before attempting to start anything on the vessel herself. Egyptian Block Alphabet is the easiest to begin with, and is also the most commonly used in general work. Once success has been achieved with this type, the more sophisticated Roman Block and Italics Block Alphabets can be attempted. Spacing is important and a rough-up of the job, if it is completely new work, is essential to adjust the spacing of the letters. W and I re-require a lot of care in spacing, as also do O and similar letters. The entire name must be laid up to see that it fits the space allotted, particularly if it is on a curved surface.

When the lettering has been marked on to the surface and the choice of colour and paint (usually a special lettering paint) has been

decided, the brush and the mahl sticks are taken out of the box. The brush is loaded with the colour required and the mahl stick placed near the first letter. The painting hand is placed on the mahl stick and adjusted until comfortable and then the first letter is begun with a short, firm, downward stroke, making the edges clean. This is repeated on the other edge of the letter, and the middle filled. The ends and then the corners of the letter will need a little practice, but short, flickering motions of the wrist are the secret in these difficult areas.

The downstrokes of the letters should always be thicker than the upstrokes, and once the vertical and horizontal strokes have been mastered, the curves come in for attention. These are the most difficult of all, and will require much patience and practice to perfect.

Once the paint job is finished it should be given good time to dry, after which a coat of clear varnish can be run over the whole area (providing, of course, it does not affect the colour scheme) and this will afford extra protection to the lettering.

Transfer Gold Leaf

The most attractive finish for lettering is undoubtedly gold leaf. Although expensive, it is well worth the extra cost if the lettering calls for a gold colour. It can be purchased

Signwriting on a boat can take many forms

No matter what the method of painting, care and patience will always be rewarded by an attractive-looking craft. Photo courtesy Power Boat & Yachting

in book form—usually 25 pages of leaf—and can vary in shade from light to deep gold. It is placed in position by the initial application of gold size—a type of varnish which dries to a tacky state in a very short time. The procedure for applying gold leaf is as follows:

The letters are painted in with gold size which is allowed to dry to the tacky stage. A leaf is taken from the gold leaf book and applied to the tacky paint. The covering tissue is rubbed lightly to ensure good adherence and the tissue then removed. Providing this is done correctly, the lettering will stand out in shimmering gold which will dry in about half an hour, when it can be gently rubbed clean with a velvet pad.

Usually the letters are outlined in black or other dark colour to give them a clean-cut appearance.

PAINTING WITH A SPRAY GUN

Spray painting is not difficult. It requires some knowledge and some practice if pitfalls are to be avoided. But where a high-gloss finish is required, particularly over a large area, no method can surpass spray painting in achieving a good result.

The preparation consists of masking-off all areas that are not to be painted. This is the principal reason why spray painting is usually limited to large areas or plain areas without many fittings. Masking takes a lot of time, but it must be done thoroughly, for the sprayed paint will creep into every corner. Windows and other glass work can be painted with a whitening coat which can be wiped clean later. The off-spray travels a considerable distance, particularly if there is a slight breeze, and care must be taken to see that it cannot touch uncovered surfaces or, for that matter, nearby objects.

The best type of paint for spray painting is already mixed for the job and is marketed as spray paint. This is usually of the right consistency; thinner than paint used for brush application and strained to ensure no small piece of foreign matter can block the fine jet of the spray. If the correct thickness is not available, however, the paint will have to be thinned with the special thinners for the job. The density of the paint is part of the secret of successful spray painting, and care, plus the close study of manufacturer's recommendations, is essential before loading the gun.

There are several different types of guns, but as always, quality is important if a good finish is required, and an expensive gun will not only give a better finish but make the work much easier for a novice than a cheaper gun.

It would be folly for a beginner to attempt to paint a boat without considerable practice and expert advice; and even when this has been obtained, it is as well to have a few "trial runs" with the gun before approaching the boat.

This not only ensures that everything is in working order, but by practising a few "swings" with the gun on an old piece of timber, the painter can get himself into the rhythm of spraying without making starting blotches on the job. Painting is done by holding the gun somewhere between eight to twelve inches from the job (depending on the type of gun) and moving it constantly. The best method is to fall into a rhythm whereby the gun is started when pointing a little to the left, is swung steadily towards the job, along the surface and to the right. This prevents sudden blotches at the start and finish of the run and presents a nice tapering-off of the paint which can be amalgamated with the next run. The gun should be held as nearly as possible at a right-angle to the surface, so this rhythm action will involve the use of the whole body.

The trigger finger is important, as the gun must be started as the swing begins and not before, or the paint will collect and congeal at the start of the run. Similarly the finger must be taken off the triger at the moment the run is completed. Thus, each run will provide a neat stripe of paint which is "feathered out" at top and bottom and also at each end. By building up a series of these stripes, merging the feathered areas together, a thin, even coat is gradually built up over the entire surface. The gun must never at any stage be held stationary as it will cause a run.

Because of the thin viscosity of the paint, more coats are required when sprayed than

when brush painting, but this in turn helps to achieve the added sparkle of spray finishing, albeit at the cost of more elbow-grease. Spray and spray again, is the motto, and in between rub back with wet and dry sandpaper. The finish will be well worth it.

Spray painting can fall foul of all the problems mentioned earlier in the general section on paintwork, and there are a few of its own, such as standing too close or too far away from the surface. However, because of the constant rubbing down and re-spraying, most problems are overcome and with practice the gun can be used as easily and efficiently as a brush or roller. Normal preparation work must be done before applying paint, whatever the method, and in some cases (primer, for example) when spraying is not recommended, the brush will have to be brought into action.

PAINTING WITH A ROLLER

The lambswool or foam roller is a tremendous asset where large areas are to be covered. Unfortunately it is not really satisfactory with gloss paint and a spray gun or brush should be used in preference. However, where the finish is not important, and where there are not too many obstacles or awkward corners, the roller is a good tool.

Anti-fouling paint can be applied by roller; it is a safe guess that the invention of this tool has cut anti-fouling time in half for those who use it. An even, thick coat is obtained that dries to a smooth (but not gloss) finish. This is ideal for anti-fouling or undercoats which should go on evenly but quickly to be fully effective.

The roller is loaded by rolling it back and forth in a small tray into which the paint has been poured. The tray should be slanted or tipped at one end so that the roller can be pulled out and freed of surplus paint, which otherwise might cause runs. It is then applied to the surface with long, even strokes; often only one stroke is required for complete coverage. This makes for very fast painting, particu-

70

Paint roller and tray

larly if the roller makes a twelve inch wide sweep with every stroke.

A word of warning. The roller is a mischievously dirty tool, particularly when working up speed. Painting cleanly and smoothly, it will deceive the unsuspecting painter into believing that he can literally go as fast as he likes. Which is true to a point. At that point the roller ceases to be docile and gleefully ejects a million tiny sprays of paint all of which seem to be aimed directly at the painter's face. The result—particularly when anti-fouling—is akin to a sudden outburst of measles.

Rollers can be cleaned and used time and time again. Usually the whole tool can be dismantled and washed in turpentine or brush cleaner to remove the surplus paint. It should then be washed in warm soapy water, dried, and stored away. Because the actual roller is interchangeable and relatively inexpensive, it is a good idea to keep one roller for each colour paint.

REMOVING OLD PAINTWORK

There are many methods by which old paint can be removed. The choice depends on the material to which the old paint is adhering and the type of paint to be applied later. Burning off, and removal by chemical solution, are equally effective in a general sense, but both have limitations on the material on which they can be used.

Burning off

This is undoubtedly the most effective way,

but must be used with discretion as considerable heat is involved. A gas or kerosene blowtorch is used in conjunction with a scraper. There are on the market combination scraper-torches, which are quite suitable if used correctly, and with the same precautions as for other torches.

The secret of effective burning off is to ensure that the flame is very hot; the hotter the better, providing care is taken not to scorch the timber underneath. The flame should be brought close until the paint begins to blister. The scraper—preferably flat-bladed —is then slid under the blister and the paint peeled off. The flame must then be moved on immediately to prevent damage to the bared surface. With some practice, the use of the torch and scraper can be combined in the one action, to burn and peel across a flat surface in one movement. Not only does this ensure the fast removal of the paint, but also lessens the chance of damage to the surface beneath. If the old paint is not too thick this method may remove all coats at the first attempt. If some paint is left after the first sweep, the process will have to be repeated, this time with even more care as bare patches may be showing which will be very liable to damage from the flame.

The gas torch heats and blisters the paint while the following blade scrapes it away. Care is necessary to prevent scorching of the surfaces beneath

If only a small amount of paint is left, it will be wise to scrape it off with a dry scraper. If the surface is to be repainted, slight scorching during the burning-off process can be sanded back and covered fairly successfully. If the surface is to be varnished, however, it is not wise to use the burning method as scorch marks will show through, and even be exaggerated by the varnish. In this case the old paint must be removed by stripper.

Following the burning off the surface should be sanded down either by hand or with an orbital sander. The use of rotary sanding discs is not recommended, as there is a tendency for these to score the surface. This will show through when the surface is repainted or re-varnished. The sanding should remove all traces of old paint and any scorch marks which may be visible. The surface is then rebuilt, beginning with primer or anticorrosive as described in the section on painting new surfaces.

Chemical strippers

Although not as effective as burning off with a blow torch the use of chemical strippers for removing old paint has advantages, particularly when the surface beneath the paint is not suited to burning off. As mentioned in the previous section, chemical strippers are particularly advantageous in stripping off varnish work, to avoid the possibility of scorch marks showing beneath the new varnish. There are several brands of chemical stripper and all work on much the same principle. Application of the stripper causes the paint to buckle and warp away from the surface beneath, whence it is easily scraped off.

Most strippers are effective only on the surface coat of paint, and therefore require more scraping than does the burning method which can remove several coats of paint at one go. In addition, when the final coat of paint has been removed, the stripper that has penetrated the surface must be neutralised. Then the normal sanding action mentioned above must be used to rub the timber back effectively before

beginning to build up with new coats of paint.

Timber surfaces

Timber surfaces may have paint removed by either burning or chemical stripper. Either is equally effective providing the necessary precautions are observed. Burning off is most suitable.

Steel surfaces

Paint can be removed from steel in several ways, burning being perhaps the most effective. If there is rust beneath the paint it should be chipped away—indeed all paint surfaces can be cleaned by chipping. Care must be taken to ensure that the steel is not pitted by the chipping hammer, and that any marking of the surface is sanded down before repainting. Chemical strippers can be used but as some of these may react with the steel, care must be taken in this regard.

Aluminium surfaces

As for steel, with the exception of chipping

With practice, large flat areas of paint can be stripped quickly and effectively, and with little scorching of the surface beneath

which is not satisfactory on aluminium. Care must be taken to ensure that the chemical stripper does not react with the aluminium.

Fibreglass surfaces

Usually, the paint can be scraped off without any need for either burning or chemical removal. However, if this is not practicable chemical strippers should be used in preference to other methods.

Plywood surfaces

These may be treated as for timber, but great care must be taken when burning off, as the heat from the blowtorch may tend to lift the top veneer. If this is likely, chemical strippers should be used.

Canvas surfaces

Canvas is probably the most difficult surface from which to remove paint, because the texture of the material will not allow burning off, and chemical strippers, while removing the surface paint, may also loosen the paint beneath the canvas. Paint should be scraped from canvas with a dry scraper wherever possible.

Scrapers

Several scrapers are available for paint removal, and each is designed for specific work. Some are shaped for long, open, flat surfaces, some to get into corners, some for curved surfaces.

The triangular scraper, flat scraper, and Swedish Skarsten scraper illustrated provide a good set for most paint-removal jobs aboard a boat.

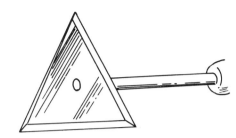

1. Triangular
for corners and stubborn paint.

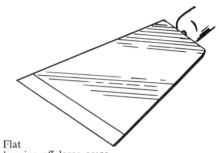

2. Flat
for burning off large areas.

3. Skarsten scraper
a good general purpose scraper.

Principal scrapers used in boat maintenance

SECTION II
Maintenance of the Hull

CHAPTER FIVE

Causes and Cures

THE TERM "maintenance" covers all aspects of boat care; therefore the factors which make maintenance necessary range from physical damage caused by an accident to deterioration caused by wear and tear. Included in this range could be circumstances which will occur only in one specific area because of local conditions. For this reason it would be very difficult to encompass in one book all the causes of maintenance problems.

There are, however, factors which are universal and which, in many cases, can create maintenance problems beyond their immediate scope, and it is with these causes that the boating man must be concerned first. Attacking the basic causes can often reduce maintenance to a minimum and even eliminate most of the smaller, aggravating factors.

Basically, maintenance depends on the materials used in the construction of the boat. In recent years, many so-called maintenance-free materials have been introduced. There is no such general term as "maintenance-free" where boats are concerned, but there is no denying that materials such as fibreglass are free from many of the problems associated with maintenance. Fibreglass, for example, is completely free from rot problems, but still requires attention in the form of cleaning, patching when damaged, and sometimes painting.

In the first chapter in this section, the principal causes of maintenance problems in boats are examined together with a brief outline of the cures usually applied. In the later chapters each of the principal boat-building materials is mentioned and the basic maintenance factors involved with each material described in detail.

DRY ROT

Dry rot is the deterioration of timber owing to the growth of a fungus. The fungus is not very visible to the eye, and is therefore somewhat hard to detect, particularly in corners and other inaccessible spots where it is most liable to be found. The mould gives off a very distinctive odour, however, and it is this stale, musty smell permeating the boat which often gives the first indication of dry rot. The fungus attacks the fibres of the timber, causing them

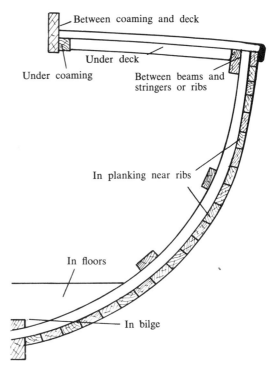

Although dry rot can attack any timber part of a boat, this illustration shows the more common areas where rot is found

to disintegrate, leaving a soft, powdery sponginess.

Dry rot is insidious and unless checked will spread very quickly, attacking all timber which has not previously been treated. It is spread by means of spores which are given off into the air and which, unless removed, will settle and grow on any suitable piece of timber nearby. The damp, often humid conditions inside a closed boat are ideal for the breeding of the spores. Thus, the best prevention for dry rot is to create a through current of air which will dry up the humidity, keep the timber in a clean dry condition, and carry away spores which may be floating around in the air.

When the telltale odour of dry rot is detected a search should begin immediately to locate the affected areas. By prodding at the various timbers with a knife or screwdriver the characteristic sponginess can be readily discovered. It is most likely to be found in corners and other spots away from through currents of air. Beams, bilges, the underside of decks, and cupboards are a few of the likely places where dry rot gains a foothold. Rainwater leaking through hatch coamings or decks creates perfect conditions for the fungus to develop.

Salt water tends to discourage the rot, and it is rarely found on the surface of the decks which are constantly washed with salt water. Fresh water provides the right condition for dry rot and it thus can be found almost anywhere where there is dampness from fresh water or condensation. Although more prevalent on the inside of a vessel, it is still not uncommon for it to spread into timbers which are open to the air all the time. Indeed, it is such an insidious disease that once gaining a foothold it may well spread, unless checked, throughout the entire interior and exterior of the vessel.

Once dry rot has gained a foothold, the only really successful cure is surgery. The affected timber must be cut out, with much of the surrounding area, and replaced with clean, and, if possible, treated timber. There are chemical preparations—copper napthenate is probably the best—which will restrict and even kill the fungus. These may be used liberally to prevent the spread of the rot and even to cure it where it is in the early stages. However, timber damaged by dry rot must be replaced in order to remove the weakness caused by the disintegration of the timber fibres. Obviously when dry rot attacks structural members, a very serious weakness arises. For this reason the fungus can cause some of the greatest maintenance problems in timber vessels, and should, therefore, be given priority in any maintenance routine.

Prevention is always better than cure where dry rot is concerned, and it is possible to begin the prevention system at the time the boat is built. By using timbers already impregnated with anti-rot chemicals, the boat owner is already halfway towards preventing this scourge. By ensuring that his vessel is adequately ventilated at all times, and that damp timber is not allowed to remain damp, he can eliminate the risk of the fungus attack. The risk is greater in tropical and sub-tropical zones, particularly during wet seasons. Condensation then provides the dampness required for dry rot to gain a foothold, and it is here that ventilation becomes the most important preventative of all.

The effect of dry rot on timber, showing (from left) clean timber, the initial mould attack and complete disintegration of the fibres

Good ventilation is necessary whatever the hull material of the boat. This steel yacht is adequately provided with good ventilation which can be trimmed on or off the wind

A Jalousie or slatted door makes an ideal ventilator when used with another opening somewhere in the boat

VENTILATION

When a boat is open and moving through the water, there is little or no need for ventilation. Air is forced into the boat by her movement through the water, and sucked out again by the vortex action of the wind blowing across open hatches and doorways. Thus a through current of air is maintained all the time and vessels that are frequently used rarely suffer from ventilation problems.

At a mooring or a marina, however, with hatches and doors locked, any circulation of the air inside the vessel depends purely on a ventilation system. There are many methods of achieving this, ranging from ventilators in the deck, or cabin top, which may be turned into the wind or off the wind as required, to the simple expedient of drilling ventilating holes or slots in hatches and doorways.

Jalousied doors are ideal for ventilation purposes, as also are the small "oyster shell" or "mushroom" type ventilators on hatches. Undoubtedly the most effective system, especially where a boat is to be completely locked up and covered with a canvas cover, involves the use of ventilators which can be turned into and off the wind. These ventilators can be used to scoop air into the boat, or to suck out stale air, and are usually fitted with rain traps to prevent rain water dripping down into surrounding timbers.

When lying to a mooring the forward ventilators should be facing forward, the after ventilators facing astern. As the boat always rides head to wind on a mooring, this will ensure that the forward ventilators are always

Ventilation equipment can be attractive and blend with a boat's decor as with this jalousie door

headed into the wind, the after ventilators away from it. This in turn creates a through draught of air from the bow through the main part of the vessel and out the stern. On a marina it will be necessary to trim the ventilators according to the direction of the wind, always remembering that some ventilators must be turned into the wind and some away from the wind in order to create a through current of air.

In tropical climates, or where ventilation is difficult, or when the boat is closed up for a long period of time, it is a wise precaution to lift some of the floorboards, and open cupboards and drawers to allow the circulating air to reach even the most hidden corner. If the boat is covered with tarpaulins, space should be left forward and aft for the air to circulate beneath the covers, otherwise the effect of the ventilators will be nullified.

Where possible portholes and skylights should be left open. The bilges should be as dry as practicable and care taken to ensure that condensation or seepage from water tanks is not allowed to provide the necessary humidity to foster the growth of the dry rot fungus. Once again, it cannot be over-emphasised that the major cause of dry rot in a boat is neglect of adequate ventilation.

WET ROT

Although caused by vastly different circumstances, the final results of wet and dry rot are not dissimilar. The wood takes on a soft, spongy appearance, and there is a deterioration

"Mushroom" vents, placed in strategic positions around a vessel, are unobtrusive and yet effective

of the fibres which results, eventually, in complete collapse of the wood structure. The principal difference between them however, is that dry rot, once it is established in the timber, spreads rapidly throughout the rest of the boat, whereas wet rot is limited almost entirely to its source and spreads only to immediate surrounding areas.

Wet rot—more commonly termed just "rot" —is the collapse of the fibres in the timber structure because of constant soaking with water, either fresh or salt. It is almost invariably caused by leakage of some kind and is more readily visible than dry rot because the seepage tends to stain the wood very dark before the rot itself sets in. Unlike dry rot, however, it does not give off any odour and in concealed areas seepage can cause quite extensive rot before it is found. For this reason regular maintenance checks should be carried out on every vessel. When it is found, however, it is fairly easy to cure and since it does not spread farther than the seepage itself can spread, usually limits itself to an area that can be easily replaced or treated.

It is most commonly found in under-deck areas, where seepage of rain water through the deck or some similar area allows a constant trickle of water over the wood, or where seams allow a constant seepage of sea water through the planks. Where the bilges are constantly covered with water, particularly if they have not been correctly painted in the first place, rot may set in over a period of time. The areas adjoining coamings, cockpits, skylights, and other openings are also susceptible places for wet rot. It can easily be differentiated from dry rot by its appearance; notably the colour, which is of a very dark nature, and the feel—which in the case of dry rot is reasonably dry and mouldy, in the case of wet rot is soft, wet and spongy.

There is no limit to the areas in which wet rot may appear, either above decks or below. It may attack the mast at the cross-trees or the keel at its connection with the outside ballast. However, areas which are constantly

Wet rot, caused by leaking fastenings is gaining a firm hold beneath the varnish on these windows

should be no further cause for concern. Correct use of primers and paints, described in this volume, will prevent further deterioration of the timber provided of course that the seepage of water giving rise to the rot is plugged.

Rot, particularly wet rot, is rarely found in small dinghies or boats which are kept out of water, since they are given a chance to dry out each time they are pulled out of the water. The possibility of dry rot comes only if they are stored where there is insufficient ventilation. However, an occasional check-up when the boat is laid up should ensure that rot has little chance to establish itself.

CORROSION

A great deal of time and money is spent by the yachtsman in protecting his craft from the ravages of the elements. Paint, plastic coverings, canvas awnings, etc., are all part of the attempt to reduce the gradual disintegration of materials by the elements. In modern times this has been reduced to a fine art, and protective substances are available for almost all surfaces which are liable to attack.

The most insidious form of deterioration, however, is often not visible to the eye, and can rarely be prevented by a covering substance. This is corrosion—a galvanic action which takes place between two dissimilar

subject to water are the most vulnerable, and the underwater areas where priming or anti-fouling may have worn off, or the timber was not correctly treated in the first place, are the most liable of all.

The cure of wet rot depends mainly on the extent to which it has spread. Because it is limited in its extent it can usually be treated by caulking or plugging the leaking areas, but if it is in an advanced stage may need the same surgical treatment as dry rot. The affected area should be cut out and replaced with new timber. Providing the area affected is successfully treated and sanded back, and the leak or seepage causing the rot stopped, there

One of the greatest features of fibreglass construction is its resistance to rot of any form. Photo courtesy Power Boat & Yachting

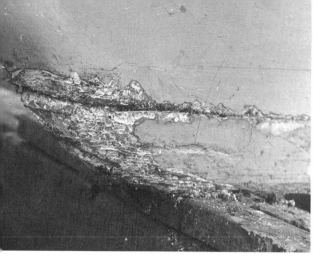

Corrosion can attack any metal at any time, but never more so than when there are impurities present. The lead in this keel contain impurities which assist the corrosion action

Where a propeller and shaft are of different metals corrosion will take place. Note sacrificial anodes on shaft and on hull above propeller

metals when they are electrically connected and immersed in a suitable electrolyte. When boiled down, these high-sounding phrases simply mean that the two metals are touching one another directly or through another metal, and are both immersed in a conductive liquid such as seawater.

It is not always necessary for the electrolyte to be a liquid as such. The salt moisture of sea air is often sufficient to cause corrosion between two unlike metals, particularly when the metals are highly vulnerable, as with zinc and copper, and it is not always necessary for the metals to be in separate locations, but may be merged in the one alloy.

To understand the process of corrosion it is necessary to look at the experiments undertaken in high school in the study of elementary electricity. If a container is filled with an acid, or similar electrolyte, and into this solution two rods are immersed, one of copper and one of zinc, an electrical current is registered immediately these two rods are connected together. If the rods are left in the solution, the electrical current will continue to flow from one to the other, i.e. from the anode (zinc) to the cathode (copper).

If the process is allowed to continue for an even longer time, a gradual wasting away of the anode will be observed until, eventually,

Electrolytic corrosion

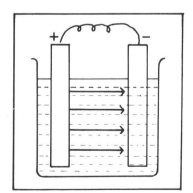

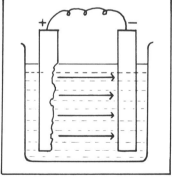

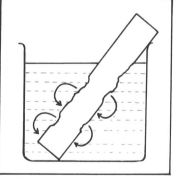

1. Current flowing from anode to cathode through electrolyte.

2. Anode gradually disintegrating.

3. Action of rust showing current travelling between anodic and cathodic regions, corroding away the anodic parts.

the anode disintegrates altogether. This is the action of corrosion, and in effect the wasting away of the zinc rod is the action of corrosion on zinc fittings or alloys in a boat where copper is in contact with zinc.

With the amount of zinc and copper alloys used for screws, bolts, fittings, masts, etc., it is small wonder that corrosion is a sizeable problem, one which cannot be ignored. The gradual disintegration of a propeller, for example, is not only expensive but also dangerous.

Steel

Rust is a form of corrosion and comes about in exactly the way described above. The difference is that the two dissimilar metals (which may be any number of elements used in the making of the steel) are together in the one alloy. The immersion of the steel in water provides the electrolyte which starts the re-action between the two substances, and gradual disintegration of one takes place in the form of rust—a ferrous oxide. The location of large patches of the anodic substance can be clearly seen by the "pitting" that is so familiar when the surface rust is cleared away.

Bronze, brass, aluminium, etc.

Since brass is a combination of zinc and copper, it is vulnerable to corroding action when in contact with salt water. The zinc and copper react together, with the zinc gradually being dispersed, either leaving small pit-marks or gradually reducing the alloy to pure copper. The latter is readily seen in the pinkish tinge of brass screws and fittings after long immersion in salt water. Pitting can be found frequently on the blades of a propeller.

When two dissimilar metals or alloys are placed in contact, the corrosion always attacks the anode. Thus a steel shaft and a bronze propeller will result in rapid disintegration of the propeller. Similarly a bronze halyard winch attached to an aluminium mast will mean rapid corrosion of the aluminium.

Steel yachts have problems with corrosion, mostly in the form of rust. Careful building and subsequent maintenance can reduce these problems

Inert metals

There are some so-called inert metals which do not respond to galvanic action, or do so to a much lesser degree than most metals. Monel is one such metal, and is ideal for use in fittings where corrosion is a problem. However, such metals are not always suitable for the location or the fitting required, and some other form of combating corrosive action has to be taken.

Preventing corrosion

There are several ways of combating corrosion in yachts and power craft. Some are electronic and highly complex—as well as very expensive. Others are less complex and can be easily fitted and maintained by the amateur handyman. Of these the most commonly used, and probably the most effective, is the fitting of what is known as "sacrificial anodes".

Since the corrosion gradually wastes away the anode, it follows that if the hull could be made the cathode, there would be no corrosion of the hull itself. This is achieved by electrical means in some steel ships, but is more easily obtained by attaching to the hull an anode of stronger negative attraction than the metal affected by corrosion.

Zinc plates are the most commonly used, and these, when placed near the bronze or brass affected, attract the current and cause it to run through the zinc anode rather than through the ship's fitting. The wasting process gradually eats away the sacrificial anode (hence its name) and it has to be replaced from time to time, but during its life it is usually sufficiently effective to reduce the corrosion problem to almost zero.

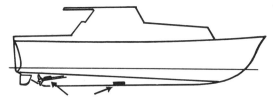

The location of sacrificial anodes is governed by the areas most subject to corrosion

It is important to note that if a sacrificial anode is used on a timber or plastic hull, it will be insulated by the hull materials, from the metal it is designed to protect. In order that the current may flow, a wire will be necessary to complete the circuit between the metal and the anode. On steel-hulled vessels this is not necessary providing both the anode and the metal to be protected make good contact with the steel hull.

Where fittings such as winches or cleats on aluminium masts are causing corrosion, the two dissimilar metals must be separated. Insulation such as bakelite can be used to break the contact between the two and thus prevent the corroding current from flowing. Lead keels do not usually corrode, but because of impurities in the lead mixture, some corrosion often takes place due to electrolytic action.

RUST

As mentioned earlier, rust is a form of electrolytic corrosion. The elements used in the manufacture of steel are often at different electrical potentials and as a result, when the steel is immersed in an electrolyte such as salt water, a galvanic action sets up in which the anodic elements gradually disintegrate into the powdery oxide commonly known as rust.

Since the interacting elements are an integral part of the composition of steel, it is impossible to isolate them and break the current or use any of the other methods of electrolytically preventing the wasting action at the anode. The only successful method of preventing rust is to seal off the steel from contact with any form of electrolyte. In the case of boats, it is invariably water which triggers off the rusting action, and sealing the steel from contact with water is usually achieved by painting, although chemical sealing such as galvanising is also widely used.

The advent of synthetic materials of sufficient strength, and the manufacture of much boat equipment from non-rusting metals, have gradually reduced the problems of rust on small boats. Fibreglass hulls eliminate the need

Rust attacking a steel stanchion plate. Note that the stainless steel stanchion is not affected

for most fastenings found in timber-built vessels, and aluminium, with its non-rusting characteristic, has made a great impact on the construction of masts and spars as well as the hulls of some boats. Brass and bronze are widely used for fittings and fastenings, and monel and stainless steel reduce the possibility of rust in rigging, handrails and other deck equipment.

There are times, however, when steel is used and rust sets in. Galvanising and painting, unless maintained properly, can become cracked or broken, and water seeps into the bare steel. Large bolts, such as are used in the heavier parts of a big vessel's construction, are often of mild steel. In short, the possibility of rust has been reduced to a minimum in modern boating, but it is still a possibility to be reckoned with when maintenance problems are considered.

Rust begins long before the steel has a chance to come into contact with water. The actual preparation of the steel, and the initial efforts made to prevent rust setting in will have a great bearing on maintenance problems in later years. There are steel boats afloat which have ridden the waves for eight or ten years

Aluminium has achieved considerable popularity amongst small boat owners because of its non-rusting properties

without even the first sign of the ominous yellow-brown stain. There are others—unfortunately the majority—that have been thrown into the water with little thought or preparation to become, within weeks, rust buckets.

THE WEATHER

Perhaps it would have been more correct to deal with the weather at the beginning of this chapter because, directly or indirectly, it is the *cause celebre* of all maintenance problems. Wet rot, dry rot, rust and corrosion—and even, to a certain extent, wear and tear—are all affected by the weather. It is because the weather plays a part in so many factors involving maintenance, that it cannot be treated as one subject.

The sun, particularly in warmer climates, is the enemy of all external materials, whether they be protective paint coats, pigments, awnings, sails and what-have-you. It is particularly the enemy of colours which, unless protected from the ultra-violet rays of the sun, soon fade and are destroyed. Exposure to strong sunlight can have a derogatory effect on most materials used in the construction of boats and many maintenance problems will result unless steps to protect the materials are taken.

Awnings and covers, whether they be of

canvas or synthetic materials, are essential when the boat is constantly exposed to sunlight. Although the awnings and covers will be affected by the sunlight, they are expendable and can be replaced easily; a different proposition to the faded colours of a fibreglass cabin or cockpit.

Indirectly the sun also creates problems by heating the interior of the boat and causing condensation and the possibility of dry rot. Stretch and warping of steel or aluminium fittings are not unknown in tropical climates, and drying out of seams, warping of timber with resultant leakage are constant problems in timber boats.

But the sun is not the only culprit. Rain, seeping down through cracks and crevices, sets up wet rot in inaccessible spots and dry rot where conditions are suitable. Sails and awnings—particularly canvas sails—suffer from the effects of rain and water as also do nonsynthetic ropes, deck timbers, paintwork, etc. Indirectly, the wind adds to the toll in the form of torn sails and covers, to say nothing of damaged hulls and equipment when storms build up.

A good boat cover is the best insurance against the ravages of the elements when a boat is lying to her mooring

The causes of maintenance owing to weather, are innumerable. The cures, though not so numerous, are varied and in most cases will depend on local conditions. The basic preventive methods of awnings, covers, etc., help to withstand much of the destructive effects of the weather, but there will always be some aspect of local conditions which will require attention if the boat is to be satisfactorily protected from the elements.

WEAR AND TEAR

Like the weather, wear and tear creates problems which are often dealt with under other headings. The chafing of sails against rigging, for example, results in the deterioration of galvanising and rust sets in. The vibration of an engine working out of alignment can cause stern-gland damage resulting in leakage or cracking of surrounding hull areas. These, and hundreds of other problems which make maintenance necessary, are usually the result of wear and tear.

Because it is such a comprehensive subject, it is virtually impossible to approach the problem of wear and tear in any set way. Most problems which are created by wear and tear are individual and need to be treated according to their individual characteristics. Loose engine bolts, loose fastenings, vibration, chafing,

The stresses and strains of sailing in hard weather
increases the maintenance problem considerably

Wear and tear on a boat can come from such simple
factors as pulling it up a landing ramp

wearing of bearings, physical wearing away of timber, are but a few of the thousands of maintenance problems which arise from wear and tear.

Perhaps only one common factor can be applied to all maintenance problems created in this way, and that is adequately described in the proverb, *A stitch in time saves nine.* Almost all maintenance problems arising from wear and tear are most effectively treated if they are caught in the early stages. Loose bolts become looser, vibration increases, any form of wearing away gets worse if allowed to continue. Wear and tear on any part of a boat will cause greater damage if it is not treated immediately. Thus the boat owner who is on top of his maintenance routine, and attacks the problems as they appear, is the owner who will have not only the best looking boat in the harbour, but also the safest.

ACCIDENT

Accidents will happen, and when they do they invariably bring with them maintenance problems.

However, these problems are almost invariably a question of physical damage and their cure lies in many directions. Repair and refitting work is described in detail later in this book, where problems arising from accident damage are dealt with.

Racing, needless to say, creates the greatest maintenance problem, particularly when wear and tear are concerned. Photo Power Boat & Yachting

CHAPTER SIX

Timber Hulls

CLEANING

SINCE TIMBER HULLS are invariably painted or varnished, cleaning a timber hull means cleaning off paintwork. Few vessels use other than glossy paint for exterior finishes—although the cleaning problem would possibly be easier if the finishes were matt or semi-matt. This is principally because any method of thorough cleaning must reduce the gloss finish of a coat of paint. Few, if any, detergents can be used effectively over any considerable area without detracting from the high gloss finish. Indeed it would be safe to say that varnish, which depends entirely on its gloss sheen for appearance, cannot be successfully cleaned without a following coat of varnish to restore the original appearance.

Since paintwork must always be washed clean before a new coat is added, the cleaning down of old paintwork is usually followed by a new coat. If not, care in the use of detergents must be taken to prevent damage to the finish of the existing coat.

Warm water made soapy with soft soap is the only cleaning material that will remove light marks from high gloss paintwork and varnish without dulling the sheen. Obviously, this can be used only to remove superficial dirt and dust, and marks of any size must be treated separately. Here, a stronger detergent solution or bathbrick should be used, carefully restricting the area affected to a minimum. This may then be touched up later—preferably with a small spray can of gloss paint or lacquer—to cover up the dull area and renew the full gloss coat.

If the hull is badly marked, a stronger cleaner is needed, regardless of the probability of a complete renewal of the gloss coat. "Sugee", the well known cleaner used on board ship from time immemorial, is better than most commercial products. It is a solution of washing soda and soap powder, and when used in hot water will remove even the most stubborn stains. It will also remove all gloss, completely and absolutely!

A bathbrick kept handy and used in conjunction with the sugee is the answer to stubborn stains or rust marks. A de-greasing solution will be required if oil or grease stains are severe, but generally speaking, sugee takes care of all but the most difficult problems. It is also fairly tough on the skin, and a bucket of fresh water should be kept on hand to wash off the sugee from the paintwork as well as from the hands when the job is done.

Brasso is an excellent cleaner where rust and similar very stubborn stains are encountered, and after all other avenues have been tried, wet and dry sandpaper is a last resort. However, these should be used only when touching up is to follow, as they damage the paint skin, quite apart from removing the gloss.

Scratches, bruises and similar marks involve physical damage of the paint skin and should be dealt with as described later in the section dealing with touching up paintwork.

PATCHING

With stoppers

The amount of patching required and the material to be used will depend greatly on the type and extent of the damage to be repaired. Large or extensive areas where the timber is

Maintaining a hull in "showroom" condition requires regular and careful cleaning

badly damaged will require surgery to remove and repair the damage. This is dealt with in detail in Section V.

Damage other than that requiring repair or renewal of the timber is usually in the form of cracks, dents or scratches. Providing these are not too large, one of the epoxy-type stopping compounds is the best repair material. The timber to be patched should be dry, and free from paint other than a single coat of metallic primer applied some hours before patching is to begin.

The stoppers are usually in two-pack form, with a limited life when mixed, and only sufficient should be mixed to cover a small area at a time. The stopper should be forced into the cracks and holes with a flat putty knife and then smoothed off flush with the surface. It should be given at least twenty-four hours to ensure a good cure, then sanded back smooth with the surrounding timber and painted with an undercoat. Further painting will depend on whether or not the

entire area is to be painted or just the damaged spots "touched up". Full details concerning painting are included in this chapter.

Where the damage is too extensive or the holes too large to fill with a stopper, yet not sufficient to warrant surgery on the timber itself, fibreglass is excellent for patching.

Fastening holes need to be patched the same as any other hole. Dowel plugs are used here and will be "faired" off later flush with the planks

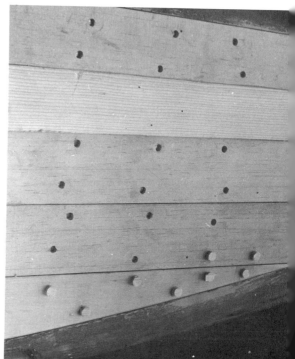

Used correctly, fibreglass is an excellent material for patching timber hulls

With fibreglass

Fibreglass is undoubtedly one of the most useful repair materials ever to hit the boating scene. Its ease of application, its ability to be applied to almost any surface, and its clean, smooth finish place it above many of the traditional patching materials such as copper, lead, canvas, and so on.

However, the fact that it is far more workable than most repair materials does not give fibreglass a blanket cover for all repair jobs; there are surfaces which will not accept the fibreglass at all. Care, thought and preparation must go into any surface before fibreglass can be applied as a patching material.

This applies particularly to timber; fibreglass cannot be applied to timber which has not been thoroughly cleaned and dried. In fact the drying process may be said to be carried to the extreme, as it is often hard to get fibreglass to take to any timber other than that in almost virgin condition. Any sign of dampness, dust or grease, and the fibreglass—although it may

take initially—will gradually peel off, leaving the hull in its original condition.

A vessel normally kept in the water will need time to dry out if effective fibreglassing is to be done to the hull. Dinghies and other small craft can be stored in a shed or garage, but a larger craft needs to be slipped and covered. This is the only drawback in using fibreglass as a patching medium.

Providing the hull is dried out properly, the next step is cleanliness. Every scrap of paint must be removed from the timber where the patch is to be applied. If chemical removers are used, the chemical itself must be washed off the timber. A good system is to burn off the area to be fibreglassed, as the heat tends to help the drying-out process.

The timber must be sanded back to bare wood to remove any primer that may have impregnated the fibres, and the surface then left slightly roughened to give the resin a "key" to grip. This roughness will not be transmitted through the "glass" as the finish is smooth and even, and can be sanded to a high gloss finish anyway.

When the surface is completely dry and cleaned of paint, dust, and dirt, the resin

Fibreglass lifts easily from surfaces which were not clean, dry or properly prepared in the first place

should be mixed. The manufacturer's instructions must be carefully followed here, as the resin can harden very quickly, according to the way in which it is mixed, and according to local weather. Once it starts hardening it cannot be used. If mixed to the normal consistency, it should not harden inside fifteen to twenty minutes.

A good thick coat of resin is placed on the damaged area and worked into the timber. If a large hole is to be covered a timber fitting piece will have to be made first. In fact, when patching a large hole it is often better to repair the hole with timber in the normal way, and use the fibreglass covering as a watertight finish. If the damage is only small, such as cracks or fastening holes, the resin will often fill them, or a small amount of the glass mat can be worked into the cavity.

The mat, whether it be woven mat, which is better for small indentations, or chopped strand, which is better for deep indentations, is then placed on the newly-painted resin, and fitted to the correct position. Immediately, more resin is worked into the glass fibres, using a short stiff brush and a stencilling action rather than a painting action. It is essential that the resin passes right through the glass fibres and makes good contact with the original coat on the timber surface. The brush should be jabbed into the mat until the fibres seem to merge with the resin. Woven mat requires more work than loose or chopped strand as, if the resin is not thoroughly worked through it, small pinholes will appear when the resin dries. Air bubbles trapped beneath the fibreglass must be worked out as they interfere with the adhesion of the fibreglass to the timber.

By making the application of resin fairly quickly, but evenly, a smooth finish will result. The resin will harden within minutes, but should be left overnight to ensure that it is properly cured before commencing any further work. It can then be sanded down by using a power sander until smooth and flush with surrounding surfaces, and then painted in the normal way. The surface should not be finished to a

A fibreglass patch is effective on almost any material. Note the rope brush used to work the resin through the glass fibre mat

really high gloss before the first coat of paint is applied, or the paint will not have a good grip. A full description of painting on fibreglass surfaces is given in the next chapter.

PAINTING

New or bare timber

With all forms of painting, no matter what the base, a good finish can only be obtained if the groundwork has been done correctly and painstakingly. More boats have a poor paint finish because time and trouble was not taken in preparation of the surface, than for any other single reason. Since primers and undercoats *must* be used, a little extra time and care in using them should not be difficult to arrange. The difference in the finish of the final coat will be rewarding.

Liberal use of sandpapers between coats is one of the most neglected aspects of painting. There is a natural reluctance on the part of an inexperienced painter to rub off, with gritty paper, the nice finish he has just obtained with a coat of paint. It is often hard to see the small bumps and blemishes which will be so obvious in the final finish, and the temptation is to go ahead and put the top coat over a smooth-looking undercoat, instead of rubbing it till it looks dull and scratched.

Like most temptations, however, it must be resisted. Fine dust, a brush hair, even the brush marks themselves will be exaggerated by every coat added, and unless it is rubbed back, each successive coat will get rougher and more uneven. The sandpaper may dull the smooth finish on an undercoat, but this is easily replaced. Far more easily, in fact, than the removal of the unevenness which will result if the blemishes in the undercoat are not removed before the top coats go on.

But the sanding of the undercoats and primer is not the beginning. Preparation starts with the timber itself, and this in turn depends on the condition of the timber to be painted. Timber that has not been painted before will need to be smoothed right back, firstly with a plane and then with sandpaper. A circular sanding disc must never be used as this will tend to score, no matter how carefully it is used. Belt sanders or orbital sanders are permissible power tools at this stage, although care must be taken to prevent scoring or marking even with these. Best of all is hand sanding, preferably with a block of timber or some other material around which the sandpaper has been wrapped.

Unfortunately, boats usually have fairly large surfaces to be sanded, particularly on the hull, and hand sanding is a long and arduous business. This is where patience is undoubtedly a virtue and it is interesting, when painting time comes around, to discover how many virtuous sailors there are.

The timber may have to be treated before sanding. A grain filler must be used if there is any sign of grain opening or cracks in the timber. Nail holes, or the aftermath of any other form of fastening, if not already plugged, must be so treated. There are many brands of fillers available—the epoxy-type is well suited for covering fastenings.

The filler should be driven very firmly into

For a racing yacht such as this, correct painting is important for more reasons than just appearance. Particularly in the underwater areas. Photo courtesy International Paints

the hole or crack and worked to ensure that it gets a firm grip on the surrounding timber. Unless this is done there may be a tendency for the filler to fall out when the boat starts working in a seaway, and no amount of paint will hold it in. Using a putty knife, or some other splaying tool, the filler can be pressed hard into the fibres of the timber surrounding the hole to ensure good bonding at this point. Needless to say the timber must be clean, dry and free from grease or oil.

If caulking has been done in the area to be painted, or if caulking seams have opened, then the unevenness must be filled and smoothed off. A putty or caulking compound is better than epoxy fillers for this job as the seams between the planks will open and close with the working of the boat and also as the planks swell and dry out when they are saturated with water. A putty or caulking com-

93

pound will remain elastic to allow such movement.

If metal fastenings have been used, care must be taken before painting to ensure that no corrosion has taken place. Galvanised steel screws and fastenings should be dipped or treated with anti-rust composition before use, and should be sealed over with a similar chemical when they are in place. Any one of the anti-rust treatments mentioned in the section dealing with rust could be used to seal over the head of the fastening before plugging.

With the timber itself treated and all cracks and holes filled and sanded off, the time has come for the first coat. This is invariably a primer; the best for new wood is a metallic primer. The traditional red lead is also suitable, but lacks many of the useful properties incorporated into proprietary brands of metallic primer. Not least among these is the ability of the primer to be absorbed by the timber, thus taking the preventive properties right into the fibres and not just building a surface protection. Also most modern primers have waterproof properties, an important consideration for boats which are permanently moored

Since painting provides protection as well as appearance, every inch of the boat must be covered, including difficult, often unseen corners.

in the water. They are designed to create good adhesion between the timber and the paint, offering a good base on which to build up future coats and make a complete seal over the bare wood.

Because of these many properties the primer should be given plenty of time to be absorbed into the timber before successive coats are added. At least forty-eight hours should elapse between coats, and further time would not go amiss.

It is interesting to note here that many shipwrights prefer to apply one coat of primer before the stopping and sealing processes mentioned earlier. This is a matter of personal preference and depends also on the type of filler used. However, by and large it is hard to go wrong by using the primer before the stopping and plugging and this can be done unless the instructions with the stopping material suggest otherwise.

Primer should be applied by brush and there should be a minimum of two coats. If, after sanding down blemishes, the bare timber starts to come through again, a third coat will not be out of order. Remember that the beautiful finish every yachtsman strives for begins at this point.

Needless to say, primer can be used only on surfaces that are to be painted. Timber to

Quality is important if a good paint finish is to be achieved. Only fresh, good quality paint should be used

ultra smooth finish that—since the final coats are to follow—is so necessary to produce a high sheen on the gloss coat. One or two coats of undercoat should be applied; if the timber is new, two coats without hesitation.

With the undercoat firmly in place and sanded back to a mirror-smooth finish, it is time for the final coat or coats. Two coats of high-gloss marine finish are best if the surface preparation has been as described above. This may be applied with a brush or spray, although undoubtedly the finish will be more attractive if the final coat is sprayed. However, spray painting requires a great deal of skill and often several more coats than brush painting (see details on spray painting in Section 1). Only the experienced should attempt spray painting, and then only with the best equipment.

The normal marine gloss paints can only be used over undercoats if they are to offer their best in terms of finishes. Sanding back between top coats is very necessary and a very hard rub back—even at the cost of an additional top coat—is more than justified. Gloss paints do not take so long to dry and twelve hours between coats is sufficient in reasonable drying conditions. The paint should be thinned to exactly the consistency required, particularly when spray guns are used. Thick paint will give rise to skin wrinkles, and thin paint will cause problems by running indiscriminately down the surface: experience is the only guide to thinning paint.

The correct thinners should be used and these with caution, as over-thinning can reduce the gloss of the paint. As a rule, *fresh* paint (bought from a store with a good turnover in this particular brand, and not from a small boatshed that may have had the paint on the shelves for years) should not require much adjustment of consistency, providing it is thoroughly stirred to ensure that the sediment is dispersed evenly throughout the entire can.

Recapitulating briefly: the essence of a good finish lies in the preparation and the build-up of the under-surfaces. However, the final coat

be varnished requires special treatment and this is dealt with separately later in this chapter.

With the primer on and sanded back to a smooth finish with medium grade paper, the first undercoat is due. As with other paints for marine use, a good, waterproof undercoat is the correct one to use for all surfaces that may come in contact with water. There are innumerable brands and the recommendation of a shipwright for both undercoats and finishing coats should be sought if one is not familiar with these paints. The undercoat can be applied by brush or spray.

Once again, time should be given for the paint to adhere and harden well before any sanding work is done. Twelve hours would be a minimum period to let the undercoat dry in good ventilation and reasonably warm weather; twenty-four hours would not go amiss. Sanding should be with wet and dry paper soaked in warm soapy water, and the slurry formed must be well cleaned off before further coats are added. This will give an

Touching up marks and damaged spots needs the same care and attention as a full paint job if a good result is to be achieved

is all important if that enviable high sheen is to be obtained. And not only the type and application of the paint itself, but the conditions under which it is applied have much to do with the final result. The weather and location can make or mar the finish. These aspects are dealt with in Section 1 of this book and are well worth consideration before taking the lid off the first can of paint.

TOUCHING-UP AND REPAINTING

As with painting new timber, touching-up old paintwork first requires attention to surface preparation. The surfaces to be repainted must be thoroughly sanded off; the more sanding the better the final result. Wet and dry sandpapering over all surfaces to be painted, with extra hard rubbing down where the old paint has flaked or peeled, is the order of the day, and if the surface has been damaged, it may be necessary to rub back to the bare timber and build up again with primers and undercoats as described in this chapter.

Power tools should be used with caution and rotary disc sanders not at all. The smooth finish to the rubbing back of old paintwork is as essential as in new work, and scores will be very hard to cover. Hand sanding with

wet and dry is by far the best—albeit the most arduous—method of obtaining an ideal surface.

Cracks, scores and other blemishes should be stopped and smoothed off, then sanded with the rest of the surface. Considerable attention should be given to ensuring that all flaking or blistering paint is sanded right out and that the edges of such affected areas are not liable to lift at a later stage. If good adhesion by the surrounding paintwork is not evident, the entire surface should be taken back and built up again. These areas, once having blistered or cracked, need thorough treatment to prevent recurrence of the trouble as well as to minimise the unevenness of the surface when the final topcoat is applied.

As mentioned earlier, there is a variety of fillers available on the market, and the one most suitable to the particular area and the section to be filled should be used. Putties, plastic wood fillers and epoxy fillers all have their uses, depending mainly on the location of the damage to be repaired and surrounding material. Filling and stopping is as important as the painting, since a filling plug which falls out some weeks after the repair has been effected, will break off the new paintwork with it. No paint will hold in an unsatisfactory filling.

If, in the course of rubbing back and repairing old paintwork the bare timber is uncovered, it will need to be treated and built up as described for new timber. Primer and undercoats will need to be used, and used with care so that they are not spilled over surrounding areas, thus building up an unevenness of the surface. If the bare timber is not uncovered, then usually one coat of undercoat over the rubbed-back areas will suffice before adding the overall top coats.

Even greater care must be taken to ensure that the old paintwork is clean and dry, than is taken with bare timber. Grease and dirt can become ingrained into old paintwork and will give an unsatisfactory base to new paintwork unless rubbed off in the course of sandpapering, or removed satisfactorily in some other way.

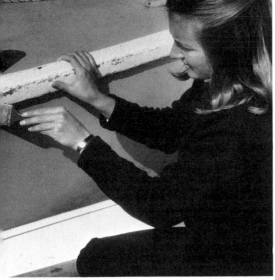

Patching up old paintwork can only be done success-fully if the areas are treated in the correct manner before the top coat is applied

The surface on to which either the undercoat or the finishing coat is applied must be clean, dust free and dry if the best finish is to be achieved.

Brush or spray may be used to apply all coats (other than primer which requires brush application) when retouching. If the brush is

The secret of successful varnishing is plain hard work — particularly in the sanding back. Photo courtesy Power Boat & Yachting

used, one top coat is usually sufficient providing the previous treatment has been adequately carried out. With the spray it is better to apply finer coats to achieve the surface required. This will be governed mainly by the conditions under which the work is done and the extent of the retouching.

Varnishing

Undoubtedly one of the hardest finishes to achieve successfully when renovating a boat is the super-gloss, mirror-like finish of good varnish work. Although the sheen is somewhat easier to achieve now that synthetic paints have appeared on the market, the final result of softly-glowing timber tones beneath the high gloss can only be achieved by patience, hard work, and strict attention to detail. Whether the varnish work is to be on a hull, a cabin, or interior fittings, the groundwork is the most important part of the whole effort, and skimping at this stage will leave a surface that will never hold a decent varnish coat in a thousand years or with a thousand coats.

With new timber the problem is not quite so acute as with previously varnished or painted timber where blemishes and marks from removing the earlier coats must be treated. However, the care and preparation required for varnishwork does not start just with the timber itself but goes back to the actual construction of the area to be painted.

For example, pencil marks, used for measuring off when building or repairing, must be removed or they will show through the varnish. Similarly scratch or "bruise" marks will become more visible when varnished. Glues must be used with extreme caution as any surplus running out of a join—even though it may be immediately wiped off—will leave a mark which shows through the varnish. Stopping and plugging must be given more attention. Wood dowels should be used to plug fastening holes, and the grain of the dowel lined up with the grain of the timber surface so that the effect of plugging is minimised. Grain filling must be done with care for the same reason.

97

Varnished hulls require a great deal of patience and skill if they are to achieve the beautiful warm glow that is characteristic of good varnish work

In short, the new timber to be varnished must be in impeccable condition before even the first coat is applied. The best way to gauge this condition is by eye. If, when it is sanded back ready for the first coat, the bare timber looks perfect, there is every chance it will look that way through the varnish. All blemishes must be removed, no matter how small, and the surface sanded smooth to bring up the grain. A wipe-over with a damp turpentine cloth will temporarily stain the surface and show up any glue streaks or other imperfections which may not be obvious to the naked eye.

With the surface ready, the eye of the painter satisfied, and the damp turpentine dried out, preparation for the varnish can be made. If there is any possibility of dust or dirt in the area it should be vacuumed, but the wet turpentine rag should have taken care of dust on the timber itself. The correct weather is important

too, more important than with painting and a warm, dry day should be chosen in preference to a day that is too hot, too cold, or wet.

There are many schools of thought on the building up of a first class varnish job. Some advocate more dilution of the varnish and a greater number of coats, and undoubtedly this has merits. However, since this book is intended to deal with general repair and maintenance and not attempt the high class artistry that may be seen on some boats, a compromise is offered in that the procedure described here for building up a good varnish coat will provide a first class job, without going to extremes.

The first coat of varnish should be diluted with about twenty percent of turpentine. This allows it to saturate the timber, giving a good base for all future work. This coat should be allowed to dry for a day or two and another coat similarly applied. The two coats must be rubbed hard back with wet and dry sandpaper, so that there are no uneven spots, no blemishes. The brush should never be loaded too heavily with varnish as runs may ensue, and in any case one of the secrets of good varnish work is to achieve as thin a coat as possible each time.

A third coat is applied, reducing the dilution of turpentine to about ten percent. This should then be given at least a week to harden. Wet and dry sandpaper of medium grade, used with warm soapy water, is the best for rubbing back each new coat at this stage, and it should be used mercilessly, taking the shiny varnish back to a dull matt. Another coat of ten percent dilution, another week to dry and another rub back, and the varnish is ready for its finishing coats.

It is a good practice to use a new brush for each coat and open a new can of varnish. This may sound a little expensive, but the remainder of the cans can be put together for

Pride of a boat painter's eye — two beautifully varnished hulls

touching up or some less important job at a later date. Varnish tends to deteriorate and the period between coats can, once the air has got to the varnish remaining in the tin, cause quite a noticeable loss when the can is opened again. Since a first class finish is required, the extra expense is well justified at this stage.

The final coats are of pure varnish, applied, as mentioned, with a new brush. Great care must be taken to see that the surfaces are well rubbed back and cleaned of all dust before the coat is applied. The wet turpentine rag can be used after rubbing off to remove specks of dust or dirt that may still linger, and the area surrounding the surface to be varnished should be vacuumed to ensure that no specks will adhere while the varnish is still wet. The coats should be as thin as possible and smoothed out as quickly as possible to prevent any unevenness when the edges dry.

The number of final coats will vary accord-

ing to the appearance of the surface, but at least two will be necessary. They must be rubbed back with fine wet and dry and soapy water after at least a week has gone by to ensure firm drying. At this stage, the varnish needs as long as possible to harden well and two weeks will not be amiss if such time can be spared. A solid, hard coat will be easy to sand back and offer a firm base for the final gloss.

Plastic and synthetic finishes

The development of plastic and epoxy finishes for clear, high gloss treatment of timber has provided the yachtsman with a new, easier to use, and often longer lasting finish. These chemicals can usually be used only on new timber, or over a previous coat of a similar liquid, and thus old varnish must be completely removed before use of one of the synthetics.

Because of the number of different brands and the different methods of mixing the solutions and applying them to the timber, it is not possible to offer a standard procedure in this book. However, the instructions given with the treatment and the publications offered

Varnish deteriorates quickly and this deterioration is accelerated if correct procedures are not followed in the application of the varnish coats

by the manufacturers are usually well detailed and simple to follow. The argument Oil Varnish versus Synthetics will not be indulged in here, but sufficient to say that each has its merits both in terms of application and appearance, and also of durability. The synthetics offer more resistance to the ravages of wind and weather, salt water and oil, etc., but a well-laid varnish surface cannot be beaten for beauty and depth of colour. The final choice must be by the boat owner.

Touching up and re-varnishing old work

As with paintwork, the secret of re-covering varnish work lies in taking back the old varnish. If it is still in good condition and showing no signs of flaking or blistering, a good rub back with wet and dry sandpaper (until the varnishwork takes on a matt appearance) is all that is required before re-varnishing with a new can of pure varnish. If, however, cracking or flaking appear, or if the surface has broken away and is showing bare timber at any point, then the varnish will have to be taken back to bare timber and built up again as described earlier.

This will also be the case if water has found its way under the varnishwork and has stained the timber. A loose or rusted fastening, cracking round edges or in corners or incorrect drying out of the wood before the varnish was applied are a few of the causes of this damp stain beneath the surface. It almost invariably appears as a dark stain and becomes almost black unless cured. It also tends to spread through the fibres of the timber, thus completely wrecking the appearance of the varnish work. The old varnish will have to be removed completely and the timber allowed to dry out or treated if corrosion or rust have added to the stain.

Removing old varnish must always be done with chemical paint strippers and never by burning. It is almost impossible to burn off timber without occasionally scorching the surface, and although this may be readily covered if the surface is to be painted later, it will

care not to score the timber either with the scraper or with subsequent sandpaper, as small scratches and scores can be grossly exaggerated when covered with varnish. Sandpapering by rubbing with the grain can reduce the possibility of scoring, but care is necessary all the time, and the use of rotary disc sanders quite out of the question.

Once the work has been stripped back to bare timber it should be wiped off with turpentine to neutralise the effect of the stripper and remove any particles which may be adhering. As mentioned earlier in this section, the application of the turpentine also has much the same effect as a coat of varnish and immediately shows up any blemishes or marks. These must be removed carefully before the final sanding, and then the re-building process begun as described earlier for new timber. If the work is to be done in the open air (e.g. on the mooring) then added care must be taken to prevent dust, dirt or salt spray being blown on to the surface before or during varnishing, as any of these, once embodied in the varnish itself, may ruin all the hard work that has gone before.

With the old varnishwork rubbed right back, the new coats should be applied thinly and carefully

stand out as a large black mark beneath varnish. The varnish should be removed as described in the section on stripping off, taking

CHAPTER SEVEN

Fibreglass Hulls

CLEANING

ALTHOUGH REPUTED to be maintenance free, fibreglass requires quite a lot of attention. Even when not painted, the surface of the synthetic material can become as dirty and marked as any other surface, and when painted, of course, is no different to any other painted material.

The dirty marks which result from rubbing against a wharf or another boat or dinghy, or from oil and other rubbish in the water, can be removed as they would from ordinary paintwork. A warm soapy rinse will take care of most superficial marks, and the use of a detergent or stronger cleaner should remove more stubborn spots.

With the passage of time, however, there is a tendency for more than dirt to mark the surface of a boat, particularly the hull. Fine scratches from objects in the water brushing the hull as it ploughs through the water, or from neglected rowlocks when a dinghy comes

Superficial marks can be removed from fibreglass by using a household detergent

alongside, can make even a clean surface look very untidy. And every now and then a deep scratch or gouge from some mishap or other will add its quota to the pattern on the boat's side.

The heavy scratches and gouges will, of course, need special treatment in the form of a filler, with sanding and finishing. This is dealt with later in this chapter. The finer scratches do not need quite such drastic treatment, and a rub down with Brasso, or similar metal polish, or a harsh scouring cleanser such as is used to remove stains from baths and sinks, will usually do the trick. For the odd stubborn scratch, a rub with fine wet and dry sandpaper should remove most of the visible signs.

Needless to say, this treatment soon causes deterioration to the super gel finish given to glass boats, and they begin to look faded. The only way to restore the appearance is with a complete coat of paint. And once paint goes on to fibreglass, it requires the same (perhaps even more) care it would on a timber boat, and thus some of the maintenance-free aspect of fibreglass has already been lost.

Cleaning a painted fibreglass hull is no different to a painted hull of any sort, and the description given under the heading "Cleaning a timber hull" earlier in this section is appropriate.

PATCHING

Fibreglass comes in several forms all of which basically consist of a glass fibre reinforcement which is set in an epoxy resin. The glass reinforcement can be in the form of strands or of woven mat. Usually, when fibreglass boats

Fibreglass, to be kept in showroom condition, needs care and maintenance like any other material. Photo courtesy Coronet Boats

are built commercially, the strand type is used in preference to the woven type. However, for patching small areas, and for amateur use generally, the woven material is easier to handle and often more effective. Much depends, of course, on the area to be patched and if a variety of patching work is to be done, the strand mat should be available as well as the woven mat. The woven material can be adapted for most patching jobs, but if a large area of considerable thickness is to be moulded, chopped strand is preferable. Where the surface to be repaired is small and shallow the procedure should be as follows:

The damaged area should be thoroughly cleaned and dried, and the edges and surrounding areas rubbed off with coarse sandpaper to give a key for the new work. It is essential that all fibreglass dust caused by sanding be brushed away, or wiped with a spirit rag, as it may interfere with the good adhesion of the new patch. The woven mat should then be cut to slightly overlap the damaged area and the

ends of the mat frayed out to give good contact with the surrounding surface. Care must be taken when mixing the resin to follow the manufacturer's instructions implicitly. Resin can cure too quickly or too slowly, and to achieve the maximum strength and durability the exact amount of catalytic agent must be added to the resin.

A small amount of the resin solution should be applied to the damaged area in order to hold the woven material in place. Then, using a fairly stiff brush the remainder of the resin should be forced into the weave of the material so it can seep right through to the resin on the underside. This should be continued until the resin has been worked hard into the cloth and has built up sufficiently to fill the damaged area and form a slightly convex surface. If the area to be patched is fairly deep, it may be necessary to lay two or more thicknesses of material, or fill the cavity with chopped strand. It is important that the depression is not filled solely with resin, as this will harden and tend to come away from the old material. The mat should be packed in fairly tightly and the edges loosened to make good adhesion with the edges of the damaged area. The filled area

Materials required to patch fibreglass: can of resin, applicator and fibreglass patch. Note: the damaged area has already been cleaned and prepared

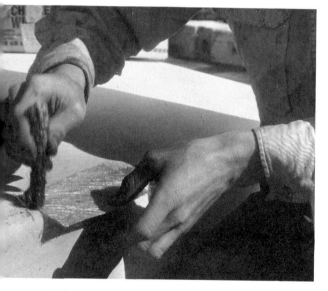

The resin has been applied to the damaged surface and a patch of fibreglass placed in position

should then be covered with a final piece of material to hold the rest in place. It is essential that when using several thicknesses of mat, the resin is forced right through all layers to saturate the entire patch, right down to the bottom of the depression. To ensure the best possible adherence of the old fibreglass to the new, where possible some of the fibres of the old fibreglass should be scraped out or separated from the resin so that they protrude into the new patch.

When the resin has cured and hardened it can be sanded back flush with other surfaces. If using a power sander take care not to score the surrounding surfaces, particularly if they are to be left bare and not painted.

Where a large area of fibreglass has to be patched, or a large repair carried out, or where the damage is of considerable thickness, it is better to turn the job·over to a professional unless experienced in this type of repair. The damaged areas must be built up with masking tape and cardboard so that the resin can be moulded into the correct shape. This becomes particularly difficult when vertical areas have to be shaped, or where the moulding has to be done on a deckhead or similar area.

If it must be done by the boatowner himself, the procedure is similar to that described earlier.

Instead of woven mat, chopped strand should be used and the strand should be packed into the area to be filled, and completely and thoroughly saturated with the resin. The surrounding fibres of the old fibreglass must be fluffed out as much as possible to entwine with the new work, as the principal difficulty always in work of this size is the firm adhesion of the new to the old. Providing this is done satisfactorily, there should be a good chance of adhesion. Again it cannot be over emphasised that work of this nature and size should be undertaken by a qualified technician—particularly where the hull skin or structural

The top coat of resin must be worked thoroughly through the fibreglass patch. Bumps and irregularities can be sanded off later

Heavy damage like this needs a moulded patch

Superfluous damage is cut away leaving fibre of the original glass sticking out for good bonding

A mould is made with cardboard (backing damage area) and glass fibres secured in position

With the resin worked right through the mat it remains only to remove the mould and sand back to a smooth surface

members are concerned. A patch or repair which comes loose or drops out when the vessel is riding in a seaway can have disastrous effects.

Where a small hole or indentation in the ship's hull has to be repaired, it will be necessary to try to retain the high gloss of the exterior of the hull on the surface of the patch. This can be achieved by placing a sheet of cellophane over the exterior of the hole and coating it with a gel layer before making the repair. "Backing pieces" of this nature are widely used where a complete hole has to be

patched, but where a high gloss is not required almost any suitable material can be used.

PAINTING

The surface preparation of fibreglass is not unlike that of aluminium, where the smooth surface has to be etched to provide a base for future coats of paint. The difference lies in that a special etching paint is not necessary for fibreglass. Sandpaper of light to medium grade when used on the bare surface will provide the necessary scoring to give the paint a foothold. If the surface of the fibreglass is

Because of its light weight and ease of moulding, fibreglass is ideal for praam dinghies and small general-purpose boats

Some people prefer synthetic paints on fibreglass, and there is nothing against this. Usually, these paints can be applied direct to the fibreglass without the need for a primer, but the instructions offered with the particular brand in use should be studied well before painting begins.

When fibreglass is moulded, the mould is treated with a chemical to prevent adhesion of mould to boat; often some of this chemical may remain on the surface of the newly-moulded boat. It is usually a waxy substance, which makes it very hard for the paint to adhere, and it must therefore be removed before new painting is contemplated. Often etching with sandpaper will remove this substance, but a wipe off with white spirit (or other agent recommended by the paint manufacturer) will ensure a clean, dry surface.

TOUCHING UP AND REPAINTING FIBREGLASS

Because of the smooth surface presented by moulded fibreglass, paint is liable to chip off easily unless good adhesion is ensured in the early stages of preparation. When, through accident or age, the paint does start to chip or flake, it is very difficult indeed to patch. Unless the edges of the affected area can be scraped or sanded away to the point where it is obvious that excellent adhesion is taking place all around the edge of the area, it is better to take the paint right off and start building up again from scratch. Hard rubbing back of bare patches will soon show whether or not the old paint is going to stay on. If there is any doubt at all, it is better to do a full repaint job, for patching up fibreglass paint often leads only to continual retouching as more and more bits flake off.

The flexible nature of fibreglass, particularly in areas where it is very thin, add to the difficulty of keeping together a flaking surface and more time and money will be wasted trying to patch it than will be worthwhile. A complete strip-down and paint job will be more than justified.

not weathered, but very smooth, then a coarser paper may be required. The amount of etching done to the surface is not important as any unevenness can be sanded out in the subsequent coats of paint.

Normal metallic primer can be placed over the etched surface without further preparation. It is best applied by brush and worked well so that it obtains a good grip. From this point on, each successive coat can be added as described for timber: undercoats and topcoats of normal marine paint, with rubbing back and cleaning after each coat has dried. The finish coat should be of high gloss and applied when the surface of the other coats has been treated to the point where only the highest finish will result.

Because of its toughness fibreglass is ideal for boats which are called on to carry out hard work

Most chemical strippers can be used safely on fibreglass. Once stripped, the surface of the fibreglass should be well washed off and cleaned so that no specks of paint or stripper remain. The surface can then be prepared and built up again with various coats of paint.

CHAPTER EIGHT

Aluminium, Steel and Concrete Hulls

ALUMINIUM

Cleaning an aluminium hull

CLEANING THE BARE aluminium of an unpainted hull can be done in various ways. The choice will depend mainly on the type and size of the marks and stains and the agent that caused them.

Scratches and eroded marks due to physical damage cannot be removed and dents and similar distortion can only be removed by repairs described later in this chapter. Other superficial marks can be removed by a strong detergent or bath brick, or other form of cleaner. Sandpaper should not be used (nor bath brick unless absolutely necessary) as

Scratching of the hull can easily be repaired with a new paint job. Unpainted aluminium could not be repaired so easily

there is the tendency to scratch the high-polished metal.

The difficulty of removing marks and stains from aluminium is one good argument in favour of painting the surface when, in the event of damage, touching-up, or even a completely new coat, can be applied quite easily. The methods of cleaning painted aluminium are the same as for all other painted surfaces, and are dealt with in this section under the heading "Cleaning a Timber Hull".

Patching aluminium

Small holes in aluminium can be repaired with an epoxy cement or a rivet hammered into place. Large holes require patching. A patch slightly larger than the hole should be cut and shaped to the section it is to cover

by placing it over the hole and gently hammering it into shape with a rubber hammer.

The edges of the hole should be smoothed off with a file or hammer, so that the new patch can fit flush across it. The patch should for preference be placed on the inside of the hull, although this is not essential. A series of holes, the same size as the rivets to be used, should be drilled around the edge of the patch at half-inch diameters, and matching holes drilled in the hull.

Patching aluminium

Tightening loose rivets is not easy in awkward corners. A specially shaped backing block may have to be made

A thin layer of caulking compound between the patch and the hull will ensure watertightness. Once this has been laid, the patch can be put on and bolted into position. Providing the patch fits well and is shaped correctly, one of the bolts can be removed and replaced with a rivet. This procedure is repeated until all the bolts have been removed and the patch has been riveted all the way round.

If a stronger patch is required, or the correct thickness of patching material is not available, then the patch can be doubled, by placing one on each side of the damaged hull. The procedure is the same as described above, except for the added plate on the outside. It is best to rivet the outside patch first, and then rivet the inside patch (which should be slightly larger than the outside patch) over the hole. The result is neat and inconspicuous.

Tightening loose rivets

Rivets often work loose, particularly when the seam or fitting they hold together is subject to strain or working stresses. Providing they are discovered before they become too loose, and thus distorted, they are relatively easy to secure. A small anvil or similar block of metal is required and a ballhead hammer.

Loose rivets are tightened by placing the anvil hard against the underside and tapping firmly but gently on the rivet head with the hammer. This should be continued until the rivet takes up securely. Where one rivet has worked loose in a seam, it is possible adjacent rivets will also be starting to rattle, and it is a good idea to tap up several of the rivets each side of the main loose one. Even if they are not already starting to work loose, the tightening action will act as a preventive.

Riveting sheet aluminium

109

Where it is not possible to get the anvil on the opposite side of the aluminium (such as with a mast or spar), a special riveter is required, and the repair will have to be taken to a workshop.

If the rivet has worked badly loose or is distorted and cannot be tapped back into place, it will have to be renewed. In this case the old rivet is drilled out with a drill slightly larger than the present hole and the new rivet, of a size larger than the old, placed into position and secured. It is a good idea, once again, to renew rivets on each side of the broken one, and it may be necessary, where a waterproof seam is to be riveted, to putty or caulk the seam where the riveting takes place.

If a considerable length has to be re-riveted, it is wise to first bolt the seam into place. After the seam has been caulked, small bolts should be placed in most of the rivet holes and tightened up. Then each can be removed and replaced by a rivet without upsetting the tightness of the seam.

Knocking out dents in aluminium

Whether or not a dent can be knocked out will depend almost entirely on where it is located. A dent in a mast, for example, would be very difficult to remove. On the other

hand, a dent in the hull, providing it is not too severe, could be relatively easily taken out. Where there is any doubt, particularly with masts and spars, they should be sent to the manufacturer, as damage can be caused by attempting the repair in the wrong manner.

Slight dents in sheet aluminium, such as is used for the hull of small boats, can be removed by using a wooden block—larger than the diameter of the dent if possible—against the inside of the metal in the manner of an anvil, and hammering the dent out with a rubber hammer. The hammering should be done evenly, using a circular movement, and, if necessary, applying some heat from a blowtorch. The hammering should be started on the outside edge of the dent and gradually worked into the centre.

Aluminium can stretch if dented too badly, and although very bad dents usually mean a professional repair, heat from a blowtorch can often remove much of the stretch. Care must be taken not to overheat the metal and the hammering should be done swiftly and evenly to move the metal while still warm.

Repairing cracks in aluminium

The first essential in repairing a crack is to

Dents in structural parts can be removed with a ball hammer and wooden backing block. A rubber mallet should be used to remove dents in sheet aluminium

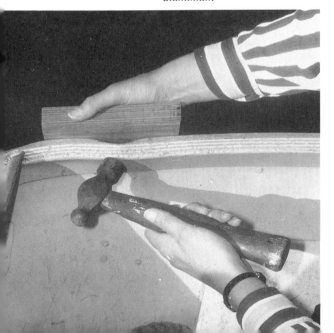

Removing dents in sheet aluminium with rubber mallet

drill the ends of the cracks with a small drill. This is the only means by which the crack can be prevented from spreading. If the crack is a small one, it may be filled with an epoxy cement, but sizeable cracks should be covered with caulking compound and then patched as described in the previous section for repairing holes.

The end of a hard season shows the need for maintenance, even on aluminium

The ends of cracks must be drilled to prevent them spreading

Painting aluminium

Painting an aluminium surface differs from painting steel or timber only in surface preparation and treatment. Normal gloss or matt paints can be used as finishing coats, as also can the synthetics. But for the initial treatment and primer, the painting of aluminium is carried out in exactly the same way as with timber.

To provide a footing for the paint, the aluminium surface must first be treated with a self-etching primer. This, as its name denotes, etches the smooth surface of the alloy and provides a base on which later coats may be built up. There are many brands of self-etching paint and most comprise two solutions which must be mixed just before use. It is essential that the surface to be etched is free from dirt and grease, and since it is not uncommon to grease aluminium surfaces for protection, de-greasing should be undertaken in every case as any grease left on the surface will impair the effect of the self-etch paint.

After it has been applied—usually by brush —the self-etching primer dries quickly and therefore speed must be made across the surface to ensure an even coat before it becomes tacky. Usually the primer takes only ten to fifteen minutes to dry, and leaves a thin film over the surface of the alloy which will readily take any following paints.

The surface tends to deteriorate if it is allowed to weather, and after four or five hours it should be covered with, preferably, a zinc chromate primer. This is applied in the usual way ensuring a good coverage over the entire surface. It should be given twelve hours to dry and then the first waterproof undercoat applied.

From here on the building-up of successive coats of paint are as for timber or fibreglass. The rubbing back and cleaning procedure between coats is the same and the type and finish of each coat need not vary. Naturally, a spray finish will give a very high sheen to an aluminium surface, but the painter should

Painting an aluminium spar. Self-etch primer covers half the spar in readiness for a base paint coat

not be deceived by the smoothness of the original surface and apply himself to the rubbing back and building up of coats as diligently as with any other material.

Touching up and repainting aluminium

The technique here is again similar to that for any other material. The surfaces must be rubbed back hard to remove blemishes, and cleaned to remove dirt and grit. Where the paint has been chipped away and bare aluminium appears, the touching-up process will begin with the self-etch primer and each section built-up to the undercoat stage before final sanding back and applying the overall finishing coat.

Where it is necessary to remove the paint, scraping or chemical paint removers may be used. Care should be exercised to see that any chemical in the paint remover does not react with the aluminium, but this is unlikely. Once the paint has been removed, the surface must be cleaned thoroughly with carbon tetrachloride and dried before applying the self-etch primer again. The successive coats are then built up as before.

STEEL

Cleaning a steel hull

Since steel in its bare form cannot be used for marine work, all steel external surfaces must be painted or treated against rust. For this reason, the cleaning of a painted steel hull is similar to the cleaning of any painted surface and this is described in detail in this section under the heading "Cleaning a Timber Hull".

Slight rust stains from seeping rust should be cleaned off with bath brick where possible, but where the stains are present because the paint has been broken and there is "bleeding", the treatment necessary will be that described later in this section for treatment of rust. This work must be carried out before any cleaning off of surrounding areas. In all probability the area will have to be chipped away and treated at the bare steel level.

"Bleeding" rust can never be successfully cleaned from paintwork without the source of the bleeding first being treated. In addition, the cleaning process requires stronger detergent than with normal wear and tear stains. Both these conditions mean that the paintwork has to be treated very severely, and cleaning down a steel hull almost invariably means touching up with paint afterwards.

Although this seems to indicate that steel surfaces require more maintenance than do other materials, in fact this is only the case when the steel surface has been allowed to deteriorate. Correct initial treatment and painting as described later in this chapter will reduce the necessity of maintenance considerably. As with all surfaces, it is the initial preparation and treatment that decides the amount of maintenance necessary in later years.

Treatment of rust

Contrary to many opinions, there is not just one form of rust, but several types, and the treatment for each is different. A careful diagnosis of any formation of rust should be made before treatment.

Most forms of rust on marine craft, however, are a result of one of two similar actions,

"Bleeding" rust streaks quickly mar the appearance of a steel boat

and as such can usually be treated with similar remedies. In both cases there is the common factor of salt air or salt moisture and it is with this factor that the treatment is concerned. The two forms of rust come about either:

1. As a result of neglect, allowing the covering surface of the steel to deteriorate to the point where it can be attacked by air and water.

2. By the flaking action of mill-scale which has the same effect of exposing the bare steel to the elements.

The former is a case for a rap across the knuckles; no material should be allowed to deteriorate to the extent that its protective covering lays it bare. The latter—*mill-scale*—is usually confined to fairly new steel and can be combated with reasonable attention in the early stages of painting.

Mill-scale is the bluish-grey sheen on new steel. When the sheet steel is rolled ("milled"), a fine scale forms on the steel which does not adhere too well to the body of the plate. As time goes on, the mill-scale tends to loosen and fall off, taking with it any protective coatings that may have been painted on. Obviously, the only treatment for this problem is the removal of the scale at an early stage before painting is undertaken.

Mill-scale can be removed in several ways. The best commercial method is sand blasting. A powerful jet of water directs millions of

grains of sand or grit on to the plate at high pressure. This blasts away the scale, revealing the clean steel beneath. The weather will do a similar job, although over a much greater period of time, hence the reason why large ships, when built on the slipway, are not painted until ready for launching. The new steel is allowed to weather so that the mill-scale falls off, leaving a coating of powdery rust which is then brushed away and the steel treated and painted.

No protective coating will prevent the scale from falling over a period of time, so new steel work, whether it be fittings or a complete hull job, needs to be treated if serious rust problems are to be avoided.

Where, because of deterioration of the covering paint, the rust has eaten into the steel plate itself, the treatment may be more drastic. The flaking rust must be chipped away, and this can be done most effectively by sand blasting, or with chipping hammers. It is important to avoid marking the steel underneath the rust with the chipping hammers as this tends to break up the new surface, making it

easier for rust to come back after it has been cured.

The remaining rust should be brushed away with a heavy wire brush until the bright gleam of the metal beneath comes through. Treatment with anti-corrosives and paint should then be begun. This is described in the next part of this chapter.

Sometimes the metal that has rusted is in a difficult position, such as with fittings or the thread of steel bolts, or is too small to attack with a chipping hammer or wire brush. Some form of rust dissolvent is then necessary. It is unlikely that the rust will be of sufficient calibre to warrant very drastic treatment, for if it has deteriorated to this stage, the fastenings are usually beyond repair.

However, if the rust has not gone too far on such fastenings or bolts, patience, together with a good freeing agent and the right tools, will usually pay dividends. Complete immersion in kerosene or a freeing oil is best if the fitting can be removed, otherwise constant application together with coaxing in a vice, or with multi-grips, should achieve the required result, and free the fitting or turn the nut.

Rust can and will attack almost any part of a boat that has a steel component. Rigging is very susceptible, and also are engines, for the heat of the engine tends to blister any paint that may have been applied, leaving the way wide open for rust to move in. Correct treatment, followed by application of the right types of paints, is the only solution, and time spent in rubbing back and building up rusted steel will pay off handsomely in cutting maintenance bills.

There are some parts of a boat's construction or fittings which· cannot be got at for maintenance at all. In a steel boat, the corners of the bilges and the stem and stern joins are all virtually inaccessible. And fittings which may be inaccessible at the top of masts or similar difficult spots, may have to go without maintenance for some time. The problem of these difficult spots is accentuated by the movement of steel as it expands and contracts with

Tell-tale signs of a rusting keel bolt. Hidden fastenings such as these must be sealed off to prevent attack by rust

Steel boats are always vulnerable to rust problems. Small marks such as seen here, can quickly deteriorate unless treated

temperature; paint treatment given to these parts during the building of the boat may crack as a result, allowing rust to seep into the bare steel.

In this case, a proprietary rustproof compound or a sealing agent such as Epi-Gard tar epoxy can be used. Since such problems are very individual it is best to contact the manufacturer of anti-rust products, as he may have a specific product to treat each specific problem.

Boat trailers, like working fittings, need special attention. Many are backed into the water to recover their boat, which brings working areas into direct contact with the salt moisture. The body of the trailer can be treated as for normal steel work, but the springs and axles, wheel hubs and winches are working parts which cannot be freely coated with paint. Here is another use for rustproof compounds, of which there are many. Correctly and frequently used, they not only prevent rust from

attacking the bare metal, but lubricate the working parts at the same time.

Painting steel

As with all materials, it is essential that steel surfaces, before they are painted, must be thoroughly cleaned and dried. In the previous chapter the methods of combating and removing rust from steel were described and, needless to say, this must be done effectively before any thought can be given to painting. When all rust has been removed and the metal has been wire-brushed to remove small flakes and dust, it should be cleaned down with a dry rag or a rag dampened with turpentine. This should leave the surface clean, although some small rust stains may remain to dull the brightness of the metal. Providing these are not loose or liable to flake off, they may be ignored.

Steel should be painted as quickly as possible after preparation in order to defeat any attempt by rust to gain a foothold on the clean metal. Any repairs or fillings necessary should be done before the final clean down. If there are signs of the metal "sweating" it should be dried off, and if necessary given time to free itself of further sweat before the last wipe-down. A coat of anti-corrosive will assist if there are any difficult corners in which some rust may still be lurking.

The first application will be metal primer. It should be applied by brush as evenly as possible over the entire area of new or cleaned steel. A heavy duty, rust-inhibiting primer containing lead silico chromates and inorganic phosphates is ideal for new steel. A good rust inhibitor applied at this stage will prevent any possibility of the rust "creeping" under surrounding paint and spreading all over the hull in the event of damage. It will confine the rust to the actual area exposed by the damage.

After about twenty-four hours, a second coat of primer should follow. This will ensure a good seal over the bare steel, and a good base on which to build up later coats of paint.

At this stage it is essential to apply at least one, and preferably two coats of waterproof synthetic paint which will offer maximum resistance to the action of salt water. Particularly is this necessary on "wetted" surfaces of the hull. Wet and dry sandpaper can be used to rub back the paint and present a smooth base for the final coats. Wet and dry is preferable to ordinary sandpaper, as it does not scratch. Used with warm soapy water, a medium- to fine-grade paper will provide a glass-smooth surface on which the final coats of gloss paint will be laid. As with all forms of painting, cleanliness is important and the dirt and slurry created by rubbing back each coat must be removed completely before the next coat is applied.

The choice of top coats is a personal one. The yachtsman has at his disposal a variety of paints and colours from which to choose, and advice on this subject would not befit a book such as this. Sufficient to say that a good quality brand of paint should always be used; a paint with an oil base and with a high gloss,

unless personal preference dictates otherwise. It may be applied by brush or spray; the latter, in the hands of a capable painter, provides the ultimate in finishes, particularly on steel.

Touching up

Providing the areas to be painted have been treated for rust and, if necessary chipped and neutralised as described in the paragraphs on rust treatment, touching up spots on steel varies little from painting the whole vessel. Slight pitting may occur if the rust has taken a good hold, and this should be plugged with one of the stoppers available on the market. At least one coat of metal primer, and preferably two, should be applied before the stopping is done, as it needs to be placed directly on the bare metal. The stopper can then be rubbed back to match the contours at the edge of the area and sealed with the following undercoats and finishing coat.

It is important to ensure that good contact is made between new work and old. The edges of the old paint should be rubbed back with sandpaper and the undercoats carried out over the edges of the old paint. It is equally important to ensure that the old paint has good

"Weathering" new steel removes much of the mill scale which is essential if the steel is to be painted

adhesion to the steel around the edges of the area to be touched up. Any flaking in this part would affect the new work as well as allowing rust to get under the old paint.

When all areas have been rubbed back, treated and stopped, the undercoat can be applied. From this point the procedure is as described above, with the adequate use of wet and dry sandpaper and cleaning rag to ensure a good, smooth finish. It is a good idea, if possible, to complete the final touching up with a complete finishing coat right over the entire area, as this will give extra sealing to any weakness that may arise between the new and old work.

CONCRETE

Cleaning a concrete hull

Concrete is never used in its bare state, but is always covered with a skin of paint. Although the concrete itself cannot be affected by water and is suitable without covering, the possibility of even the smallest section of the wire reinforcing showing through the concrete would be disastrous after contact with the salt water. The corrosive action of the water would begin a rust spot which would "run" along the wire mesh beneath the surface of the concrete.

Once started this sort of rust action is impossible to stop, and therefore security can only be obtained by correctly sealing off the bare hull from contact with salt water by means of the correct coatings of paint. Thus the question of cleaning off a painted concrete hull becomes the same as that described in "Cleaning a Timber Hull", in the earlier part of this section, and should be followed in detail.

Patching concrete

Like fibreglass, a concrete hull is formed by the addition of a liquid bonding to a shaped reinforcing material. For this reason it is— also like fibreglass—relatively easy to repair minor damage to hull and other skin surfaces. Major damage resulting in replacement of the reinforcing is a professional job since (in this case, *unlike* fibreglass) the wire mesh used for reinforcing is knitted together throughout the entire hull, and any breaks cannot simply be patched by slapping another piece of reinforcing into position. It must be knitted to the remainder of the reinforcing to provide a homogeneous strength and this must be done painstakingly, twisting each strand of the new wire to each one of the old. Since some hulls have up to six layers of mesh, this can be quite a job.

Smaller surface repairs that do not require major work on the reinforcing can be carried out simply. Loose ends of wire that may be sticking out of the damaged section should be pushed back into place, and a batch of cement mix prepared. This is usually a combination of pure sand and Portland cement in the ratio 2:1, with about twenty percent Pozzolan added. However, since different types of concrete mix may not bond well, the consistency of the original mix should be checked.

The damaged section should be wet all over with loose slurry and the mixture forced into the cavity. A trowel is all that is needed to finish off, and the mixture left to cure. Sanding back, priming and painting should then be carried out as though the vessel were to be painted overall.

Maintenance of Masts, Spars, Rigging and Sails

CHAPTER NINE

Masts and Spars

MASTS (General)

THE FUNCTION OF A MAST, basically, is to act as a spar holding the sails in position. During sailing, the greatest load coming on to a mast is the downward pressure of the weight of wind in the sails. This pressure creates what is known as *compression* strain on the mast, and if this strain is sufficient to force the top of the mast downwards and bend it, failure will result.

For this reason, most masts are hollow, for the tube structure is far stronger than a solid spar when this type of pressure is applied. The greatest strain (going to windward) comes on the after end of the mast, so the cross-section of the mast tends to be longer than it is thick. And because the thwart-ships rigging is always heavier and better set up than the fore and aft rigging, this longer fore and aft section of the mast gives added strength where the rigging is weakest.

Some masts are round section (the older type) and some rectangular, or box section. The latest and most efficient trends in mast design compromise between these two by creating a pear-shaped, or oval section, which has many advantages, including streamlining and forming a smooth flow of air on to the sail, as well as added strength and flexibility.

Spars, such as the boom, are sometimes shaped in similar sections to the mast, although of recent years there has been a trend to shaping booms in such a way that they can be bent with tackles to create different shapes in the sail. This somewhat technical aspect of yacht design is not suited for a volume of this kind. Crosstrees, spreaders and other spars aloft are also rounded or shaped, but this has little to do with strength and is mostly connected with streamlining and reducing wind drag.

Masts may be stepped on deck or on the keel. There are advantages in both methods, although stepping on deck is coming more into favour because of the ease of lowering the mast for maintenance work, and the added roominess of accommodation below decks. There are other features in favour of stepping on deck, not least of which is the lessening of the risk of damage to the hull if the mast carries away. Usually the mast breaks above the deck line anyway, but when stepped right down on the keel, sudden stresses which cause the mast to break can be transmitted to the structure of the hull. Also, by mounting the mast on a *tabernacle* on the cabin roof, the need to pierce the deck, with subsequent leakage problems, is eliminated.

Naturally, the cabin deckhead must be strengthened to take the load of the stepped mast, and this can be resolved in a number of ways. A short steel pillar transmitting the load from the mast directly to the keel is efficient, but takes up valuable cabin space. A more popular method is to transmit the load through deck beams of steel or similar metal to the sides of the vessel, whence it can be distributed through the hull structure.

MAINTENANCE OF MAST STEP

If the mast is stepped directly on to the keel, little maintenance will be required on the mast step itself. An occasional check is necessary to see that rot of any form has not worked its way into the timber (particularly if the mast

Small boat masts sometimes come in sections for portability. This type is a gunter rig

Typical tabernacle of modern small yacht. The stepping of the mast is simple and makes for easy maintenance

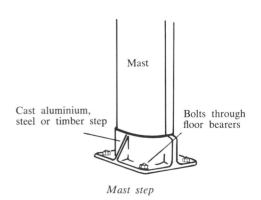

Mast step

step bridges two or more floors and leaves a gap beneath) or, in the case of aluminium, that the step—which is usually cast and therefore more vulnerable to corrosion—has not been corroded by electrolytic action from nearby keel bolts or fastenings.

In either case the treatment should be that described in the respective sections for rot and for corrosion.

MAST COLLAR

More maintenance problems arise when the mast is stepped on the keel, at the point at which it pierces the cabin deckhead, than from the mast step. Here, a hole has to be cut to allow the mast through and this allows working and possible leakage, with resultant maintenance problems. Rot can quickly take hold in this zone as it is very difficult to treat the actual area where the mast penetrates the deck without removing the mast altogether. In addition, the working of the mast can set up strains around the cabin deckhead area which cause fracturing, or working of the fastenings and beam corners.

All these areas should be checked frequently, particularly the mast collar. The mast is secured in place in the collar by means of a circle of wedges hammered into the gap around the mast itself. These serve to strengthen the area and give some rigidity to the mast, and also to transfer any strains to the adjacent deck beams. Some boats do not have this wedging, thus allowing the mast to move freely in the hole, supported solely by the rigging, and transferring all the stresses right down to the keel. This is an acceptable method, but gives rise to considerable maintenance to the other parts of the mast collar, particularly the canvas covering which is so liable to crack and allow leakage.

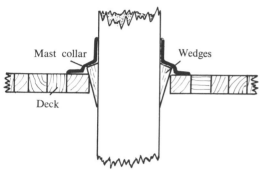

Cross section of mast collar

Often synthetic materials are used for the mast collar, and many of them are quite efficient. But the old canvas collar has much to be said for it, being waterproof, elastic, and easy to paint. However, ready-made mast coats can be purchased, usually made from synthetic plastic or rubber. Providing they are a good fit and can be readily applied, they are quite efficient.

FITTING A MAST COLLAR

To make a new collar, the canvas must be cut very carefully. Because of the shape of the fitting, it is virtually impossible to cut a well-fitted collar from one piece of material, and the old method of using a good wide strip of canvas still has merit. The canvas should be marked so that a hole the exact diameter of the mast can be cut out. Note that the tighter the fitting of this hole the better the collar.

A wider circle should then be cut, concentric with the first and not less than about nine inches between circumferences. This size will vary with different boats, of course, but allowing three inches around the deck, three inches

up the mast and a reasonable turn-under is the very minimum for any size of boat.

If the mast is unstepped, the collar can be placed in position as it is, but if the mast is stepped, the collar will have to be cut to allow fitting round the mast. This is no great problem, as darts will have to be cut later anyway, to make for a good fitting, and the cut made to place the collar round the mast can be used as a dart later.

Once in position the collar should be turned under all round the outer edge. This may necessitate the cutting of darts, but the minimum number should be cut, and their fitting must be very carefully done if complete waterproofing is to be assured. A good tuck under all round the circumference of the collar for at least two inches is a good guide. The deck beneath should be treated with red lead or some other waterproofing composition and the collar then tacked in place with copper tacks.

A mast collar. Note the tight fitting around the mast

If the deck is of fibreglass or aluminium, the copper tacks will be neither suitable nor desirable, and an aluminium or nylon deck ring should be used to clamp the collar in position. There are patent rings made for this purpose, but if one is not found that is suitable, a little ingenuity may have to be applied. Providing the seal on the deck is efficient, almost any method is permissible, although care should be taken to ensure that metals which can corrode aluminium are not used. Copper or brass fastenings cannot be bolted through an aluminium deck or used anywhere that may bring them into contact with an aluminium mast.

With the deck section fastened down it remains only to secure the collar surrounding the mast. This can be done in a number of ways, preferably by lashing with tightly-bound cord or securing with stainless steel clamping band. It is better not to tack the collar into a wooden mast, in case splitting occurs. Once again, the imagination can be put to use to devise all kinds of methods of making a waterproof binding. Providing the wedges are well covered and the seal at the mast completely watertight, there is no restriction on the type of fitting used.

CROSSTREES AND SPREADERS

Of the many mast and boom fittings, the crosstrees—or spreaders as they are often called—and their attachments should be given top priority for maintenance. When the mast is unstepped they should be overhauled and examined in detail. This is because for the greater part of their working life they are out of sight, and wear and tear or loosening of fittings which would normally be noticed down near the deck level may not be seen at crosstree level from one season to another.

These fittings are mostly important for keeping the mast in position and spreading evenly the strains and stresses which come on the mast when sailing. Often, if a crosstree fails, the mast will be endangered, and then—

apart from the personal risk to crew—there might be considerable expense for the owner. An annual overhaul of the mast and its fitting is a wise precaution.

All mast fittings are open to the weather and because of the tendency of the mast to bend, come in for a fair share of the stress. Rust and corrosion, as well as wear and tear also take their toll. With the advent of aluminium masts, some of the maintenance problems are eased, but since most of the mast fittings are similar to those used on timber masts, there is little reduction in the maintenance required by these parts.

Spreaders should be examined first at their inboard ends to see that strain has not worked the mast fastenings loose. There are many ways of fastening the crosstree to the mast, some having permanent fastenings where plate holding the crosstree arm is bolted

The cross trees are important in spreading the rigging strains. Many fittings are usually congregated around the cross-tree area

directly on to the mast. Some have flexible fittings, some hinged fittings. Whatever the arrangement, there must be a secure fastening to the mast as it is this fastening which takes most of the strain. The spreaders are designed to hold the shrouds at a good angle at the mast cap, and as a result considerable stress comes on the spreader when the windward shrouds take the full strain.

Flexible or hinged fittings are the best and relieve the immediate strain on the fastenings. They may be of rubber or leather or, in the case of hinges, just metal. They should be examined frequently for wear and for any sign of deterioration caused by weather or movement of the crosstree arm. The fastenings should be checked to see that they are not working loose. These may be bolts, in the case of a timber mast, or rivets, in the case of aluminium. Other fastenings may be used, but care must

Rigging terminals are found in many locations up the mast. These are important to the strength and safety of the mast

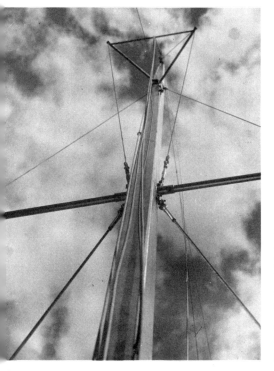

be taken to prevent electrolytic corrosion between aluminium and copper-based metals.

Any corrosion or rust should be treated and if necessary the fitting replaced. Fittings are usually of stainless steel or galvanised steel and are easily replaced. It should be borne in mind when making an examination that the fittings and fastenings may not be examined again for another year. Wherever bolts are used they should be secured with a lock nut or split pin, for the constant working of the parts in the area may cause the nut to work loose.

The outer ends of the spreaders are grooved to carry the shrouds. These areas should be closely watched for any signs of chafing which may wear away the strands of the wire or, in the case of galvanised rigging, wear off the galvanising and allow rust to set up. In both cases some form of anti-chafe is necessary. The easiest and most effective form is insulating tape, which should be placed between the crosstree and the shroud, and then, when the shroud has been pinned in position, carried over the top to help prevent chafe of the sail which may touch the end of the spreader when close hauled. Liberally used, this insulating tape can be effective in many ways for anti-chafe purposes. If there is a tendency for the colouring of the tape to mark the sails, white tape should be used.

PVC is generally a good material for any form of chafing is concerned and can be used liberally around mast and rigging wherever there are signs of chafing.

THE MAST CAP

At the very top of the mast is one of the most important fittings of all. The mast cap is the point at which most of the rigging is attached, thus the point at which much of the strain comes on the mast. Also in this vicinity, although not necessarily part of the mast cap, are the halyard blocks for main and jib (in the case of a masthead vessel). In a two-masted yacht the triatic stay also fastens at the mast cap as does the spinnaker block and other extras such as flag halyards and mast-head light fittings.

In short, the mast cap is the seating point for many important fittings, and so must be kept in good condition throughout the yacht's sailing period. Because of its location, the mast cap can only be examined properly when the mast is unstepped, although an eye can be cast around the fittings each time a hand is sent aloft for any reason. At least once a season a thorough examination of this area must be made, one way or another.

As with spreaders and other mast fittings, the two principal faults lie in loosened fastenings and rust or corrosion. The mast cap is usually made of stainless or galvanised steel, and much the same remarks apply here that applied to the spreaders. Bolts should be locked with locknuts and pins, and care taken to ensure no electrolytic action can take place. Where fittings designed to carry blocks or shrouds protrude from the mast cap, the weld at the mast cap should be closely examined for cracks or rust. A failure here could mean the loss of the mast. The actual fastening of the cap to the top of the mast varies a great deal, but whatever the method used working of fastenings can occur and should be checked at intervals.

More often than not, the main halyard is separate from the mast cap, particularly with aluminium masts and internal halyards where a sheave, let into the mast itself, is the only halyard fitting. The sheaves should be checked for wear of the pin, and for freedom of movement. Most sheaves are designed to be self-lubricating, or of synthetic material which does not need lubricating. But as the pin (or the internal part of the sheave) wears, more and more stress is placed on the movement of the sheave under strain, and often this can cause jamming.

Wear on the outer edges of the sheave should be checked also, for it is not uncommon for the sheave to wear to the point where the halyard can slip down the side of the sheave itself and jam. When this happens the sheave, halyard and mast can be damaged, to say nothing of the difficulty of hoisting or lowering a sail.

CARE OF MASTS AND SPARS

Aluminium, like fibreglass, has created a revolution in the world of boats. Because of its light weight and tensile strength it has found tremendous favour for the construction of small hulls, and only its great expense has limited the number of larger hulls made in this alloy. It is used most prominently in the manufacture of masts and spars for racing yachts. Aluminium masts are now as common as—perhaps even more common than—timber masts, and associated spars and many of their fittings are made from the alloy also.

There are many reasons for this great swing to aluminium masts, including a considerable saving in weight aloft and reduction in maintenance. A saving in maintenance has been one of the most sought-after factors in the search for new boat-building materials, and the added advantages of reduced weight and

The mast cap. Showing some of the many fittings at this point, ranging from shroud terminals and halyard blocks to light fitting

ease of handling make aluminium a number one choice.

However, timber masts still have many points in their favour, and they are far from being eliminated from the scene. Apart from the maintenance factor, aluminium appeals particularly to the racing yachtsman because of the reduction of weight aloft. For cruising there is no benefit in the reduced weight, and considerable disadvantage in the extra cost involved. Repairs to aluminium masts are not as simple as to timber, and this, too, is a factor to be considered by the boat owner who does most of his own maintenance.

From a maintenance point of view, both

Aluminium mast and spars reduce much of the weight aloft—an important factor in ocean racing yachts

aluminium and timber masts will be dealt with in this section.

ALUMINIUM MASTS

Aluminium masts and spars are extruded in sections and either welded or riveted. Although they are generally considered free from corrosion, this is not entirely the case. Corrosion will always take place to a degree, depending mainly on the type of alloy used. The stronger alloys are less resistant to corrosion and must be treated, whereas the weaker ones are almost free from attack by corrosive elements. In most instances, the manufacturer strikes a happy medium, achieving the strength he requires with as great a resistance to corrosion as possible.

Some masts are anodised when made, and this gives them a high resistance against corrosion. The anodising is a bath treatment which can only be done before the fittings are riveted in place. The anodising forms a protective surface over the alloy which keeps the corrosive elements of the air and sea from contact with the alloy itself. Paint can be used to the same effect although special requirements for painting aluminium must be followed. These are listed in the previous section.

But corrosion by the elements is not the end of the problem. Aluminium, being a metal, is vulnerable to corrosion caused by the electrolytic action of dissimilar metals in contact with one another. Aluminium and copper, for example, if placed together in a salt solution, would cause very rapid corrosion. Thus copper, when in contact with an aluminium mast or spar in the salt-laden sea air, can cause serious corrosion and neither painting nor anodising will prevent it. Since brass, bronze and copper are three very common metals on board ship, the extent of the problem can be easily judged.

Prevention is better than cure, in this case, and time and trouble spent in preventing electrolytic action will be rewarded many times over in costs alone, for once it has gained a serious hold, there is little that can be done to repair corroded aluminium. Often the mast or spar is extruded in a very thin section and the eating away of this section by electrolytic corrosion can weaken the spar beyond the safety margin. Corrosion from the atmosphere is not serious and can be treated quite easily; it is the electrolytic action that causes the damage.

Prevention of electrolytic corrosion in aluminium

Since there is no cure for badly-corroded aluminium, the prevention must start at the very beginning—when the mast is first stepped in the boat. All fittings of brass, bronze or copper must be insulated to prevent the flow of a current between the metals and the aluminium. For example, if bronze halyard winches are to be fitted, they must be mounted on insulating material. Timber, tufnol, mica or other synthetic is suitable for this work and

Care must be taken to match the metals used for fittings on aluminium masts and spars or corrosion will take place

Effects of corrosion on the foot of an aluminium mast

Treatment of surface corrosion on aluminium

Most forms of corrosion show up as a white powder on the aluminium. This is the case with corrosion from electrolytic action and also corrosion due to the weathering of the alloy in the elements. As mentioned, the former can cause deep indentations in the alloy and reduce its strength to danger point, but this is unlikely in the case of corrosion by the elements. As a general rule, this form of corrosion only affects the appearance of the surface by causing shallow pitting which—at least in the early stages—can be ignored from the point of view of safety. However, nothing looks more unsightly than masts and spars that are pock-marked and patchy, and the corrosion needs to be checked and treated if only for appearances sake and to prevent it eating further into the alloy.

A light brushing with a wire brush or steel wool will remove the surface powder. However, it will soon re-form unless treated, and the best method of treating is to give the spars a coat of clear lacquer. Painting will also cover the marks and prevent further attacks, although the question of painting becomes a personal one, as most owners prefer the attractive brightness of the aluminium spar in its natural

should be made up in the form of a pad on which the winch or fitting can be mounted. Good allowance around the edges of the fitting should be made as sea water, thrown up as a spray, can "jump" the insulation unless it is well spaced.

The fastenings holding the fittings in place must also be insulated, but because this is very difficult to achieve, it is better that the fastenings be made from some less-electrolytic material, such as stainless steel. Indeed, if it is possible, all fittings should be made of stainless steel, thus reducing the possibility of corrosion to a minimum.

Attention must be given to the parts of the mast or spar which come in contact with the boat itself. The mast step, for example, and the collar, if the mast is not stepped on deck. Bronze or copper fastenings and bolts may be in the timbers on which the mast is stepped and these will quickly attack the foot of the mast or, if it is stepped on an aluminium casting, attack the vulnerable casting even more vigorously. In this case a timber step provides a better arrangement with stainless steel bolts or fastenings.

The collar is also a vulnerable spot for much the same reason; copper or bronze fastenings bound in the area where the mast comes through the deck. In this case a rubber collar or sheath to protect the mast from actually coming into contact with the deck would ensure safety from electrolysis.

Mast corrosion due to fittings. Even stainless steel winches can cause some corrosion, as seen here

colour. Painting aluminium is described in detail in the section on painting, earlier in this book.

Another method of brightening and maintaining natural-colour aluminium is by using spray wax, as used on vehicles. Most garages supply this as a protection for chromework on cars; it is simply sprayed on and rubbed up to a shine. Needless to say, this will not last as long as a lacquer or paint, but it is surprising how long it does last, and the repeat performance is no great drudge. In addition, it eliminates the re-painting problem that must come when paintwork on the mast begins to flake and peel—a long and arduous job if the smooth finish of the aluminium is to be retained after a series of repaints.

General maintenance of aluminium

Broadly speaking, the principal maintenance routine concerning aluminium masts and spars —outside their fittings, which are mentioned separately in this section—lies in the checking of corrosion, particularly corrosion by electrolytic action. The masts and spars should be checked frequently for signs of corrosion and the source of the trouble found, or the corrosion treated as described.

Metal fatigue is rarely heard of in yacht masts, but it can occur if rigging is slack or the mast improperly tuned. The mast should be examined for small cracks which will usually occur at the point where the maximum bending occurs. Welding should be given attention, as first signs of cracking are often seen close to a weld.

Fittings should be checked to see that their fastenings are not becoming loose, particularly in the case of rivets. There is a tendency for slide tracks and other vulnerable points to work loose as time goes on, and these must be refastened before they pull out altogether, or enlarge the fastening holes.

TIMBER MASTS

The making of a mast is a somewhat ambitious project for amateur boat builders, but it sometimes happens that a small spar has to be repaired or replaced, and this is a job that the amateur should be able to handle quite easily.

Solid spars are obsolete and are better left that way. They had disadvantages, not least of which was their weight and the tendency to split. Modern masts, whether of timber or aluminium, are hollow and often rectangular or pear-shaped. Aluminium masts, as mentioned earlier in this chapter, are extruded and can be bought in prepared form for finishing. Timber masts, on the other hand, can be built up from basic planks without a great deal of effort.

Hollow timber masts and spars are made up in one of several ways. One system involves the use of two heavy pieces of timber whose combined thickness is greater than the final diameter of the mast or spar. These two timbers are gouged out on one side to a concave shape considerably less in diameter than the finished diameter of the spar. By gluing the two gouged faces together, a "hollow log" effect is achieved, and the spar can be finished to size, taking care to keep an even thickness of timber around the entire circumference and along the entire length.

Obviously, this is a very lengthy process and a somewhat difficult one as well. The need to take great care with the gouging to make an even surface throughout the length and diameter of the mast (and the subsequent weaknesses if this thickness varies at all) carries this method beyond the ability of the average amateur, and into the realm of professional spar making and professional machines.

The built spar—which, as illustrated, can be made up in two different ways—is far and away the most popular method of making masts and spars. Tremendous control over the construction of the mast is available in this system and its ease of construction makes it available to the amateur who requires only sufficient space to lay out the full length of the spar. Neither method is better nor easier

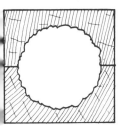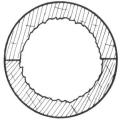

Cross section of built spars. Left, spar made from two gouged planks. Right, two forms of spars built up from four basic planks

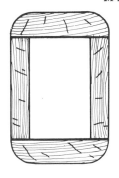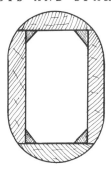

than the other to make, and there are even variations on these two basic themes, so that either may be adapted to suit the requirements of the individual. For square or pear-shaped masts, the four (or five) section spar is more suitable. The multi-section allows more variation in the type of mast or spar to be built, particularly if it is to be of the "bendy" type.

In both cases, the timber is cut slightly longer than the length of the spar, and shaped to section. The amount of taper required can be induced by tapering each of the sections, and the amount of flexibility and weight controlled partly by the type of timber used and by the number of sections involved. Obviously, at this stage the builder can literally decide exactly what type and weight of spar he will build, and what characteristics it will have, by adjusting his materials and methods.

It is preferable to use pieces of timber that run the entire length of the mast or spar, but if this is not possible, the additional length can be gained by scarfing (see Section V). The scarf joint must be extremely well made, and with very low slope faces to spread the weakness as much as possible over the length of the spar and not concentrate it in one sector.

When all the sections have been shaped and finished, a "dry run" will ensure that they all fit perfectly. A high-quality marine glue must be used, and each section laid up after gluing both faces, and clamped with G clamps until the glue is absolutely cured. It is preferable to do this work indoors, as variations in the weather, particularly humidity, can cause

changes in the timber, and these may lead to an unevenness between surfaces before the final sections are glued together. Rain, of course, will put paid to the job altogether, and since it may take some days to glue all sections together, it is asking a little too much of the weather to stay constant over that period.

Some professionals have moulds into which the sections are placed and glued up altogether. This is the ideal, and there is nothing to prevent the mast being glued up in one operation. But under normal backyard conditions, trying

Timber masts are still widely used in cruising yachts. The conglomeration below the cross trees is a radar scanner

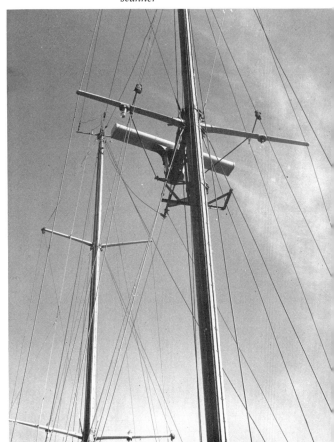

to hold five or more pieces of glued timber together while clamps are put in place would be far too difficult, and would probably wind up with the operator securely glued into the mast structure! The chances of obtaining accurate results would be, to say the least, doubtful.

The types of timbers used for making masts and spars are discussed elsewhere in this book but by and large, spruce is one of the best, or oregon, if a good quality in this timber can be obtained. Generally speaking, strength with lightness should be aimed for in selecting timber for this type of work. Virtually any kind of timber *can* be used, but if heavy timber like gum or teak are considered then one might as well build the spar of steel and be done with it.

MAINTENANCE OF TIMBER MASTS

Since timber masts and spars cannot be left in their natural state but must be either painted or varnished, maintenance is the same as for any painted or varnished surface.

Details of mast fittings and rigging are dealt with elsewhere, as also is the use of the bosun's chair for maintenance and repair aloft.

The description given in Chapter 6 concerning maintenance of painted and varnished timber is applicable in full to timber masts and spars.

STEPPING AND UNSTEPPING THE MAST

If the mast is stepped on the keel there is only one possible way to lift it out of its position and that is by means of a crane, or gantry, or some other lifting mechanism. This being the case there is little need to dwell at length on the subject here as it entails the use of ship-yard equipment. The crane is made fast in an appropriate position, the weight is taken and the rigging let go, then the mast is lifted straight out, taking care not to allow it to swing and damage the cabin on the way up.

If it is stepped on deck, however, there is

Small yachts with deck-stepped masts, can lower them simply by easing back on the forestay

132

no need to go to the trouble and expense of a crane or gantry, and provided the boat can be berthed in a convenient position (preferably on a slip) where she can be held steady, the mast can be lowered quite easily by means of a block and tackle. This will have to be a fairly large tackle, not so much from the point of view of mast weight as for the distance the mast has to be lowered. If a winch or similar power mechanism is available then the tackle can be dispensed with, but whatever the means used, a long length of rope will be necessary.

The tackle should be connected to a wire rope leading to the top of the mast, where it can be fastened securely around the mast cap or top spreaders. It should be led forward over the bow and the tackle (or winch) located fairly well ahead in order to give a good angle

Stepping the mast on the keel involves the use of a crane or derrick. Photo courtesy Power Boat & Yachting

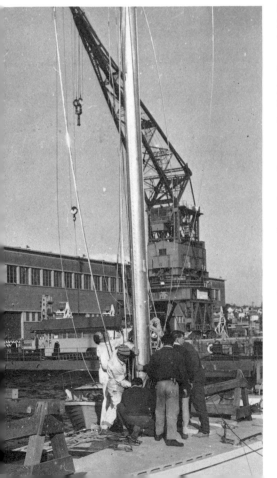

of pull. When all is set, the forestay can be released together with all shrouds, other than the two after shrouds. These can be left in place to steady the mast as it is lowered.

By slacking away on the purchase, the mast can be lowered backwards, pivoting on a single bolt in the tabernacle. If there is more than one bolt in the tabernacle, all but the most convenient for pivoting must be released. As the mast is eased back any tendency to swing either side will be corrected by the shrouds left in place, also two hands can be positioned, one at each shroud, to steady the mast should it begin to swing. It can be guided down until reasonably close to the deck when a prop or crutch can be used to take the weight.

It is important to note that unless a good angle is obtained on the purchase by having it well forward (and if possible, high up) there will come a point as the mast is lowered when the holding tackle is virtually in line with the mast and will thus not take any further weight. Unless a prop is placed under it at this time, the mast will crash to the deck. Once lowered on deck the remainder of the rigging can be released and the mast taken out of the tabernacle.

To re-step the mast, the reverse procedure will apply. The foot of the mast must be stepped and bolted by one pivot bolt into the tabernacle. The after shrouds can be secured and the top of the mast connected to the purchase. It will probably be necessary to manually raise the mast a few feet in order to give sufficient angle for the purchase to pull the mast upright. This will be a matter of practice. Once upright the remaining shrouds and the forestay can be connected, and the purchase removed. The rigging can be tuned.

MAST FITTINGS

Slide tracks

There are several ways of attaching the mainsail to the mast, although two are principally used in modern yachts. The luff groove is a recess in the after side of the mast into

133

which the luff rope of the mainsail is fed and this is a most satisfactory and simple method. If there is no luff groove, then invariably the mast has some form of internal or external track attached to it, on which small nylon or brass slides can run. The slides are fastened to the luff of the sail by means of leather strips or nylon cord.

In the case of the luff groove, there is little or no maintenance. Whether the mast is timber or aluminium, there is little that requires maintenance unless the groove becomes damaged by a heavy blow, in which case it must be opened out again in order to allow free passage of the luff rope. In the case of the tracks, however, some attention is necessary. The slides or the track can become damaged, causing them to jam, or the track can become bent due to a bend in the mast or warping of the mast timber. In these cases removal and replacement (if straightening is not possible) of the tracks becomes necessary.

Nylon slides do not as a rule become jammed as a result of the action of the weather since they are corrosion-resistant. However, brass or aluminium can become slightly corroded, creating friction which may jam the slides, and in this case the use of one of the patent spray lubricants is recommended. By lowering the sail and thus piling all the slides at the foot of the track, the lot can be sprayed together. If the main is then hoisted, the lubricant is carried up the track by the slides, eliminating the necessity to go aloft to lubricate.

"V" spreaders

These are no different in use to any other form of spreader; their aim is to spread the shrouds to give a greater angle and thus greater efficiency at the mast head. Whereas normal spreaders, or crosstrees, stick out from the mast at right angles, "V" spreaders, as their name denotes, stick out in a partly forward direction and at an angle to one another, forming a "V" shape, with the angle of the "V" at the mast.

Because they serve the same purpose as

any other form of spreader, and are made of the same material, they are subject to the same stresses and the same wear and tear. Maintenance is exactly the same as that described in the earlier chapter dealing with spreaders and crosstreees.

The boom

The boom is fast becoming the subject of much speculation in yachting circles. There are schools of thought on extra long booms, or extra short booms, on bendy booms, on rigid booms and even on no booms at all. However, this is a question of design rather than of maintenance, and in this volume, the assumption will be that there *is* a boom, no matter what shape or size.

The foot of the mainsail is attached to the boom in much the same way as the luff is attached to the mast. Grooves to take a foot rope or tracks with their slides are the accepted methods in use, although there may be variations on these themes, including loose-footed sails which are attached only at the ends. Maintenance is the same as that mentioned for masts in the earlier part of this chapter.

The importance of the boom and its fittings can be seen in this photo where much of the action is concerned with boom gear

Stainless steel fittings at the gooseneck eliminate much of the risk of corrosion at this vital spot

Booms may be of aluminium or timber and in each case require the maintenance described for that material. The boom end fittings vary, and may be of the type which allows the cap at the end to turn and thus enable roller reefing, or may be fixed. Likewise, there are several fittings used to pull the end of the sail out along the boom—referred to as "outhauls" —and almost all of these fittings are of metal. The best fittings are stainless steel, although brass and bronze may be used in the case of timber booms. In no circumstances must bronze fittings be used on aluminium booms, or corrosion will occur.

Maintenance of the fittings consists mostly of lubrication. As they are moving parts, they should be stripped down once a year and examined for wear or corrosion, as any such deterioration can cause jamming which, in the middle of a race, can mean trouble and probably the loss of the race.

At the other end of the boom, attaching it to the mast, is the gooseneck. This is usually made of stainless steel or bronze, and is a most important part of the boom fittings. If the boat is fitted with roller reefing gear it will be incorporated with the gooseneck fittings. There

are many forms of roller reefing and gooseneck fittings, but no matter what shape or design, they should all come in for close attention when maintenance work is under way. Once a year the whole fitting, roller reefing gear as well, should be stripped down and prepared for a new season by oiling and cleaning all working parts. Any wear or corrosion should be attended to and replacements made if necessary. When the fittings are back together they should be tested for freedom of use as there is little time or inclination to adjust these things when about to reef down for heavy weather.

Spinnaker fittings

The actual spinnaker fittings found attached to the mast are limited to the spinnaker ring and a couple of blocks for topping lifts. However, since the spinnaker pole is a boom of sorts, it will be included in this section.

Spinnaker poles are invariably made of aluminium these days for timber is rather heavy, particularly for large vessels. For this reason they require only the maintenance mentioned earlier for other aluminium spars and the mast, and since they do not carry a groove for a bolt rope, need little attention at all. In the case of a timber spar, painting or varnishing is the only requirement.

The fittings at the ends of the pole can vary considerably, but the most common forms are quick-release parrot-beak types which can be pulled open together or singly by means of a release cord. The fittings are invariably stainless steel and thus require next to no maintenance other than occasional lubrication to keep the sliding bolts moving freely.

Topping lift and sheet and brace fittings are usually in the form of blocks, and reference should be made to the section on these fittings later in this book. The blocks are fitted all round the boat at suitable points and thus may be attached in any number of ways. As a rule they are swivel blocks requiring lubrication of the swivels fairly frequently, as they often become immersed in salt water when sailing hard, particularly when on a "shy run".

Winches

Halyard winches are merely deck or sheet winches fitted to the mast to assist in tightening the luffs of the various sails. Details of maintenance of the winches will not be mentioned here as it is covered in a later section, but it is important to mention at this stage, when fitting winches to an aluminium mast, that due care must be taken to prevent corrosion. Many winches are made from bronze and this metal must not be placed in contact with aluminium

Much of the spinnaker gear can be detached when not in use and is thus easy to maintain

or severe corrosion will begin immediately. The winch must be mounted on a timber or synthetic pad which insulates it from the aluminium of the mast, and stainless steel bolts should be used to fasten the winches in place.

REPAIR OF TIMBER MASTS

Masts can be easily damaged by the many strains placed on them. Failure can be due to several causes, such as inability of the metal (or timber) to take the strain, or failure of the rigging. In the former case the damage usually occurs high up on the masts, in the latter close to the deck. Aluminium masts bend and then crack across, timber masts usually crack in a vertical line and then splinter across

Halyard and sheet winches may be made of any non-corrosive metal or of synthetic material

In either case the loss of the mast is complete. The repair or replacement of the aluminium mast is a job for a professional workshop and far outside the scope of this volume. Indeed, damage to an aluminium mast, other than superficial denting or bending, should be repaired at a professional yard, as the straightening process is difficult and can cause more damage if done incorrectly.

Timber masts, however, can be repaired by an efficient amateur, provided the damage has not gone too far. A completely broken mast is a big repair job and not recommended for amateurs, but cracking, due to the stresses and strains mentioned earlier, or to the failure of inefficient glues, can usually be treated successfully.

In the case of a solid timber spar, the cracking may also be caused by the use of unseasoned timber, and these cracks can simply

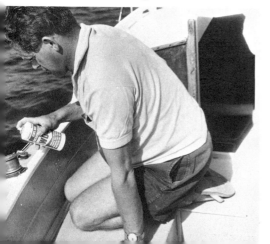

Frequent lubrication helps keep the working parts of winches in turning condition

be puttied over and painted or varnished. Where the cracks are due to strain or failure of glues, however, it is necessary to rejoin the parted timber.

Masts are made in sections which begin to come apart when glue fails. To make a thorough repair job—since the glue will continue to deteriorate in other sections even if one section is renewed—it is as well to rebuild the mast as a whole by taking it apart and cleaning off all the old glue.

This requires a long room or shed, but is not difficult. When the sections have been opened out, a scraper will remove most of the old, brittle glue, and clean the timber at the join. This should be left slightly roughened to give the new glue a good key. The choice of marine glue is a wide one. The manufacturer's advice should be sought if in doubt, or if the advice of a professional shipwright is not available. Many glues which are well suited to normal "shoreside" work are unsuitable for marine work, particularly in the gluing of a mast or spar where flexibility is essential.

With the cleaned surfaces re-glued, the mast should be held together with G clamps for as long as possible, to ensure a good grip. If the mast is to be varnished, care must be taken to ensure that glue does not run from the seams as the G clamps apply pressure. This will show up through the varnish and spoil the whole appearance of the mast. Needless to say, all fittings will have to be removed from the mast before gluing, which gives an excellent opportunity to scrape back the varnish or paintwork and have a virtually new mast when the work is done.

If the cracking is localised and is due to stresses and strains rather than glue failure, it can be cured without the need to unstep the mast. The cracks should be opened by inserting a thin chisel so that a liberal application of glue can be fed in. A great deal of care must be taken not to aggravate the crack too much, and cause the split to run too far. But it is equally pointless to try and poke small amounts of glue into a fine crack and hope that it takes

137

Repair work—other than general maintenance—should be done with the mast unstepped. This also allows close examination of the less accessible areas

up, as this will do nothing whatever to bind the timber surfaces. The crack will only break wider the next time it is subjected to strain.

When the crack is filled with glue, the chisel is taken out and the crack closed by means of G clamps. Once again care must be taken with varnished masts to see that the glue does not mark the surrounding timber. Pads of plywood should be placed under the jaws of the G clamps to ensure that they do not bite into the wood of the mast itself.

Small cracks and holes should be treated in this way, as the mast, when under severe strain, has enormous compression forces acting down its length, and these will quickly enlarge even the smallest weakness to a dangerous point.

Other mast fittings

The fittings attached to a mast vary from vessel to vessel. Fast modern ocean racing yachts have a mass of antennae at the mast-

head that looks like a Christmas tree gone wrong. These are connected to instruments in the cockpit and detect wind directions, speeds and relative velocities.

Similarly, most vessels have masthead lights, spreader lights, and perhaps navigation lights on the mast, to say nothing of blocks and other gear connected with flags, radio aerials and so on. All these fittings are dealt with in their respective sections of this book, but it is worth pointing out that whenever maintenance to the mast is in progress it is as well to include all fittings in the routine.

Light fittings should be checked to see that they are not corroding or chafing or that water is seeping into the globes. Aerials should be checked out against chafing, particularly where

A useful style of cleat for running rigging

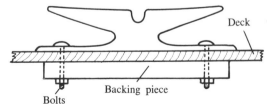

138

Modern ocean racers are fitted with a mass of gear, most of which is connected in some way with the mast and rigging

materials are proving ideally suited for sea-going conditions in that they are highly resistant to all forms of corrosion and wear, as well as being much lighter and easier to handle.

Two principal types of blocks are used on small craft. Metal blocks—in which both the shell and the sheave are of metal—are used for running wires, and the blocks mentioned above with a combination of stainless steel and a synthetic sheave for use with ropes. Whatever the use of the block, the most important factor when fitting it is to ensure that it is the right size for the rope it is to hold. The throat of a block that is too tight for the rope will cause chafe and wear; if it is too loose the rope will work about and often get between the sheave and the cheek, thus fouling the block. Since modern synthetic ropes do not swell or shrink when wet, there should be little difficulty in selecting the right block for a particular use.

Blocks are usually shackled to the part where they will work, but sometimes a general purpose block is required which can be fitted to any part of the boat, and in this case a rope tail is attached. Some blocks are made for a specific purpose, having an inbuilt swivel, or

they may come in contact with sails or halyards. And all fittings should be examined for rust or corrosion. If the mast is unstepped, this is a relatively easy task, but since most masts are unstepped only once every year or two, the opportunity should always be taken, when sending a hand aloft, to run a maintenance check over all fittings. These objects are virtually out of sight but should never be out of mind; failure to maintain them will invariably result in an uncomfortable experience somewhere out at sea.

BLOCKS AND TACKLES

Modern developments and research are constantly improving the quality and durability of blocks. Synthetics have wrought these improvements. Nowadays wooden blocks are seen only on the older vessels and then only rarely; they have been replaced mostly by stainless steel blocks with a synthetic sheave. And the newer

Synthetic blocks, with stainless steel fittings are popular for running rigging and all but wire ropes

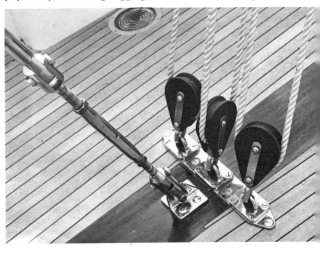

Combination of single, double and treble sheave blocks can be arranged where their use is necessary

as the weight of whole blocks in that position can seriously affect the performance of the boat, but there are also disadvantages. One of them is the tendency for the mast or surrounding surface to chafe the wire halyard and score its own surface. Aluminium masts can be badly scored unless this is prevented, and timber masts tend to wear away from the sheave, allowing the halyard to drop between the sheave and its surrounds, and jam: a most unhealthy prospect when sailing in a heavy sea.

Tackles—their mechanical advantage

Blocks are frequently used singly as guides for ropes and wires, but they can also be used in number to form a purchase. This purchase,

Masthead blocks such as spinnaker head blocks need close attention or they may jam when strain comes on them, an unhealthy situation, particularly during a race

jam cleat; some are for permanent fixture, others for use in many parts of the boat. Undoubtedly one of the handiest is the snatch block, which can be opened on one side and snapped on to a rope that is already in position, thus eliminating the need to thread the rope through the block.

The strength of a block is of importance where heavy loads are to be taken. In the case of larger blocks, such as those used on cranes or derricks, the safe working load is usually stamped on the cheek of the block. Smaller blocks do not have this as a rule, and the manufacturer's catalogue should be consulted if there is any fear that the block may not take the load.

Frequently the need for a block is eliminated by the use of a recessed sheave. This is particularly the case with masthead halyards where the halyards are roved internally. Small sailing dinghies also have a sheave fitted into the mast to eliminate the need for a block. There are advantages in using fixed sheaves

140

depending on the number of blocks and the reeving of the ropes through them, can give a mechanical advantage of a very high ratio. For example, an engine which could not possibly be lifted from its bed by two or three men can be raised easily by one man using the right combination of blocks and tackle.

Small tackles—known as *handy billies*—can come in for use at any time on any kind of craft. They are as useful as the toolbox in the locker below, and are usually made up in advance and kept in just such a locker. They may be used for anything from hoisting a man up the mast or lowering a dinghy over the side, to pulling a grounded vessel into deeper water. The term "handy" is more than appropriate.

THE HANDY BILLY

The actual number of blocks in a handy billy is not important. What is important is that it is made up of relatively small blocks that are fairly light in weight. The rope to be reeved through them should also be light and of good strength. In this way the handy billy can be used for a multitude of purposes.

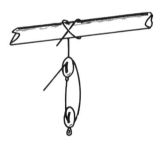

The handy billy

The most convenient purchase form would be one giving a mechanical advantage of three. This keeps the purchase light and manageable and yet by enabling the user to increase his strength by three times, as it were, provides a very useful asset for all forms of shipboard work. The billy should be set up as shown in the diagram, as the most useful form of purchase is one with a downhaul action. A tail

on the upper block allows it to be attached to anything (even another rope), and the swivel at the bottom allows any sort of fitting to be shackled on without the risk of twisting the purchase.

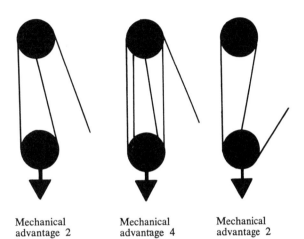

| Mechanical advantage 2 | Mechanical advantage 4 | Mechanical advantage 2 |

Purchases and their mechanical advantages

A small handy billy in the toolbox is a must for a vessel of any size, and even the smallest sea-going craft find them invaluable when trouble occurs.

The purchase diagrams illustrate the types of purchases which can be made up for any job. Naturally the larger the mechanical advantage gained, the bigger and heavier the purchase; therefore most of these purchases would not be made up, but either kept in a boatshed, or (if the vessel is large enough) on board, but not reeved—the blocks are separated so that any form of purchase can be made at a moment's notice.

Although there would be a thousand and one times when a purchase would be handy on board, undoubtedly the most common use is in the removal of an engine. Here a heavy tackle with a large mechanical advantage is necessary, to handle the weight of the engine with safety.

Wire purchases are quite common, although they are really specialised equipment, unlikely to find a place on a boat. Some of the bigger racing yachts, such as the 12 metres, use wire tackles in their running rigging, but this is the exception rather than the rule. Most blocks on the average-sized craft are roved with rope, and are of a convenient size to handle.

RIGGING THE BOSUN'S CHAIR

Rarely seen on board a power boat, the bosun's chair is an invaluable part of a yacht's fittings. Without it a crewman could not be sent aloft (unless he climbed the rigging) to unsnarl fouled ropes or replace broken fittings or even paint down the mast. Any work that has to be done aloft requires the use of the bosun's chair; he is a foolhardy sailor who will go aloft at sea without one: it provides not only a means of ascent, but a protection, when aloft, from the whipping mast and flapping sails which can so easily dislodge a foot or handhold.

It provides a seat for anyone working aloft in an area where there is hardly room for a seagull to perch, and its wrap-around protection makes it virtually impossible for a man

to fall. To go even further: despite its traditional appearance and use, it can become fully "automated". The hand working aloft can raise and lower himself without any assistance from the deck. Indeed, sailors invented their own automatic lift in the bosun's chair long before buildings rose above three stories.

And yet, despite all modern adaptations the bosun's chair has not lost its reputation as the last remnant of the hard days "when ships were wood and men were steel". Because of its shape, the bosun's chair makes it impossible for its occupant to linger too long on the job. Its hard, flat seat is so uncomfortable even the most professional malingerer would hurry through the job to get down and get out of the damn thing.

If the main halyard is in position, much of the hard work can be eliminated by shackling on the bosun's chair to the halyard and hoisting by means of a halyard winch or by manpower. The chair itself is simply a board with a hole in each corner and a rope passed through all four corners, crossing beneath the seat and forming a bridle over the top. It is to the eye

The Bosun's Chair, a simple but useful contrivance for use on board yachts

Secured in the Bosun's Chair, a crew man is able to raise or lower himself at the top of the mast

of this bridle that the halyard is shackled. Using the halyard, the hand aloft can be raised or lowered by calling down to those on deck.

Sometimes however, it is not possible for the halyard to be used. The reason for sending a man aloft may be to replace the main halyard. On the other hand if he is going to paint the mast down, he may prefer to raise and lower himself at will and not depend on someone being available to operate the winch. In this case the chair will be hoisted by rope (not wire) and a block at the head of the mast must be used. This may be already in place or another sent aloft for the purpose.

Using the Bosun's Chair

When he is ready, the hand to go aloft can be hoisted by someone on deck, or can hoist himself by sitting in the chair and pulling himself up with the downhaul. By assisting with his legs where possible this is a reasonably easy job. Once in position he should adjust the rope until he is comfortably settled and then fasten himself in position with the bosun's chair hitch.

With his left hand he takes a firm grip on the two ropes just above the bridle of the chair, thus jamming them together and holding himself in place. Reaching down with his right hand he picks up the now slack downhaul and draws it up in front of him, passing the bight up through the bridle and over his head. The bight then has to be worked down his back, outside the chair and around his feet, after which the slack is taken up and gradually worked back up to the peak of the bridle.

When the two ropes gripped in the left hand are released, the weight of the chair will come on the hitch and jam it in place. It is a

The Bosun's Chair hitch. Adjustment of the small rope around the bridle of the chair allows the crew man to raise or lower himself at will

perfectly secure hitch and the crewman can begin his work. When he is ready to lower himself, he simply takes the slack end of the downhaul and feeds it into the hitch. By manipulating the hitch he will thus lower himself steadily downwards for as long as he feeds in the loose downhaul. To go up again, he pulls himself up as before, re-adjusts the hitch, and allows the weight to come back on the rope.

Thus by careful adjustment he can work up and down the mast for any period of time he desires, with no problems other than a very sore behind if he stays aloft too long.

143

CHAPTER TEN

Rigging

STANDING RIGGING

THE QUESTION OF maintenance, wear and life-span of rigging can be decided to a certain extent when it is first fitted. Two principal forms of standing rigging are used on modern yachts—stainless steel wire rope and galvanised plough steel wire rope. Each has its advantages and each its disadvantages and it would be as well to examine them separately before attempting to discuss their maintenance and repair aspects.

STAINLESS STEEL WIRE ROPE

Stainless steel wire has become more and more popular in recent years, particularly with racing yachts. It has advantages which appeal to the racing man. Principal among these is its greater strength. Thus far thinner wires can be used for rigging when made up of stainless steel, and this reduces windage, a factor to be reckoned with when racing.

Another advantage is its resistance to rust, and thus its longer life. However, these advantages are offset by the tendency of stainless steel in this form to become brittle with age and snap without warning, and also by its greater cost. Galvanised wire gives plenty of warning that its useful days are nearing an end by "whiskering"—the breaking up of the strands into short hairs which stick out from the main body of the wire.

Stainless wire does not rust and, if fitted with stainless steel mast and deck fittings, eliminates most maintenance problems for much of its working life. Usually it is laid up in the following forms:

1x19, which is a solid core around which nineteen similar strands are woven in a long spiral. This is the stiff, non-flexible form used for standing rigging in larger vessels;

7x19, which comprises seven strands, each made up of nineteen smaller strands, woven around one another to give a very flexible form of wire; mostly used for rigging small craft and for running gear on larger boats;

7x7, which comprises a seven-stranded wire centre, around which six other similar seven-stranded wires are laid. This is a good all-purpose wire for standing rigging, it has a little flexibility, although not sufficient for running rigging. It is the wire mostly in use for average-size vessels.

GALVANISED WIRE ROPE

Galvanised wire's main advantage is that it can be as little as one-third the cost of similar stainless wire. However, its life is less and when the shorter life and the cost of renewing rigging more frequently is balanced against the initially higher cost of stainless there is possibly little difference between them over a period of time.

The ability of galvanised wire to "tell" when it is nearing the end of its life is a great advantage. Wire rusts in the first instance in its inner cores and the deterioration is hard to see. However as soon as the strands begin to part they spring out from the main body like hairs and can be seen (and felt) quite readily. To check a rusted wire for safety, it should be folded double in a short curve. If it is beginning to deteriorate, the rust whiskers will show at this point.

To reduce air drag—"windage"—the finer gauge stainless steel rigging is essential for racing boats

Where speed is of less consideration than cost, galvanised wire has a definite place in yacht rigging.

ROD RIGGING

Undoubtedly one of the most efficient systems of rigging is metal rods for shrouds and stays. The advantages include greater strength for size, less windage, longer life than wire, and greater safety. Unfortunately the one main disadvantage of rod rigging is cost.

Several metals can be used for rod rigging; tungum alloy and stainless steel or monel are ideal. The very names of these metals indicate the cost involved in using them. Stainless steel is probably the most popular but should never be set up by an amateur, for working it may tend to lower its temper and create a weakness.

The rods are usually fitted with a rigging screw so that they can be tightened up, and since they do not stretch, virtually no alteration to their original setting should be required.

SPLICING WIRE ROPE

The days of splicing wire rope by hand are, fortunately, fast disappearing. Only one who has experienced the blistering agony of laying up a "Liverpool splice" in a large-diameter wire rope can know the frustrations associated with this art. It is still practised occasionally at sea, but in the world of modern yachts, splicing rigging wire is now almost invariably done mechanically.

Several methods are in use. Each has certain advantages. Most require the use of a powerful tool or a machine, for each depends on pressure to force the splicing ferrule on to the wire. The Talurit system is perhaps the most common and can be done by the amateur providing he has the necessary tool.

The wire is passed through a ferrule, around a thimble and back through the ferrule and then adjusted to the size of the thimble. The tool is clamped around the ferrule at enormous pressure which forces the ferrule around the wire and forms the splice. A few factors are relevant here, notably:

1. The choice of the correct size of ferrule for the wire to be spliced.

2. The choice of correct metal for the ferrule. Copper ferrules must be used for stainless wire and alloy ferrules for galvanised wire or electrolytic action will be set up between the two dissimilar metals.

3. The choice of correct size of thimble. In the finished splice the thimble should just be movable.

145

4. Correct alignment of the wire in the ferrule so that the wires do not cross, and the tail is outside the completed splice.

Talurit splice

This splice, correctly made, is stronger than a hand-made one, and, providing the splicing tool is available, much quicker, simpler and easier on the hands.

Among other forms of mechanical splicing in use on modern boats are the Swage splice, which is used for stainless steel wire only. Here the wire is inserted into a special fitting and the fitting rolled down on to the wire. It is even stronger than the Talurit splice. Its disadvantage is that expensive special equipment is needed to make an effective splice, and usually this splice has to be ordered with new rigging from the riggers yard. This is a risky business as measurement of rigging wire is difficult and if the splice is made before the rigging is fitted to the mast, any error means that the lot has to be sent back to the factory.

Maintenance on standing rigging

Since stainless steel wire is rust- and corrosion-resistant, maintenance concerns the galvanised steel wire. In smaller craft signs of rust or deterioration should be the signal for replacing the rigging immediately, and this is where the advantage of the low cost of plough wire comes in. In large vessels, however, the rigging can be treated as for normal rusty steel, providing there is no sign of

Swage splice (right), Talurit splice (left). Note: the swage terminal is on stainless steel wire, the Talurit on galvanised steel wire

"whiskering". Large-diameter rigging can be wire-brushed to remove surface rust and if necessary painted, preferably with a rust-killing paint.

Turnbuckles

Turnbuckles nowadays are made of stainless

Small turnbuckles are best adjusted with a spanner. Note: Locking nuts above and below main body of turnbuckle

146

steel; the old galvanised "bottle-screws" are fast disappearing. Where still found, they are usually liable to rust and seize up, for the galvanising is taken off the thread when they are adjusted, and, as they are virtually immersed in water each time the yacht puts her lee rail under, the metal has little chance to resist the rust. This is even more the case inside the body of the turnbuckle where preventive chemicals cannot be used. The only real way to keep the turnbuckles in use is to pack the inside with a mixture of white lead and tallow so that salt water and air cannot get to the metal.

Stainless steel turnbuckles, like their partners in rigging wire, need little attention, and a squirt of freeing oil will release any over-tightened or jammed thread.

Stainless steel, however, can become brittle with use and a close eye should be kept on both rigging and fittings to ensure that cracks do not appear. A six-monthly check around the chainplates and turnbuckles, and a trip aloft in a bosun's chair to check the fittings and shackles at the masthead and crosstrees, are a part of every wise yachtsman's calendar.

Because of the enormous strains that come on the rigging when sailing, careful maintenance and renewal of rigging are an important safety factor.
Photo courtesy Power Boat & Yachting

This is also an opportunity to check the mast-cap and the various blocks aloft, many of which are made of stainless steel.

RE-RIGGING A MAST

One of the major jobs in rigging maintenance, whether it be stainless or galvanised wire, is the replacement, periodically, of the full set of rigging. This can be done with the mast stepped or unstepped, and since the taking out of the mast is dealt with earlier in this section, a description of renewing the rigging with the mast stepped in position will be sufficient at this point.

If the boat is small enough, or if the cruiser or motor sailer has a mast sufficiently short and well footed to stand of its own accord, there is no problem. For that matter many yachts, alongside a jetty in calm water, could release most of their rigging without danger of the mast falling. However, it is not just a question of releasing the rigging; it is a question of going aloft to release and re-secure the top fastenings, and there are few men who would care to risk their 150 lb weight at the top of an unrigged mast.

So the problem becomes one of replacing each section of rigging piece by piece. Any top rigging, such as diamond stays, jumper stays, triatic stays, etc., can be changed without

trouble, as the main shrouds and backstays support the mast while this is being done. Runners too, can be taken down, measured and replaced without problem.

When the main rigging is changed, the difficulty arises of measuring for the new shrouds and stays. A piece of string run down the length of the old stay will assist, but invariably this somehow gives a different measurement when the new rigging is set up. Another system is take each piece to the rigger's yard as it is removed, have a new piece made up identically, and then replace it on the boat before moving on to the next shroud or stay. The disadvantage here, of course, is that only one piece of rigging can be done at a time, and half the day is spent running backwards and forward to the rigger's yard.

The best system of all, if a Talurit swaging tool is available, is to have new rigging cut in advance and spliced at one end, with the other end left open and the wire extended by a foot or so over the required length. Using this system, the rigging can be changed over at the masthead, and then the bottom splice made on the boat at the exact spot where the turnbuckles are to be fitted. Talurit swaging tools are not expensive; in any case a boatshed or club probably has one to lend or hire out for an afternoon.

Working in this way, each piece of rigging is renewed in place on the boat and the margin for error is minimised. As each new shroud is set up, its partner on the opposite side can be released. In this way the new rigging should be almost an exact replica of the old.

TUNING NEW RIGGING

There is bound to be some stretch in the first few weeks of use, but rigging is made these days so that the stretch should be small enough to be taken up by the turnbuckles. If not, the rigging will have to be re-spliced above the turnbuckle.

Setting up the rigging is simple, but tuning it to get the best results requires a lot of

Small boat rigging can be fitted or changed on the relative comfort and stability of dry land. Photo courtesy Fibremakers

experience. The golden rule always is that when in doubt have it too slack rather than too tight. The mast will bend to take up any slack in the rigging, but if the shrouds and stays are consistently tightened to violin-string

Fine tuning of the rigging can only be done when the boat is under canvas. This is a job for the expert if unnecessary strains on mast and gear are to be avoided

pitch, there is a strong possibility that the mast will be driven down through the bottom of the boat.

Firstly the mast should be tuned into an upright position, without sails. When the rigging is changed, the mast can easily get out of plumb, and the eye cannot always detect this. A good check is to tie a tape-measure to the main halyard and hoist it aloft, keeping the end on the deck. When the tape reaches the top, the measurements can be read to the main chain plate on either side of the boat. If the mast is upright the measurements will be identical. If not, the rigging must be adjusted.

Tightening a lower shroud alone will tend to pull the top of the mast in the opposite direction, and similarly tightening an inner forestay can set the top of the mast back. These are but a few of the vices of a yacht's rigging, and a few more will become evident as the tuning progresses. Basically, the forestay must be tight, for it needs rigidity to keep the luff of the jib tight. Using this as a basis, the mast can be set up by gradually tightening or easing the other shrouds and backstays, remembering once again not to set any rigging too tightly. The art of tuning the mast for racing is outside the scope of this manual and involves much experience both in sailing and rigging—it must be done when the vessel is under way with full canvas set. It is sufficient at this stage to set up the mast and rigging for normal sailing.

ANTI-CHAFING GEAR

The constant wear and tear of sheets and sail-cloth can rub away the galvanising on standing rigging. Once the galvanising has gone it is only a matter of time before rust sets in and the wire begins to deteriorate. The worst-affected places are low down on the shrouds where the jib sheets wear constantly, on the forestay (if it is not stainless) where the jib hanks wear off the galvanising, and near the crosstrees where the sail, when running "dead square", chafes at the shrouds.

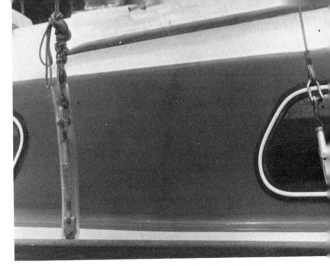

PVC hose is ideal for preventing chafe on isolated areas, particularly turnbuckles

In larger vessels lengths of lambswool are wrapped round and round the affected areas of the rigging. This does not look good however. Modern plastics, PVC hose or other forms of covering, are gaining popularity. A good basis of protection is to slip the PVC tube over the rigging before splicing into place. It cannot slip off, and can turn around the

The PVC tube must be fitted before the rigging is secured if it is to be secured without cutting. Tape holds it in position

wire to prevent the sheets or sailcloth chafing the plastic itself.

RUNNING RIGGING

Other than standing rigging, running rigging forms most of the ropes and wires used on board a boat. It can be generally defined as any wire or rope used in the handling of the boat which is not permanently fixed in one position. It can vary from halyards used to hoist sails to light cordage for flying a flag hoist. It is invariably in one of two forms; flexible wire rope or normal synthetic or fibre rope. Frequently it is a combination of both.

FLEXIBLE WIRE ROPE

As mentioned in the section on standing rigging, flexible wire rope is usually made up of 7x19 wire, comprising seven strands of nineteen-strand wire woven around one another. It may be of stainless steel or galvanised steel wire, each with merits of its own. It is spliced in the same way as standing rigging; the Talurit splice is the most popular and easiest to apply. Halyards, liferails, braces and downhauls may all be made up from this type of wire, which depends on its thickness for its degree of flexibility, but which can be coiled by hand into a reasonably small loop.

Because of its constant working, wire running rigging usually has a shorter life than that of standing rigging of the same diameter. The tremendous strain at the block when a sail is hoisted and tightened or a brace is winched home, tends to flatten and spread the strands of the wire, causing them, over a period of time, to loosen slightly and thus allow salt air to penetrate more readily. In the case of stainless steel, fatigue can be induced by this constant application and release of pressure and although the rust problem is not so prominent as with galvanised, there is nevertheless a need to keep a constant eye on stainless running rigging and not take it for granted that it has indefinite life.

Wire running rigging should be examined at not less than three-monthly intervals for signs of rust or whiskering. Chafing in the halyard blocks can whisker even stainless wire. This occurs at the very top of the halyard when the pressure is winched on, but the entire length of the wire must be examined, and not just the lower sections. More often than not, the eye splice in the ends of the halyards will not pass through the masthead blocks and the wire must be examined from each end separately. This being the case, care must be taken to ensure that the *middle* section of the wire is not missed.

A good procedure here is to examine the halyard when the sail is set, working from the foot of the mast up to the first crosstrees. The sail can then be lowered and the halyard run out to its end. A similar examination from the foot of the mast to the first crosstrees on this section will ensure that the entire length of the wire has been sighted. More care is needed with internal halyards.

Because it is constantly running through blocks, the life of running rigging is reduced by tension and friction and must be replaced fairly frequently

"Marrying" the old and new halyards can allow a change without having to climb to the masthead. Care is needed to see that the connection is secure

CHANGING A HALYARD

If the eye splice in each end of the wire halyard is too big to pass through the block at the peak, then there is no way to change the halyard and re-splice the eye other than with a Talurit tool. The wire must be passed through the block before it is spliced and then the eye spliced in later. The procedure is as follows:

The old halyard is cut just above one eye splice. The new halyard is prepared to the correct length and an eye spliced in one end. The free end is lightly whipped to prevent it unravelling. This free end is then "married" to the free end of the old halyard; i.e. the two loose ends are butted together and bound by sailtwine so that they cannot separate. Adhesive tape can be used here providing it is of sufficient strength: it would be a nuisance to get the new halyard as far as the block, only to have it separate from the old and both come tumbling down on deck. This would necessitate going aloft to re-reeve the halyard.

With the new and the old halyards married,

There are a thousand and one uses for rope aboard ship, the principal use being in connection with rigging. Photo J. M. Falls

All depends on the size of the vessel. An average yacht will have a main sheet of rope because of the freedom required and the flexibility through the purchase. A larger yacht, particularly a powerful racing yacht such as a 12 metre, may well adapt the flexible wire rope for her sheets.

However, at some stage even the largest vessels resort to normal synthetic or natural fibre ropes, and since small vessels rely on them for ninety-nine percent of shipboard tasks, ropes and the smaller cordage are an integral part of every vessel's equipment.

Natural fibre ropes

Synthetics have made inroads into the use of natural fibre ropes. In the relatively few years since synthetics became available to the boating public, the sale of natural fibre ropes has declined almost to nothing. On larger vessels they are still used quite extensively, but even here the inexorable march of synthetic fibres goes on. For this reason it is not intended to deal at great length with natural fibre ropes, other than to point out their qualities which are individual rather than general.

There are several different types of natural

ropes; basically the following are the principal ones used on small craft.

Manila is a fairly hard laid rope made from plant fibres. It is the most popular of the natural fibre ropes in that it is very durable and long-lasting. It is popular for use in hawsers and similar work where large-diameter ropes are required, but is not so popular for sheets and purchases because of its stiffness. It will deteriorate if stowed wet or allowed to lie out in the sun and weather, but because of its relatively large fibres, dries easily and is not difficult to preserve.

Hemp, like Manila, is a vegetable fibre rope. It has the advantage over Manila of being softer and more pliable. Italian Hemp in particular is sufficiently pliable to be suited for block and tackles. Its disadvantage, besides that of all natural fibres, deterioration, is that it has not the long life of Manila, though it is of high tensile strength and its fibres are similar and closer-woven. For this reason it needs more attention when drying out and stowing as it is liable to rot. Some forms of Hemp are tarred to reduce this vulnerability, but it can never be eradicated altogether.

Sisal is a very "hairy"-looking rope and is not widely used for several reasons. The most important is that when wet it tends to swell, which causes it to jam in blocks or leads.

Coir, like most other ropes, is made from the fibres of a plant. The fibres are woven into a thick, rough cordage which is elastic and very light. It has relatively low strength and for this reason is not over-popular among yachtsmen. Its only unusual characteristic is that it floats and it is probably for this reason more than any other that it still maintains a place in ocean-going vessels.

Cotton ropes are used widely on small vessels. They are soft and pliable and easy to use in purchases. Their main disadvantage lies in their hardness when wet and relatively short working life.

Whether the vessel is a crack motor yacht (background) or a fast racing sailboat (foreground) ropes are an essential part of her equipment. Photo courtesy Power Boat & Yachting

Care and maintenance

As mentioned above, all natural fibre ropes are vulnerable to rot, and this is undoubtedly their biggest disadvantage. After use they must be dried before stowing away, or else stowed in an airy spot in a loose coil so that the air can circulate and dry the fibres. Some fibre ropes are tarred or treated, which has a definite staying process where rot is concerned, but cannot eliminate it altogether.

In larger vessels with plenty of room this may not be such a disadvantage, but in smaller modern vessels, where space is at a premium, the need to be able to toss ropes haphazardly (and wet) down into a locker is the main reason for the popularity of synthetics.

Natural fibre ropes are almost always laid up in three or four stranded ropes, and because of their fibre basis do not stretch overmuch. This is their one advantage over synthetics, which can stretch considerably, especially when in the form of laid rope. But in all other

ways they lose, particularly in terms of long life. Even though carefully treated and maintained, fibre ropes cannot approach the longevity of the synthetics.

SYNTHETIC ROPES

As is usual with a relatively new discovery, the range and characteristics of synthetic ropes change almost by the day. It would be impossible in a volume of this kind to even attempt to list the various types of synthetics and their properties. Probably by the time the book came off the press they would be obsolete. Sufficient at this stage to look at the general range and the uses on board small vessels.

Broadly speaking, most synthetics fall into two brackets: nylon and terylene (dacron is similar to terylene for the purposes of this book). The ropes are made up of manufactured fibres twisted into ropes of various forms, the most popular of which are the laid ropes and the braided ropes. Laid ropes usually have the same three-stranded lay as natural fibre ropes, and braided ropes are laid up in what is virtually a continuous platt.

153

Synthetic ropes may be laid (dark rope) or braided. There is little to choose between either for general work. Photo courtesy Power Boat & Yachting

The advantages of the synthetics over the natural fibres are enormous. They have a soft pliability that could never be achieved in fibre ropes, by virtue of the rough nature of the fibre themselves. Synthetics need no drying and are almost impervious to salt air, sun and other deterioration agents. They have an incredibly long life, are tougher and stronger for their size than any other material and in general can do all the things fibre ropes can do, and do them better.

It is only natural that for such tremendous advantages, the boating man is going to pay more money, and synthetics are, indeed, considerably more costly than natural fibre ropes. However, their long life and their ease of handling, more than repay the extra initial outlay.

There is no maintenance with synthetic ropes. They will deteriorate gradually if left out in the weather and sun, but the rate of deterioration is very slow and since it is a natural process, little can be done about it.

The normal care of ropes, when applied to synthetic material, will give almost a lifetime guarantee.

In addition to the normal development of ropes for running rigging, the new materials have been developed for specific purposes. Floating synthetic ropes are commonly seen, as well as ropes with greater or less stretch for certain jobs such as towing.

Splicing synthetic ropes

Braided ropes are somewhat difficult to splice, but the normal laid synthetic rope can be spliced in the same way as natural fibre; and they have the added advantage that the frayed ends of the strands need not be whipped. During the splicing operation they should be held in place by a small round of cellotape or other adhesive material. When the splice is completed, the ends of the strands should be held in the flame of a lighted match. The synthetic material will melt and the strands will fuse together, thus eliminating the need for whipping.

Braided rope cannot be spliced in the normal way. When an eye has to be made it should be formed by means of a knot and whipped. The knot is not always necessary as the eye may be just whipped into place. However, synthetic ropes tend to be shiny and slippery and the addition of a half hitch to the eye will ensure that it does not slip out from beneath the whipping.

As with laid rope, the ends of braided rope may be fused to prevent them from unravelling. In this case the strands are not fused separately, but the entire end of the rope placed in the flame until the material melts and the strands fuse together. This should be continued for about quarter of an inch along the rope to ensure that the strands are securely fused.

To cut a synthetic rope requires care, as its elasticity causes the ends to fly apart and unravel quickly. The area to be cut should be marked, and a round of adhesive tape placed on either side of the spot. When the rope is

154

There is a variety of synthetic ropes available to suit every purpose on board ship

cut it will unravel only as far as the tapes, and each end can then be fused with a flame and the tapes taken off.

CORDAGES

Cordage is generally referred to as the "small stuff" of the ropes on board ship. There is no definite limit on size or construction, but cordage is used mostly for temporary work or for repair. Various small forms of natural fibre cordage such as marlin and sail twine have been greatly replaced, like their bigger brothers, by synthetic cordages. Here the variety is of size; sail twine, in the synthetic version, is just a fine nylon or terylene twine, and the larger lashing and whipping materials are graded up from this.

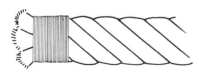

"Whipping" the end of a rope using sail twine prevents it from becoming unravelled

The choice of cordage depends on the job it has to do and this is dealt with individually throughout this volume. The synthetic cordages are, of course, more expensive than natural fibre materials, but here again the disadvantage is outweighed by the advantages of longer life and ease of use.

LIFERAILS

Because of the vicious nature of a small boat in a seaway, liferails are essential in any craft which puts its bow into open waters. This is particularly the case in ocean-going yachts where, in addition to the movement of the craft over the waves, and the heel, it is extremely difficult to secure a good foothold. Liferails are designed to prevent any one from falling over the side, but they have several useful sidelines, not least of which is that they provide an anchor on to which a safety harness can be clipped when men are working forward.

There is a tendency—particularly in smaller boats—to try and fit liferails where either they cannot be fitted because of the limited deck space or else to fit small stanchions. This is a bad policy, for short rails tend to defeat the object they are meant for; instead of holding a falling body inboard, they catch it right behind the knees and assist it over the side. And rails of such small size cannot be built sufficiently strong—or even attached to the boat with sufficiently secure stanchions—to withstand the shock of a body against them. Thus they give a false sense of security and can cause an accident rather than prevent one.

It can be seen that if liferails are to be fitted at all, they must be of a size and strength to withstand considerable strain. If such rails cannot be fitted, it is better to do without rather than use smaller, scaled-down stanchions to "suit the size of the boat". Where the boat is small and rails are impractical, a good cabin handrail can be substituted, and this if properly secured is quite safe, for, because it is inboard, it tends to keep the weight of the person using it in towards the boat instead of outwards towards the ocean, where a slip can mean an accident.

Fitting liferails

The liferails are usually of stainless steel and are often covered with plastic to prevent chafing. They are held in place by fore and aft pulpits and a series of stanchions secured at intervals along the deck. Various other means can be used to hold the forward and after ends of the rails, but the solidly built and secured pulpit is undoubtedly the best, and since it is here that the greatest strain comes on the rails, it is unwise (and unattractive, too) to try to compromise.

The pulpits are made from one-inch piping, either of galvanised steel, stainless steel, monel or aluminium alloy. If money is no object, undoubtedly monel is the best available. They are bent into shape to conform to the shape of the boat's bow and stern, and secured around uprights of the same metal. The uprights take the form of stanchions and have base plates fastened to the deck. Obviously, with the various sizes and shapes of boats, pulpits are for the most part made to order, bear-

Liferails, including fore and aft pulpits, should be designed to fit each individual boat

ing in mind not only the shape of the curves, but also the accessibility of the deck where the uprights are to be secured. A well-made pulpit serves no purpose whatsover unless it is well secured through the deck.

The forward pulpit may—in the case of a yacht—be required to extend out around a bowsprit. This will require special fittings around the bowsprit itself, and each individual job will have to be measured and fitted on the spot. Where the pulpit comes inboard how

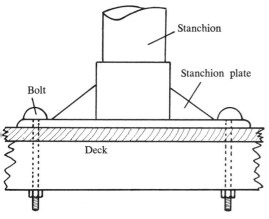

Cross section of stanchion fitting showing fastening through deck beam

ever, fairly standard fittings are used. The base plate of the uprights should be drilled for four bolts and if possible, should be bolted through the deck in the way of a beam, so that the full stresses falling on the pulpit can be transferred to a major structural part. If there is no beam handy, then the plate will have to be bolted to the deck, and in this case the underside of the deck should be built up with a square of timber and, if possible, a matching plate. Unless this is done there will be a tendency for the pulpit to tear out of the deck when a heavy weight is thrown on to it.

If a beam is not immediately available but there are several nearby, a bridge may be built across the beams and the bolts secured through this bridge. It is important to ensure that the uprights of the pulpit are secured wherever possible to a major structural member as the stresses they will be subjected to may be far greater than just that of a body. In the event of an accident, the pulpit may well need to take considerable strains for which it was not originally intended.

With the pulpit in place, the stanchions should be fitted at regular intervals down the sides of the vessel. This will vary greatly, according to the size of the boat, but distances much greater than five feet between stanchions will weaken the general structure of the liferails. The stanchions govern the height of the

liferails and should be at least two feet high with holes drilled to take the rails near the top and about halfway down the stanchion. Usually two rails are sufficient if placed at this height, and care must be taken to see that the edges of the holes drilled in stanchions are smoothed off to prevent chafing of the wire.

Once again the securing of the stanchions is all-important. The method used for securing pulpits can be adopted; each stanchion is secured over a beam. In this way the yachtsman can be sure that his stanchion will have to bend or break before it will tear out of deck.

Fibreglass boats often have few beams and so the stanchions must be secured through the deck. This, in turn, is much thinner than a timber deck and a wide wooden block must be secured on the inside to distribute the load and prevent possibility of buckling the deck.

With the pulpits and stanchions in place the rails can be fitted. They can be shackled on to the stern pulpit direct, but should be fastened to the forward pulpit by means of a turnbuckle so that any stretch occurring as they are used can be taken up. Liferails are always subject to stretch, and besides the inital fitting, the turnbuckle is always handy for slackening or tightening the rails according to requirements.

It is wise to fit some form of quick-release clip to the rails near the cockpit, so that they can be dropped between two stanchions for

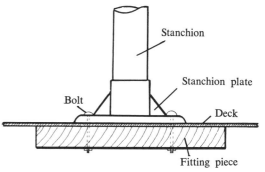

Cross section of stanchion fitting through fibreglass deck. Note fastening pad underneath deck

157

*Pulpits and stanchions have to bear the full weight
of a man and should be solid and well secured*

loading or unloading heavy gear without needing to undo the turnbuckles and re-reeve the wire. This is also handy when the boat is running dead square downwind, as the main sheet tends to chafe on the rails if running for any distance.

Some owners prefer to have completely removable stanchions, and this involves making the base plate separate from the stanchion, and securing the stanchion into the base plate socket with a pin or bolt. Care is needed to see that this fastening does not come undone when the vessel is working in a seaway.

The maintenance of rails and stanchions will vary according to the metal in use. Stainless steel, monel and aluminium require little or no maintenance, but galvanised steel may tend to rust where the galvanising has worn off. Stanchions and pulpits may be treated and painted to prevent this, but it is unwise to use a galvanised steel wire for the liferails as the constant chafing with running gear and the stanchions will soon wear off the galvanising or paint.

CHAPTER ELEVEN

Sails and Canvas Work

THIS HEADING CAN cover a multitude of sins. Many sails are made of canvas, many are not, but quite apart from the sails themselves there is a great deal of canvas used on both yachts and motor cruisers. Awnings, covers, blinds, are a few instances, and there are many others ranging from sailbags to canvas cots. Obviously, canvas work is of considerable importance when the question of maintenance and repair on board arises.

With the advent of synthetics, the old cotton canvas is fast disappearing as a sail material, and, indeed, so popular are these synthetics that almost all canvas work is giving way to the use of dacron, terylene and nylon materials.

A giant spinnaker needs a great deal of space in the sail loft when the hundreds of panels are sewn together. Photo courtesy Power Boat & Yachting

The principal advantage here is that they are virtually rot-proof, a tremendous asset when compared with the very vulnerable canvas which can be easily rotted either by water or sun.

CARE OF CANVAS SAILS

Day-to-day maintenance of sails depends on the material of which they are made. Cotton canvas sails—still popular in many craft today —require careful attention each time they are used as they readily fall victim to rot. After use they should be washed off with fresh water and dried carefully. Hosing them off on a lawn or similar open space is sufficient, providing the salt is removed from the material.

Drying can be done in the sun, although

*Well kept canvas sails can be as attractive and as
effective as those made from synthetics*

too much sun, particularly when the sails are
still impregnated with salt, can rot the stitching
and affect the yarn of the cloth very quickly.
However, stretched out on a lawn, with boxes,
or similar props underneath to keep a circulation of air passing on both sides, the canvas
will soon dry. Some skippers prefer to "hang
the washing" by hoisting the hosed-off sails
on their halyards and spreading them across
the rigging. This also is a good system.

Provided the sails are washed clean of salt
and dried thoroughly, they can be stowed
almost anywhere that is dry. Canvas is liable
to mildew and a damp corner will start a
mould creeping over them unless carefully
watched. It is a good practice, regardless of
where they are stowed, to air canvas sails
once in a while if they are not in use. This
rids the weave of any spores of mildew which
may have lodged there waiting for a chance to
develop. Needless to say, any small amount
of dampness in the canvas will trigger off
mildew and rot.

When stowed, the sails should be folded
rather than rolled and placed in a good sail-
bag. Nylon is ideal as it allows the canvas to
"breathe", and provided it is subsequently
stowed in a clean dry spot, will reduce any
possibility of mould forming. Care must be
taken to see that any ropes, such as sheets or
lanyards, that are to be stowed with the sails,
must also be dry. They themselves may be
impervious to rot, but the moisture they contain can cause mildew in the sail.

CARE OF SYNTHETIC SAILS

As mentioned earlier, synthetic sails are
virtually rot-free and thus need little care in
normal use. They may be stowed away wet,
although this is not recommended, for dampness can cause mould to set up on the material.
The mould is only superficial and can be easily
cleaned off without harm to the material, but
it is unsightly, can mark the material, and,
of course can spread to other materials in the
vicinity. If the sail has been sewn with cotton
stitching the mould will attack and rot the
stitches with resultant damage to the sail.

160

Terylene and dacron sails should be dried and folded before they are stowed, and placed in sailbags of similar material. Once again, the accompanying ropes should be perfectly dry. It is a good practice, particularly if the sails are to be stowed for some time, to ensure that everything that goes into the bag is clean and dry.

Synthetic sails can be left in place on the boat, particularly mainsails, which can be protected from the elements by a cover of similar material. This is a great advantage when the boat is in constant use, but when only used occasionally, it is far better to take them down and stow them away below. In addition to the precautions mentioned above, taking the sail off regularly offers the opportunity to check any wear that may be taking place aloft.

CLEANING SAILS AND AWNINGS

Sails become dirty with use. In addition, the location of the sails—touching rusty rigging, dirty paintwork, etc.—soon wears off the pristine newness they have when they come from the sailmaker's loft. Providing the dirt does not become too ingrained, it can usually

Modern synthetic sail materials are so impervious to rot that they can be stowed in position on the boom with just a light cover to keep off the sun

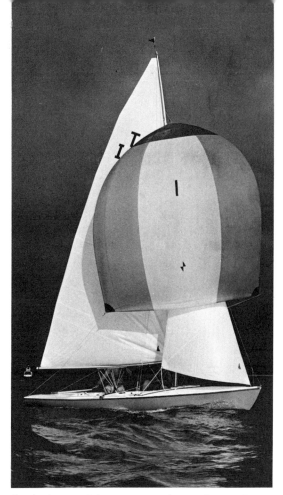

Synthetic materials are easy to clean and give a bright, sparkling appearance to yacht sails. Photo courtesy Power Boat & Yachting

be cleaned off fairly easily. It is good practice to clean fairly frequently as canvas, in particular, can absorb the dirt to the point where any chemicals in the dirt begin to stain the material permanently.

This is particularly the case when the boat is sailed in waters next to a large city or industrial zone. It is not uncommon to see even synthetic sail go completely yellow in one season because of chemical contamination from the atmosphere. In this case little can be done to return the sail to its former whiteness, but constant attention and frequent cleaning can prevent the contaminated air from gaining a foothold on the material.

Some laundries are geared to clean sails,

161

Regular cleaning prevents stains becoming ingrained in the material

particularly large ones, although care should be taken to ensure that the particular laundry knows exactly what it is doing. It has been known for sails to come back completely misshapen or even discoloured because of inexperience in the handling of this type of material. The safest way is to scrub the sails down with light detergent, either by spreading them out on a floor or lawn and using a light scrubbing brush, or, if they are small enough, by ducking them in a large tub. One 12 metre crew, wishing their sails to be the brightest on the day of a race, spent the previous day scrubbing them (complete with detergent) in a goldfish pond. The goldfish were removed first.

Awnings and sails can be scrubbed quite hard without affecting their appearance. Actually, this is essential, as the looser-woven material absorbs grime into the weave of the cloth more readily and a good scrubbing is

162

the only way to remove it. Synthetic materials are often coated with a surface which prevents too much dirt getting into the weave, and in this case the scrubbing should not be so hard as to damage the surface.

Once washed off with detergent, the sails should be hosed off with fresh water and hung out to dry. Wrinkles will soon come out when the sail fills with wind, so no ironing is necessary! They should then be bagged and stowed in a dry place until required.

The method used for cleaning sails can be applied to awnings and other canvas work. Smaller items, such as covers for winches, bunks, ropes, and sailbags, should be washed in a washing machine or tub, as they cannot be laid out flat for scrubbing. A day's work cleaning all the canvas work on board ship can be very rewarding when next the sails are set.

REMOVING STAINS

The stains found on sails and canvas work on board ship can be many and varied, and not all will be easily removed. The most common stain is rust, and with care this can be taken

Because of the amount of handling they receive, sails soon become marked. Careful cleaning will usually restore them to their original newness

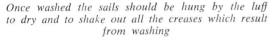

Once washed the sails should be hung by the luff to dry and to shake out all the creases which result from washing

Localised stains can be removed before washing the sail as a whole

out of canvas or synthetic material without too much effort. An oxalic acid solution is best for removing rust stains. It should be diluted as much as possible before use. By starting with a small, diluted quantity, and gradually building up the strength, the stains can be removed with the least effort, and with the least risk of damage to the sail.

Many patent stain removers are available, but care should be taken, particularly for synthetic sails, to ensure that they do not contain a chemical which may damage either the material itself, or the surface coating. Oxalic acid, used carefully, is safe for both canvas and synthetic materials.

Oil and grease stains can be removed with perchlorethylene or similar chemical. It should be applied sparingly, and quickly washed off as soon as the grease has been removed. Particularly is this the case with synthetic sails where the chemical may, over an extended period of time, damage the surface coating.

Bloodstains are hard to remove, although oxalic acid will take them out if they are not too old. Some patent cleaning fluids are able to remove these stains and can be used providing the care mentioned earlier is taken.

Whatever the stain, it should be removed as quickly as possible and the area then washed off thoroughly to remove all traces of the cleaning agent. The sail can then be washed as a whole, or dried and stowed away, as the case may be.

DARNING SMALL TEARS

Where a sail or awning has been torn shortly and cleanly the tear can sometimes be darned successfully. In any case, if it cannot be sent immediately to a repair depot, it should be darned to prevent the hole becoming enlarged; this is particularly the case if the tear occurs at sea, and the sail has to be used before it can be sent to the sailmaker. Thread should be used for darning, using a fairly robust needle, although too thick a needle should be avoided as it will make large holes in the weave of the cloth.

The procedure for darning is as follows:

1. Hold the two edges of the tear together.

2. Place the needle under the canvas at a point about a quarter of an inch from the tear and level with the end of it. Push up through the canvas, down through the tear

163

Canvas sails become dirty quicker than synthetic as the material tends to absorb moisture and dirt

RESTITCHING SEAMS

A common repair job on canvas, and particularly on parts of a sail which are subject to chafe, is the restitching of a seam where the original stitching has worn away. This requires the use of a palm and needle, as some force is needed to drive the needle through the thicknesses of the material. This stitch is carried out entirely on top of the canvas; the procedure is as follows:

1. With the palm and needle, drive the needle down through the material and back up again in one movement so that it comes through the seam. Pull tight.

2. Repeat the process at intervals of about one sixteenth of an inch, arranging the stitches so that they "lean" slightly in the direction of stitching.

It will be seen that this form of stitching is normal hand sewing, but with the thickness of material used it requires more dexterity to ensure an even and strong stitch.

Tears in a sail will usually need patching although darning will sometimes take care of small tears

and up through the canvas on the opposite side in a similar position.

3. Bring the needle back over the tear and push it down through the canvas immediately alongside the first point of the stitching.

4. Bring the needle up through the tear behind the crossover stitch just made and draw tight. Pass it over the crossover stitch and down through the tear again and push it up through the canvas immediately adjoining the first stitch on the opposite side.

5. Bring the needle across the tear to the near side, push down through the canvas, up through the tear, cross over, down through the tear and back up throuh the canvas on the near side. Continue until the tear has been darned.

164

PATCHING

There are many methods of patching and many types of material for patching. Recent developments in the field of synthetics have produced a patch that needs only to be pressed on to a tear; its self-adhesive qualities keep the patch in place. Other methods require the use of a hot iron to fuse a patch into place, and these are often quite successful, particularly in small craft.

But undoubtedly the best—albeit the oldest—instruments for a patch are the good old needle and thread. Almost without exception a well-sewn patch will outlast any quicker and easier method of closing a large hole or tear, and is often stronger and will wear better.

The size of the patch—particularly in a sail—governs the type of patch to be used. If the material is torn for the greater part of a panel, then it is often better to remove the panel and stitch in a completely new one. A patch over existing material can cause the shape of the sail to be altered, with the result that the boat's performance may be affected. In this case it is always better to get the sail-maker to do the job as skills beyond the make-do-and-mend stage are required.

For small patches, however, whether they be for canvas or synthetic material, the following method of stitching is best:

1. Cut the patch larger than the hole or tear and where possible keep it to a square or rectangular shape. The patch should, if possible, be made from the same material as the torn section and should be so cut that the weave is at right angles to the edge of the cut, and that it also coincides with the weave of the material to be patched.

2. Place the patch in position over the tear, turn in the edges all round, and with a pencil or chalk, mark the position of the patch edges on the sail. A few definite marker points should be made across both patch and sail so that it can be placed exactly in position later.

3. Using the stitch mentioned in the pre-

vious section, sew the edge of the patch all round, being careful to see that the registration marks coincide.

4. Turn the sail over and cut out the damaged section, leaving a reasonable margin in from the previous line of stitching. Turn this edge under and sew as on the opposite side.

5. If in the course of patching, the patch overruns a seam, or into the edge tabling, the seam or tabling must be lifted to incorporate the patch, and then be re-sewn.

REPAIRING A TORN BATTEN POCKET

This is done as described in the previous

Terylene and other synthetics reduce the need for maintenance and repair of yacht sails. Photo courtesy Fibremakers Ltd

section. Where the cloth is torn, it must be patched, and if the sail has torn as well as the batten pocket itself, then the pocket must be lifted and the sail patched under it, before the pocket is patched and replaced. All stitching in this operation is the normal straight stitching as mentioned in past paragraphs.

RENEWING THE LUFF WIRE

One of the most common repair jobs with jibs is the renewal of the luff wire. This tends, by virtue of the strains put on it, to rust and collapse far earlier than the material of the sail or, for that matter, the stitching. The test for a weak or rusty luff wire is to bend it double and pinch the eye; if the wire frays or breaks inside the material it should be replaced.

In any case, rusty luff wires stain the material of the sail, making it unsightly. For this reason plastic-covered wire should be used where possible.

The following is the procedure for renewing a damaged luff wire:

1. Cut the stitching holding the wire in place and remove the old wire.

2. Cut to shape a new piece of sailcloth or tape about four inches wide. Stitch this to the sail along one edge, so that it overlaps the old luff at about the halfway mark.

3. Place the new wire in position and fold the tape over. Stitch in place with a zig-zag type of stitch as close to the luff wire as possible. To ensure that the material is close around the wire, the stitching can be done with a piece of light cord instead of the wire. When the stitching has been completed, the wire can be joined to the string and pulled through.

SEWING AN EYE INTO CANVAS

There are two ways of making an eye in sails or canvas, one of which is the fitting of an

Testing a sail for its ability to withstand wear and tear. The cameras in the test photograph the crosses on the sail to show abnormal strain on the cloth when under wind pressure. Photo courtesy Fibre-makers

eyelet by means of the proper eyelet punch. This is dealt with later in this section. The other method, which is more common for sails, is to sew the eye into place. Sewing is also the correct method of repairing an eye that has pulled badly or damaged the material surrounding it so that a punched eye may not hold well.

The ring to be sewn into the sail should be placed on the material and a circle drawn around its inside circumference with a pencil. The ring should be removed and the position of the mark checked; then the procedure is as follows:

1. Draw a second ring, inside the first, concentric with it but with about half the diameter. Cut this inner ring out.

2. With a palm and needle, sew the brass ring to the cloth, using round stitches close together and about the same size as each other.

3. If the eye is for ornamental use, it can be left as such, but if it is to have anything connected through it, a brass eyelet should be punched into it to provide a firm metal surface and prevent chafing of the stitching. This will require the use of a special punch and die as described in the next paragraphs.

PUNCHING A BRASS EYELET INTO CANVAS

This is the most common method of fitting an eye to canvas, and is particularly useful where boat covers, awnings and other canvas work is concerned, for it is quick and easily replaced. It requires the use of a special punch and die which must be exactly the same size as the brass eyelets to be used. Failure to match the die with the eyelets will result in a loose eye.

The die comprises a punch and a female die. They are not expensive and are much used in boat maintenance. The procedure is as follows:

1. Place the canvas over the female member at the point where the hole is to be made. With the punch cut a hole at this spot.

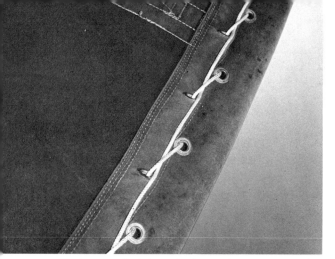

Eyelets punched into the hem of a canvas awning provide a neat and effective method of securing

2. Place the thimble on the die, and place the canvas over it so that the hole fits snugly over the shank of the thimble.

3. Place the eyelet ring over the shank of the thimble and with the special punch, splay it out so that it turns back on the ring and grips it firmly.

It is important to note that when punching a hole in canvas, particularly near an edge, a seam or hem should be made so that the eye is punched into a double thickness of canvas. Too much strain can easily pull an eye from single-thickness canvas, and even if it is not

A typical home made overall awning in canvas. Such a cover provides excellent protection for varnish and paintwork beneath

pulled right out of the canvas, it can be stretched and damage the material surrounding it so that it is difficult to punch another eye in the same spot.

BOAT COVERS

Canvas work for boats varies greatly according to the type of boat concerned. Apart from sails, a yacht requires an overall cover, often a spray dodger, skylight cover and numerous other bits and pieces, possibly including an awning. Cruisers, on the other hand, require a similar overall cover, but often need in addition blinds, or side curtains to close in the cockpit area or the well deck. These, of course, must be specially shaped and fitted so that they are snug and do not flap in a breeze, since they may be kept in place when the boat is under way. They may be cut from a number of materials, of which canvas is probably the all-purpose champion, although from the point of view of looks, vinyl is rapidly gaining favour. There are also several plastic and similar synthetics available. The choice offered a motor yacht owner is varied and interesting.

To make any sort of cover some skill is needed, and the proud owner would be well advised to leave such workmanship to a skilled tradesman. Although he may save money by making it himself, unless he has the right machines for stitching and uses skill in the making, the end result can look very tatty. And since boat covers and awnings are on show to the world, as it were, a bad cover can mar a nice-looking boat as readily as a good cover can make one.

Patching and similar repair work can easily be done by the amateur, however, and the various sections in this chapter deal with the most probable types of repair that will be encountered. Anything requiring major alterations and repair should be left to the professional, for the result of amateur work in this regard could be worse than the original damage.

AWNINGS

Sun awnings are not a permanent fixture for a boat, and are quite easily made. These, indeed, can be put together by an amateur without too much trouble and since they are only brought out for an hour or two when lying to an anchor, there is no great problem if they are not completely professional looking.

An awning can be made for a yacht or a cruiser, although in the latter case, if it is to be a semi-permanent awning over a flying bridge or similar spot, it will require careful measurement and cutting to shape. But for an all-purpose square awning, the following steps are a guide:

1. The awning should be cut from a piece of reasonably light canvas or synthetic material. A rectangular shape is the easiest to handle.

2. Once shaped to fit the boat, allowing sufficient on the edge of the canvas to turn a hem under, a strengthening piece should be inserted right down the centre of the awning in a fore and aft direction. This will fit along the boom, in the case of a yacht, or along a spar in the case of a cruiser. If there is more than one spar it is not necessary to sew strengthening pieces for all, only for the centre one. A strip about six to eight inches wide of the same material can be used, and it should be sewn along both edges after turning them under. The ends should be turned into the pocket made by stitching the sides, and stitched level with the end of the awning.

3. The hem should now be turned under and sewn all round with two rows of stitching, one where the edges of the canvas are turned under, and one at the edge into which eyelets can be inserted.

4. At intervals of three to four feet, a batten pocket must be sewn on to the underside of the awning. This is done by cutting a strip of the material about six to eight inches wide, turning under the edges, and stitching it across the underside of the awning from side to side. The ends should be turned into the

A more elaborate awning, these should not be attempted by amateurs if a good fit is required. Note gap left for ventilation

pockets and one end sewn up to the awning to close it off, the other sewn back on itself to leave the end open. The sizes of battens used are of no consequence providing they are sufficient for the size of the awning, and they do not have to fit snugly into the pockets.

5. Eyelets are punched into the canvas

The simplest form of boat cover and one well within the scope of the handyman

A sun awning used as a boat cover. Note battens and strong centrepiece of awning. Raised at the stern this would provide good shelter for the boat's cockpit

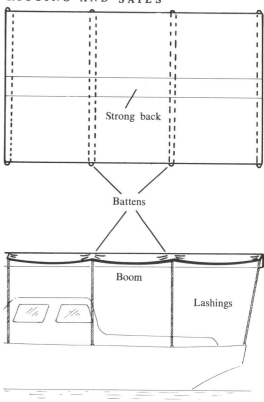

Illustration of sun awning. Plan of awning (above) Method of securing in position on yacht (below)

at the batten pockets, ensuring, of course, that in punching the eyelet on the open end of the batten, it does not close the hole or restrict the entry of the batten.

6. Lanyards of suitable length should be spliced into the eyelets, and battens of sufficient thickness to remain stiff when supported only in the middle, shaped to fit the pockets. The awning is now ready to be put into place; the strongback section is placed along the boom or awning spar, and the battens are tied down to the side of the boat with the lanyards.

The size of awning obviously depends on the shape and size of the area it is to cover. Other fittings, such as an eyelet at each end to keep the awning stretched along the boom, will be inserted according to individual needs. If the awning is for a cruiser in which some structure is already in place, then once again it becomes a question of measurement and shaping for individual needs. The awning described here is simple and basic, to be put up almost anywhere, and rolled up and stowed in a relatively small space when not in use.

170

CHECKING SAILS FOR WEAR AND TEAR

At the end of each season, or more frequently if the boat is competing in races, the sails should be checked carefully for signs of wear and tear. At this time a stitch in time saves a darn sight more than nine! A single broken stitch in the seam of a sail drawn tight with wind will soon develop into a completely unstitched seam unless repaired or strengthened in time.

The best way to check out a sail is to spread it out on a lawn or floor when it can be gone over methodically. In the confines of a boat only a section can be examined at a time and the tendency is to miss spots that show up later as greatly aggravated damage.

The mainsail should be examined thoroughly,

piece by piece, starting at the headboard. A great deal of chafe occurs in this vicinity, mainly from backstays which touch the head of the sail when the sheets are freed out. Stitching can carry away very easily here. The headboard itself can be worn, particularly the eye where the halyard connection is made. The board moves around a great deal when the yacht is sailing, and with the strain on the halyard shackle, considerable wear takes place.

The leather or nylon fastenings on the slides are vulnerable to wear, and should be tested one by one. Weak connections should be replaced, and the slides also examined and replaced where necessary. Nylon slides can become worn, and brass slides dented, although this often shows up if the slides jam in the track when the sail is hoisted.

The eyelets through which the slide fastenings are attached should be examined for signs of chafe, and repaired as described earlier in this section. If there are no slides, the luff rope should be examined for signs of it parting from the sail itself. This, of course, also applies to a luff tape. Leather sewn on to the corners of the sail can come in for a fair amount of chafe. If there is any sign in any of these

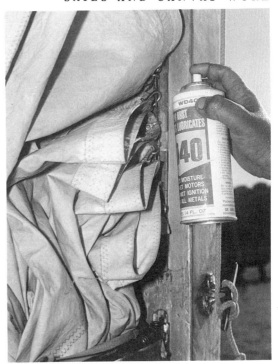

Freeing oil squirted on the sail slides will reduce friction and thus wear and tear

areas of excessive chafe, then the mast should be examined with a view to preventing a reoccurrence once a repair has been effected.

The stitching of a sail needs a thorough, inch-by-inch inspection, as one stitch broken is not easy to detect. However, the areas round the batten pockets are always the most vulnerable and the stitching here should be thoroughly examined and overstitched if there is any sign of some stitching giving way. If an area has come unstitched, a repair will have to be made.

The point at which crosstrees touch the sail always needs attention, and providing it does not add too much weight to the sail, particularly a light weather sail, a strengthening patch can be sewn into position before the chafe has worn right through the sailcloth. Also, areas where the sail chafes on runners or after shrouds should be inspected regularly to see that the material is not deteriorating.

Sail numbers are usually stitched only

Subjected to enormous stresses when full of wind, the sail will quickly aggravate any light damage

171

Considerable strain comes on the corners of a sail as can be seen by the drawing of the cloth in this picture. Photo courtesy Power Boat & Yachting

The clew itself is probably the most chafed area of any sail on the boat, and for this reason is heavily strengthened when originally made. Wear and tear in this area may necessitate replacing the eye, strengthening it, or even fitting a completely new corner over the old. Because of the difficult angles in this area, it might be wiser to leave this job to a professional sailmaker.

The luff wire is also vulnerable, and must be examined for signs of rust or corrosion. Bending it severely will indicate whether or not the luff wire is in a weak state. If it breaks or whiskers it will have to be replaced. The method of renewing a luff wire is described in this chapter.

Jib hanks get a great deal of wear, and often have to be repaired or replaced. The spring-loaded piston hanks, usually in brass or bronze, need lubricating to keep them in working order. The nylon type need less attention but are more liable to wear. These, and their connections to the sail (usually twine

Every part of every sail bears strain and tension when racing. Only careful maintenance will keep the sails in good shape and appearance

lightly and may need strengthening as also may insignia on the sail. The leach should be carefully checked, for a slight flap here can burst the stitching; likewise the outhaul and the foot of the sail, where the connections are similar to those on the luff.

To prevent too much creasing, and consequent wear of the material, the mainsail should always be folded when stowed away.

The jib comes in for much the same problems as the main and should be examined all round for stitching wear. Considerable wear comes on the foot and leach of big Genoa jibs where they sheet around the shrouds, or bear on the crosstrees. Similarly the edges of the sail come in for some rough wear when going about as the sail flaps violently along its leach, and is often dragged mercilessly across from side to side, around shrouds, mast, or perhaps inner forestays. All of this plays havoc with the leach, foot and clew of the sail.

172

Because of their size, spinnakers like this can easily become fouled and tear. Their light material also makes them vulnerable

or stitching) should also be examined and renewed where necessary.

Spinnakers require a considerable amount of attention. Because they and their fittings are kept as light as possible, and because of their free-flying nature, they are very liable to twist and foul or tear. The patching gear should always be kept handy when the spinnaker is in use, and many a yacht has won a good race with a spinnaker patched like Joseph's coat of many colours.

The sail itself should be examined in the usual way for signs of stitching wear and chafe, although since it is only attached at the corners and flies free from the mast and rigging, chafe is less of a problem than with other sails. More wear comes on each corner and the

fitting there. This may be simply a ring or (usually at the peak) a swivel, and both the fitting and the way in which it is fastened to the sail should be watched for signs of wear.

One of the most vulnerable spots in the stitching of a spinnaker is at the edges of the strengthening pieces. It is sometimes worth the effort to double-sew these edges, for once there is a break in the stitching, the tension on the sail causes it to run very quickly. Most strengthening pieces are at the corners and this is where the real strain comes.

Mizzens and extras require much the same attention as the sails mentioned above. Most of these sails—mizzens, mizzen staysails, fishermen, cheaters etc.—are versions of one of the standard sails, and the methods of inspection described above hold good for all.

Repair of large tears in a spinnaker is a sailmakers job if the shape of the sail is to be retained

Care and Maintenance of Marine Engines

CHAPTER TWELVE

Routine Maintenance

THE REPAIR OF marine engines requires technical knowledge. Although many amateurs like to dabble with repair work on engines—some quite successfully—generally speaking it is a subject beyond the scope of all but the qualified professional man. Quite apart from the technical know-how required to repair any kind of motor, from the smallest motor mower to the most hotted-up car, marine engines have their own peculiar technical problems, which do not as a rule come under the scope of normal engines. For this reason, the repair of marine engines is best left to a professional mechanic, and for this reason also the subject is beyond the scope of a book of this kind.

Minor repairs to superficial equipment such as leads, terminals, etc., can be successfully handled by the amateur, but major repair work involving the stripping-down of the engine is something which, when handled by an inexperienced person, can often result in problems far greater than the original trouble. Undoubtedly the services of a professional marine mechanic will hit the pocket fairly hard, but an attempt to repair the motor without the required technical knowledge and tools may well result in a far more expensive job by the mechanic anyway.

For this reason the subject of marine engines will be limited in this volume purely to their care and maintenance. This is the side of the subject into which an amateur should dig his teeth deeply. The correct care and maintenance of an engine is the best insurance

The power plants of fast craft such as these must be maintained and tuned to perfection if they are to give top performance. Photo courtesy Coronet Boats

against the problems mentioned above where major repair work is involved.

Unlike people, engines thrive on work. In addition to work, they require the care and attention that are necessary to any mechanism when it is subjected to the streses and strains, the wear and tear of constant working. Like the boat in which it may be mounted, the engine requires regular and considerate treat-short and its demands for mechanical attention high. The correct care and maintenance can reduce to a minimum the need for major work on the engine or its auxiliary equipment.
ment. If this is not carried out, its life will be

Three kinds of motors are generally in use for marine work: inboard engines, outboard engines, and the combined inboard-outboard engine. The choice of which to use in a boat depends on a great many factors principally the size of the boat and the speed required.

INBOARD ENGINES

In large craft, from about twenty feet upwards, particularly power boats, the inboard engine gives the best performance and operating economy. The question of horsepower in this type of motor depends almost entirely on the design of the hull. It is never a question of speed, since greater horsepower does not necessarily mean greater speed. Indeed, it can mean exactly the reverse. A vessel designed to reach a maximum hull speed with a certain drive, will probably slow down if a greater thrust or drive is put on the propeller than has been calculated for this designed hull speed. There is a tendency for over-powered boats to "dig a hole" in the water, causing the bow to rise, the stern to sink beyond the designed planing inclination, and a large stern wave to build up behind the vessel. An extreme case of this over-powering can look quite ridiculous with the vessel almost vertical in the water, sitting down on her stern, with a mountain of frothing water pushing out behind her.

The question of power and speed is for the designer. In addition to designing the maximum hull speed, he should design also the size and specifications of the propeller that is to drive her. With these specifications in mind, an engine is purchased which will give the correct revolutions to the propeller to obtain maximum thrust for the hull speed. In this way engine and hull are matched up through the propeller, so that maximum speed is obtained with minimum operating economy.

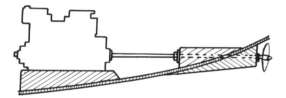

Inboard engine

The inboard engine is usually mounted fairly centrally on heavy bearers in the bottom of the boat. Details of mounting an inboard engine are given later in this section. Because of the design or size of the boat, however, the engine may be mounted in the stern and drive obtained through "V" gears. Once again this is a question of design, and it is rarely practical to take any hull and just drop any engine into it in any position. The design and layout of the engine must all be combined in the designer's calculations if the boat is not only to obtain maximum speed at economy, but also to ride properly in the water.

Diesel Engines

Inboard engines may be of two kinds: diesel or petrol. Undoubtedly the diesel is the most suitable for marine work as, principally,

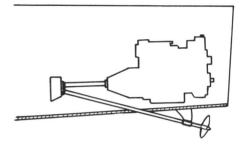

Inboard engine with "V" drive

it eliminates the need for electrical equipment which is so vulnerable in salt air conditions. However, diesel engines are frequently more expensive than petrol, and have limitations which make them impractical for many pleasure craft. Thus the marine petrol engine has been developed to a high state of performance, and can be obtained in all sizes, shapes and horsepowers to suit virtually every vessel afloat. Another feature in the popularity of diesel engines for marine work is the elimination of fire hazard, ever-present when petrol is carried in the boat. However, once again modern design has eliminated much of the hazard of petrol fires and with reasonable care and caution petrol engines can be successfully used in almost any vessel.

Marine engines range in size from huge diesels to tiny yacht auxiliaries such as this

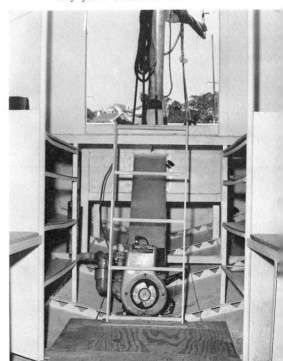

The careful choice of engine is the only way to obtain maximum results from the boat. This racer would actually move slower with more powerful engines astern. Photo courtesy Power Boat & Yachting

Petrol Engines

The petrol engine group can be broken down even further; two prominent types are fitted in pleasure craft—the fully-designed marine engine, and the converted car engine. Needless to say the fully-designed marine engine is always the best, since it is manufactured for the purpose it will serve. The "marinised" or converted car motor is not originally designed to be fitted in a boat, and can run into problems because of its incorrect environment. However, some manufacturing firms have overcome most of these problems and can convert car engines with reasonable success for marine use. Perhaps their greatest advantage and the reason for their popularity lies in the relatively low cost. Many old model cars have been stripped of their motors which, although not suitable for the road, may still have many miles in them when converted for marine use.

OUTBOARD ENGINES

With the enormous boom in small craft, particularly lightweight runabouts and dinghies, the outboard engine' has come into its own in recent years. Designed specifically for these types of craft, the engines range from as low as one horsepower to greater than 100 horsepower. The more powerful engines are not necessarily designed for larger vessels, rather are they designed for high speed work on small boats. Apart from the high-revving motor, and the small propeller associated with outboard engines, the difficulty of mounting them on the back of larger craft is one of the reasons for their restriction to small boats. However, as an auxiliary for yachts, and as an emergency engine in case of failure of the main inboard engine, outboards are sometimes carried on large craft.

There are many hundreds of types of outboard engines available on the market. Generally, they are designed to suit specific boats for specific purposes. Low horsepower, two-stroke engines are used for small fishing boats and the like, whereas the larger multicylinder engines are designed for high speed work either in racing or for towing water skis. In all cases, the engine is a complete unit and its installation requires nothing more than clamping to the stern. Some of the more advanced models have remote controls, remote fuel tank, etc., but the engine itself is a self-contained unit within a fibreglass or metal cover and permanently fixed to its drive.

INBOARD-OUTBOARD ENGINES

This form of engine is finding increasing

179

popularity, particularly among the medium-class type of motor vessels. They are virtually useless in yachts because of the peculiar design of the motor and its drive. However, they are convenient, compact, and usually sufficiently powerful for craft up to a good size. In this case the engine is separate from the drive and is mounted inboard. The drive itself, comprising gears and propeller, is mounted outboard in much the same way as the outboard engine itself. The transmission takes place through the transom of the boat, usually above the water line. This design has one considerable advantage over the fixed inboard marine engine with its shaft secured beneath the boat, that in the event of running into shallow water the drive unit can be lifted up to prevent damage. Another advantage is that the engine is located close to the transom, in much the same position as a "V"-drive engine, but without the extra apparatus of the "V"-drive. This makes for a great deal more room inside the vessel and also eliminates the unpleasant fumes which can permeate from an engine mounted in the cabin.

Large horsepower engines are not always required. This boat would sink by the stern with a much bigger motor

CHOICE OF ENGINE

The question of choice of engine is so wide that little advice can be given in a general manner. The type of power unit to be installed in a vessel will depend on a great many factors, the principal of which will be the type of use for which the boat is built, the design of the hull, and the availability of space inside the hull. Yachts and sail boats, by virtue of their narrow hulls and restricted space, require very small motors. This, however, is usually quite acceptable, since yachts are designed to sail anyway and the motor is usually just an auxiliary to motor through difficult areas such as moorings, or to motor home when the wind has died. Ocean-going yachts pay more attention to the quality and power of their motor since it may well be their saviour in time of emergency. These vessels, being larger, can afford more space into which to fit the engine,

although if they are racing boats the question of weight is also borne in mind as a limiting factor to the size of power unit to be installed.

Power vessels in the large, ocean-going class upwards of thirty feet invariably fit inboard power units, usually twins, in order to obtain speed and drive against the seas in the offshore areas in which they are used. With the additional hull space available in these larger craft, diesels are the most popular choice because of the factors mentioned earlier. If space is limited, however, petrol engines may have to be fitted, although modern developments of some diesel engines have reduced the size of the motors by slanting the engine block out of the vertical. In this way even a fairly large, heavy engine can be mounted in a limited space beneath a cockpit floor. Motor boats in the twenty- to thirty-foot range can adapt either an outboard-inboard or a fitted inboard engine for their use. Here the question will be principally one of speed and available space. Sailcraft of this size will probably be restricted to either very small inboard engines, or the adaptation of an outboard on the stern or

180

dropped through the hull well. The engine will most likely be limited to petrol, although some inboard-outboard diesels are available, and modern developments of single-cylinder diesels have made them sufficiently compact to fit in boats of this size.

CARE AND MAINTENANCE

As mentioned earlier the question of care and maintenance of a marine engine is a most important one.

Unless properly looked after, an engine will be more trouble than it is worth. A neglected marine engine is a mechanic's nightmare, since in lying idle it has had an opportunity to breed all kinds of ills, particularly corrosion; an ever-present problem where salt moisture lies heavy in the air. When an engine is stationary its protective oil runs down to the bottom of the sump and leaves the vital working parts relatively unprotected. It needs only one small spot of corrosion to start on the highly machined working parts for trouble to begin and spread quickly. Indeed, it is no fallacy that the worst possible thing to do to a marine engine is to leave it idle, and regular running, even for a few minutes weekly, will breathe a steady and valuable breath of life through the engine.

But keeping the engine turning over is not the sole answer. A well-run motor will be subject to wear and tear, and although it may run beautifully for many years, sooner or later parts will begin to wear and faults will begin to show up. If the engine is properly cared for and subject to regular routine maintenance, this wear and tear will not only be kept to a minimum, but will be spotted immediately it begins to take serious effect on any part of the engine. If it is not corrected at an early stage, wear and tear can result in serious damage not only to the part immediately affected but to other parts in the vicinity. Any-one familar with the problems in a car engine, and its need for regular maintenance, will appreciate that the marine engine, working under far more difficult conditions, will necessarily require more attention and care.

Because the maintenance routines for petrol and diesel and also for outboard engines are considerably different, they are dealt with separately in this section. However, inboard engines and inboard-outboard engines can be grouped as one. Their transmission varies somewhat, but the power unit is usually fairly standard.

Naturally there are differences also between different models and makes of engines. The routine maintenance for one make of diesel engine may be different to that for another. Quite often lubrication points, belt tensions, etc., are in different places on different models. However, there is a basic routine which, when applied to virtually any engine, will keep it in good running order. It is not suggested that the maintenance routines described in this book should override the manufacturer's recommendations—quite the reverse. The maker's suggestions, together with the routine laid down here, should keep any marine engine in first-class running condition.

Engine Log Book

A properly kept engine log book can be of great assistance to both an amateur and a professional engineer when it comes to fault finding. It should contain such items as: Hours run, lubrication, oil pressure and temperature, ammeter charge and water temperature. With the aid of this book an amateur can see, for example, a gradual drop in lubrication oil pressure over a long period of time, which could mean the spring losing its tension in the relief valve. This in itself is no great problem and can be rectified with little cost and effort, whereas if it were allowed to carry on, the main bearing could be ruined—a very expensive repair job.

ROUTINE MAINTENANCE OF DIESEL ENGINES

A diesel engine, like any other engine, needs

181

to be used often to be kept in good condition. If it is not actually used for driving the boat, it should be started and run for a few minutes weekly. Failure to do so will lead to the complications mentioned earlier in this chapter, and in turn will involve expensive overhauls when the engine is required again. When in use the engine should be subject to a general maintenance routine along the following lines:

Daily

1. Check water level in header tank, and check entire cooling system for sign of leaks.

2. If the engine is fitted with an open cooling system, open seacocks.

3. Check oil levels in engine and gearbox sumps. Top up where necessary.

4. Check level in fuel tank.

5. Check lubricating oil pressure.

6. Check ammeter for battery charging.

Every 150 Hours

1. Check tension on engine belts and adjust where necessary.

2. Check batteries and top up with distilled water where necessary.

3. Check charging ability of generator, clean contacts, etc., where necessary.

Every 300 Hours

1. Renew lubricating oil filter.

2. Renew air filter.

3. Drain oil from gearbox and engine sump and renew.

Every 600 Hours

1. Check the fuel system through in case of sediment build-up, including lift pump chambers and filters. Clean and renew where necessary.

2. Check generator, lubricate where necessary, as indicated in the service manual.

3. Drain cooling system (closed system) and refill with fresh coolant and filter.

4. Check cooling system throughout for leaks or loose connections.

Every 1000 Hours

1. Remove atomisers and send for cleaning.

2. Check valve clearances.

3. Check lubrication of rocker shaft.

4. Inspect brushes and commutator of dynamo.

5. Drain and clean fuel tank.

TROUBLE SHOOTING (Diesel engines)

Engine Will Not Start

Starter fails to turn engine

(a) Battery run down. Check and replace if necessary.

(b) Check all wiring and terminals.

(c) Check switches, including solenoid switch, to ensure they are working.

(d) Check commutator and brushes on starter motor to ensure they are clean and making good contact.

(e) Check starter motor for faults.

Starter turns but engine will not fire

(a) Check that all conditions as mentioned in starting section of operating manual are correctly made.

(b) Check that atomisers have fuel. If not, check fuel system, pump, and fuel tank that all taps are turned on and fuel line is free.

(c) Check working of fuel lift pump.

(d) Check fuel level in tank.

(e) Check possibility of air lock in fuel line.

(f) If there is fuel at atomisers, the atomisers may require servicing. Valve or pump timing may be incorrect.

(g) Check engine compression for possibility of severe piston wear.

Engine starts, runs then stops

(a) Check fuel feed pipe and filter for possible blockage, and ensure fuel tap is open.

(b) Check capacity of fuel lift pump for possible weakness.

(c) Check that vent hole in fuel tank is open.

(d) Check for possible restriction in induction or exhaust systems.

(e) Check fuel lines for possible air lock.

Engine misfires or runs erratically

(a) Check fuel system for air lock. This is the most likely cause.

(b) Check fuel lines for possibility of water in fuel pump, or leaks around connections.

(c) Check atomisers. Replace where necessary.

(d) Check valve and pump timing for correct adjustment.

(e) Check valve clearance against manufacturer's recommendations.

Loss of power

(a) Check fuel pump output and examine throttle linkage for possible weakness.

(b) Check fuel filters and lines.

(c) Check atomisers. Replace where necessary.

(d) Check air clearance against possible blockage.

(e) Check compression (see end of this routine).

Smoke from exhaust

(a) Check air breathing system against restriction of air into engine.

(b) Check fuel pump for possible defects.

(c) Check valve and pump timing.

(d) Check atomisers and replace if faulty.

(e) Check tension of propeller gland as excessive load on the engine can cause a smoky exhaust.

(f) Excessive oil consumption and wear and tear leading to poor compression will give rise to smoky exhaust. Check compression as described at the end of this routine.

Low oil pressure

(a) Check gauge and oil warning light against possible faulty reading.

(b) Check level of oil in sump. Top up where necessary.

(c) Check oil line against possible leakage.

(d) Check the correct grade of oil is used and that level in sump is correct.

(e) Check that oil filter element is working correctly and is not choked.

(f) Check compression.

High oil pressure

(a) Check that the correct grade of oil is used and level in sump is correct.

(b) Check that the pressure gauge is working properly.

(c) Check that the pressure relief valve is working.

Overheating

(a) Check thermostat unit for faults.

(b) Check tension on driving belts to water pumps.

(c) Check water cooling circuits against possibility of blockage, particularly damage to exterior cooling pipes.

(d) Check that water pumps are working correctly.

Dynamo not charging

(a) Check tension of belt drive and tighten or renew as necessary.

(b) Check all wiring and terminal connections including battery terminals.

(c) Check that commutator and brushes are clean and there is no sign of burning or charring on wiring.

183

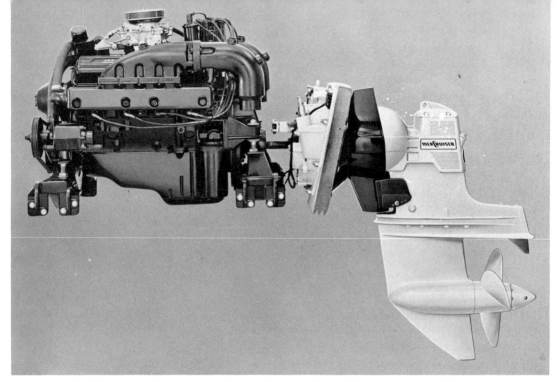

A typical inboard/outboard layout. This versatile arrangement is very popular with medium/large motor yachts. Photo courtesy Power Boat & Yachting

(d) If no results are obtained through the above checks, remove the dynamo and send it ashore for checking.

Poor compression

Poor compression is a sure indication of serious engine trouble. Feel the compression when turning the engine by hand; starting will be difficult and sometimes impossible if much compression has been lost. The causes are numerous: worn piston rings, worn liners, leaking valves, are among the major suspects. There is no quick remedy for this condition. A top overhaul may possibly remove much of the trouble, depending on just which part of the engine is concerned. More than likely a complete overhaul will be necessary if the lost compression, which is so vital to the efficient running of a diesel engine, is to be restored completely.

Colour of exhaust smoke

The colour of the exhaust smoke can often indicate the nature of internal problems.

Black smoke indicates dirty atomisers, overload on engine.

Blue smoke indicates worn piston rings, liners, etc.,

White smoke often indicates water in the fuel.

ROUTINE MAINTENANCE OF PETROL ENGINES

Marine petrol engines fall into two principal categories: two-stroke and four-stroke. Both types are quite suitable for any size of vessel, but the general rule seems to be that the larger vessels have four-stroke motors and the smaller power craft carry two-strokes, as also do sailing craft. Size has a bearing, since generally the two-stroke is the more compact motor. But in terms of performance each is equally efficient and each, provided it undergoes the routine maintenance and care, will give many years of good service.

The basic difference between the two is that the two-stroke motor fires at every stroke of the piston. In terms of practical use, the main difference is that the four-stroke generally uses petrol, and most two-strokes use a petrol-oil mixture. For this reason there are several differences in routine maintenance of the two types. They will therefore be dealt with separately in this chapter.

Maintenance Routine (Two-Stroke)

Daily

(a) Check fuel tank to ensure sufficient fuel.

(b) Check fuel lines for blockages and leakages.

(c) Visibly check fuel filter in case of water or undue amounts of sediment.

(d) Check water cooling system to ensure that taps are open and there are no leaks.

(e) Check that correct fuel-oil mixture is made when filling fuel tank.

Every 25 Hours

(a) Check oil level in gearbox and top up if necessary.

(b) Check battery level and top up if necessary. Use hydrometer to check the charge.

Every 50 Hours

(a) Oil all linkages and bearings or fill grease cups where provided, using the manufacturer's manual to check grade of oil.

Every 100 Hours

(a) Drain gearbox oil and replace with fresh oil of suitable grade.

(b) Change the fuel filter, and check out all fuel lines.

(c) Remove plugs and check for excessive carbon or other signs of wear.

(d) Open magneto and check the breaker points and other parts for wear.

(e) Check wiring, terminals, brushes and commutator of generator. Clean, and tighten up terminals.

Every 500 Hours

Have engine completely checked out by a qualified marine engineer.

Maintenance Routine (Four-Stroke)

Daily

(a) Check oil level in crankcase by means of dip stick.

(b) Check fuel lines for possible leaks or blockages. Visibly examine filter bowl.

(c) Check fuel tank to ensure there is sufficient fuel.

(d) Check all taps to ensure that water cooling system is open and there are no leaks.

Every 25 Hours

(a) Check oil level in gearbox. Top up if necessary.

(b) Check the condition of the battery with the hydrometer. Top up if necessary, using distilled water only.

(c) Oil all linkages and bearings or fill grease cups as provided.

Every 50 Hours

Pump out sump oil and replace with fresh oil of the correct grade. This is best carried out when the engine is hot, as the oil will easily drain out and carry with it any sediment that may have gathered in the chamber.

Every 100 Hours

(a) Drain gearbox oil and replace with fresh

(b) Change the fuel filter.

(c) Change oil filter.

(d) Remove the flame arrestor and clean with suitable solvent. Dry thoroughly and replace.

(e) Check operation of fuel pump and carburettor, and check fuel lines at the same time. Examine sump of petrol tank, empty sediment and clean.

Every 250 Hours

(a) Clean and adjust contact points to correct gap and lubricate distributor cam.

(b) Remove spark plugs. Clean and reset gap or replace with new plugs if necessary.

A typical small two stroke engine—compact and reliable when properly maintained. Photo courtesy Stuart Turner Ltd

(c) Check ignition timing.

(d) Check carburettor adjustments.

(e) Inspect all wiring for loose connections or worn insulation. Clean terminals and coat with vaseline. Check operation of generator.

(f) Check valve tappet clearance.

(g) Clean exterior of engine completely.

Every 500 Hours

Have engine completely checked out by a marine engineer.

TROUBLE SHOOTING (Petrol engines)

Two-Stroke

Engine fails to start

(a) Failure of starter motor or allied equipment. Check batteries, leads, switches and starter itself.

(b) Choked exhaust. Check exhaust line for possible blockage or water in exhaust line.

(c) Incorrect mixture. Check to see that petrol-oil mixture agrees with maker's recommendations.

(d) Check magneto to ensure that spark is obtained. Remove plug and hold against side of engine while turning engine by hand to obtain spark at the plug. If there is no spark, check wiring and timing of magneto.

(e) Insufficient turning of the motor, particularly if it is not fitted with an impulse-starting magneto. Impulse-starting magnetos will fire the engine at a very slow turn.

(f) Flooding. Remove spark plug and if wet turn starting handle several times to dry out plug before replacing. Close throttle and choke.

(g) Dampness in ignition cables, switches, or magneto itself. When left on board a boat, moisture may find its way into the magneto and cause a short circuit. Magnetos should be disconnected, opened and dried.

(h) Dirt or paint under the magneto. This will cause a weak spark which may not be sufficient to fire the mixture in the cylinder.

Low power

(a) Choked exhaust. Check that exhaust bung is out and there is no blockage in the pipe.

(b) Poor compression, usually as a result of worn pistons. An overhaul job.

(c) Magneto timing incorrect. Check the points in the magneto and the timing.

(d) Defective spark plug. Remove and examine spark while turning engine by hand. Replace if necessary.

Overheating

(a) Water pump failure. Check action of water pump, check cooling system for leaks. Check thermostat.

(b) Choked water inlet or seacocks closed. Check all round.

Backfiring

(a) Too weak a mixture, probably because jet or filters are blocked by sediment.

(b) Air lock in petrol pipe. Check lines and filter throughout.

186

(c) Water in petrol system. Check filter bowl and fuel lines.

Failure to Two-Stroke

(a) Too rich a mixture. Check carburettor float against persistent flooding, commonly caused by dirt under float needle.

(b) Too much oil in mixture.

(c) Choked exhaust.

Note: Because of the oil-fuel mixture used in two-stroke engines, one of the commonest problems is the oiling of the plug, particularly when starting from cold. Much of the art of getting the best out of a two-stroke is to get to know the motor well. The motors are extremely efficient, but they vary slightly from model to model, and getting to know the motor and the adjustment of fuel air intake is the best guarantee against flooding a cylinder at each start.

Four-Stroke

Engine will not start

(a) Check electrical, battery, and starter equipment as described for two-stroke engines.

(b) Dirty or corroded distributor contact points. Check and clean where necessary.

(c) Flooded carburettor. Check for possible sediment or dirt in jets.

(d) Dirt or water in fuel line and fuel pump. Check fuel line from tank to carburettor. Check operation of fuel pump.

(e) Faulty coil or condenser. Remove one spark plug and turn engine to see if spark is obtained. If not, coil or condenser is suspect.

(f) Faulty ignition cables. Check high tension cables for possible cracking or "tracking". Replace where necessary.

(g) Incorrect spark plug gap. Check and adjust gap or replace plugs if necessary.

Engine starts then stalls

(a) Idling speed set too low. Adjust idling screw.

(b) Idling mixture too lean or too rich.

(c) Faulty coil or condenser. Check as in previous paragraphs.

(d) Incorrect choke adjustment.

Engine missing

(a) Spark plug gap incorrectly set. Remove, check and replace if necessary.

(b) Distributor contact points incorrectly gapped. Check and adjust gap, clean points.

(c) Partial fuel blockage, or water in fuel. Check fuel system throughout.

(d) Defective coil or condenser. Check and replace if necessary.

(e) Cracked or disfigured distributor rotor. Check and replace if necessary.

(f) Dirt in carburettor jets. Remove carburettor and blow out jets.

(g) Incorrect timing. Check and adjust where necessary.

Loss of power

(a) Dirty or badly-adjusted spark plugs. Remove, adjust gap or renew as required.

(b) Partial blockage of fuel line or water in fuel. Check fuel line from fuel tank to carburettor.

(c) Incorrect ignition timing. Check and adjust.

(d) Defective fuel pump. Check and replace if necessary.

(e) Defective coil or condenser. Check and renew if necessary.

(f) Worn distributor rotor. Check and replace.

(g) Burned or pitted valves. This will mean a valve grind or top overhaul.

(h) Blown cylinder head gasket. This again will entail a top overhaul.

Low oil pressure

(a) Check oil level in sump. Top up if necessary.

187

(b) Check that correct grade of oil is used.

(c) Check oil pump relief valve. This may have stuck.

Excessive oil consumption

(a) Worn, scuffed or broken rings. This will entail removing the head to check the state of the rings.

(b) Excessive valve stem to guide clearance.

(c) Excessive wear of cylinder walls, leading to "piston clatter".

Overheating

(a) Blockage at water intake or cocks closed. Check cooling system throughout.

(b) Failure of water pump. Check and repair as necessary.

(c) Incorrect timing. Check and adjust as necessary.

(d) Low oil level in crankcase. Check with dipstick and fill where necessary.

(e) Overloading. This can come about in several ways, including incorrect propeller for engine, binding of the stern gland, propeller fouled, etc.

Misfiring engine

(a) Loose, broken, or crossed spark plug wires. Check and replace where necessary.

(b) Damage or dirt in distributor. Check and correct.

(c) Badly-fouled spark plugs. Remove and check, renew where necessary.

(d) Valve trouble. Usually associated with sticking or burned valve, or broken valve spring. This will necessitate an overhaul.

(e) Incorrect gap at distributor points.

(f) Incorrect fuel mixture. Check carburettor.

Note: Petrol motors depend on two principal systems for their operation. Basically, an engine that will not start or run correctly is lacking either in the electrical system or in

Outboard motors are well sealed against moisture and the amateur should be well informed before he attempts any but routine maintenance. Photo courtesy
Power Boat & Yachting

the fuel system. A complete run-down first on the fuel system from tank through to engine intake, followed by a complete run-down of the electrical system from battery to spark plug will usually indicate where the fault lies. Otherwise, a qualified marine engineer will have to be called in.

ROUTINE MAINTENANCE
(Outboard Engines)

Because of the compact nature of outboard engines, and many unique features which are not included in the more common petrol engines, and also because the outboard engine is so readily portable, routine maintenance is carried out on only very simple parts. Lubrication, greasing, and general attention to wearable parts—these are the principal features of outboard maintenance. It is wiser to drop the outboard into the local official dealer to have it checked over by a qualified mechanic every 100 hours of operation, than to attempt to fiddle with it oneself. Unless qualified in this particular field, the amateur should shy away from attempting to do any but the simplest maintenance on an outboard. Much of it is sealed against the possibility of moisture and salt water, and to attempt to carry out any interior maintenance may result in damage being done.

Thus maintenance of outboard engines falls into two simple categories: (a) Return to qualified dealer for check-up and maintenance every 100 hours running, and (b) simple lubrication of moving, accessible parts.

Perhaps the most important part of care with outboard engines is ensuring that the correct mixture of petrol-oil is used. With different makes of engines and different recommendations for fuel mixtures, and also many patent mixtures marketed as outboard fuels or outboard oils, the newcomer to outboard engines can be understandably confused. However, the manufacturer of the engine usually goes to great length, both in his Operation Manual, and also with information printed on the engine or petrol tank, to ensure that a recommended brand of oil and the correct mixture of this oil is used in the fuel. Only these recommended brands should be used, unless completely certain (with the approval of the manufacturer's agent) that alternate fuels may be used.

Mixing the fuel

Mixing fuel for the outboard consists of placing oil and petrol together in the tank. As mentioned above, correct mixing is of the utmost importance if the engine is to give not only a good performance but also long life. Thus once the quantities of oil and petrol have been determined, the tank should be prepared. The oil should be placed into some of the

petrol, never into an empty tank. The best system is to put one gallon of petrol in the tank, then add the oil in full; the tank should be shaken vigorously to ensure good mixing, and then the balance of the petrol added. A further shake will ensure thorough diffusion of the oil throughout the petrol.

Fitting the engine

Since outboards can be fitted on a variety of boats, it is not intended to go into great detail about the actual fitting. It is important for the running of the engine, however, that it be placed in such a position that all auxiliary equipment can function normally. If the engine is mounted with insufficient water over the propeller and cavitation plate, there will be a tendency for the water pump to draw into the cooling system air as well as water, with resultant overheating. And a propeller thrust too deep into the water can place undue load on the engine.

Other auxiliary parts cannot work properly if the engine is incorrectly mounted. Care should be taken with all equipment, including the flexible petrol hose, so that when the engine is started, the equipment will function normally. The manufacturer usually recommends in the Operation Manual the best position for placing the motor, but broadly speaking, providing the cavitation plate is well immersed and the motor is in a fairly vertical position, it should function to its best ability.

Shear pins

Most outboard motors have a shear pin fitted to the drive shaft so that in the event of the propeller becoming fouled or striking a submerged object the shock will be taken by the propeller itself and the pin sheared in order to prevent the shock being transmitted through the gearbox to the engine. The pin acts in much the same way as a fuse in an electrical system and for that reason spare pins should always be carried on board. Replacement of a sheared pin entails only the removal of the propeller, punching out of the old pin and replacement with the new.

Flushing-out

Although many of the older types of outboard engines are designed to run in fresh water only, or else to be flushed out with fresh water after use in salt water, the trend is to make motors non-corrosive, and thus resistant to salt water. The motor should always be drained when taken out of use, but unless specifically stated in the Operation Manual, there is no necessity to flush out the cooling system with fresh water.

If the motor is of the type which requires internal flushing, a fresh water hose should be placed at the entrance to the water intake and the tap turned on full to force fresh water through the cooling system. If this is not successful because of water pump or valve resistance the engine should be placed in a tank of fresh water and run briefly to completely eliminate any traces of salt water.

Generally speaking, it is important with any motor not to tilt it above the horizontal, or raise the lower unit above the motor itself before all water has completely drained from the cooling system.

Carbon removal

Like most engines, outboards are subject to an accumulation of carbon at the top of the pistons and cylinder head. This may increase or decrease, according to fuels used and the mixture required. Because of the detrimental effect on the running of the engine this carbon deposit should be removed somewhere around the 200 hours mark. It is an operation which should be carried out only by a qualified mechanic approved by the motor manufacturer.

Spark plugs

One of the commonest problems with outboard engines is the tendency for spark plugs to become "wet", particularly when starting the engine, giving rise to difficulty in starting.

Also, spark plugs can deteriorate with use. Attention to these points is well within the capability of the amateur. In order to keep the engine running at its best performance, plugs should be examined periodically, cleaned where necessary and the gap adjusted to the recommendation of the manufacturer. Severe deterioration of the plug will necessitate replacement with a new plug. Once again, only the correct plug recommended by the manufacturer should be used.

Breaker points

Breaker points deteriorate with use, and can be renewed in most motors without much dismantling. Usually the breaker points are beneath the flywheel, fitted in such a way that they are sealed from moisture. Care must be taken in cleaning or replacing the breaker points to ensure that this seal is not damaged, as salt water getting to the breaker points will create considerable problems in the starting and running of the engine.

Fuel Filter

Some manufacturers incorporate in their engine a "visible fuel" filter bowl, which can be examined periodically to see if any deposit or sediment is building up. Other types do not allow immediate visible inspection, but can be readily examined by removing the cover plate and examining the filter inside. In all cases care should be taken when refitting the filter bowl or plate, to ensure that a good seal is made.

TROUBLE SHOOTING
(Outboard Engines)

Motor will not start

(a) Fuel connections not made properly Check fittings at tank and engine.

(b) Fuel line pinched. Check throughout length.

(c) Lack of fuel supply. Check that carburettor has been primed correctly. Check level of petrol tank.

(d) Insufficient choking. Check choke fitting.

(e) Overchoking. Check that motor is not flooded. If so, turn off fuel supply and crank engine until flooding is cleared.

(f) Water in fuel system. Check filter bowl or fuel lines.

Motor will not idle

(a) Incorrect carburettor adjustment. Adjust according to Operation Manual, or contact mechanic.

(b) Defective spark plugs. Remove plugs, check and replace where necessary.

(c) Improper fuel mixture. Check manufacturer's instructions.

Motor loses power

(a) Defective spark plugs. Check and replace where necessary.

(b) Fuel system restricted or fuel contaminated. Check fuel lines throughout, check fuel filter, check fuel tank.

(c) Overheating. Check cooling system, check water discharge, check operation of water pump. Failing these, take motor to mechanic to have thermostat checked out.

(d) Engine in need of overhaul. Return to approved mechanic for carbon removal, or other internal overhaul as required.

Irregular running

(a) Incorrect fuel mixture. Check manufacturer's instructions.

(b) Incorrect carburettor adjustment. Check manufacturer's instructions or return to mechanic for adjustment.

(c) Wrong propeller. Check manufacturer's instructions.

TUNING UP A MARINE ENGINE

Tuning-up an engine is basically just another term for giving all systems a thorough checkout. An engine is designed to work with its

The complex electrical system of a motor is only one of the systems involved in tuning. Photo Gordon B. Sinclair

electrical, fuel and timing systems synchronised to a point of perfection. With running, however, some parts become worn or fouled and the systems begin to get out of synchronisation. Although this deterioration is relatively small, as soon as the engine gets out of balance, its running efficiency and power output are affected.

The best indication of the need for a tune-up is the number of hours of running since the engine was last tuned. At this stage the deterioration in performance may not be noticeable, but if the engine is run further, marked deterioration will become obvious. The engine will be hard to start, run unevenly, particularly when idling, and will lose power rapidly. There may be some misfiring or hesitating, and vibration will become noticeable.

Continuing to run an engine when unbalanced can result in extensive wear and tear of all parts. The actual "feel" of a well-tuned engine running smoothly and quietly is an indication of less wear and tear than when the engine is rattling and coughing like a "bucket of bolts".

Tuning up any engine means checking out each of the systems thoroughly and synchronising them. Because of the different types of engines (diesel, petrol, outboard) to say nothing of the different makes, it would be impossible to give a complete run-down on tuning any particular engine. And since tuning is a fine and delicate art, only the correct procedures and measurements as designed by the manufacturer for this particular engine can be followed. This means the close study of the maintenance manual issued with every engine.

Basically, however, there are routine procedures which apply to all engines and these can be summarised as follows:

Fuel system (diesel and petrol). Check quality and purity in tank and open entire fuel system to remove residual fuel. Thoroughly check pipes for blockages or water, change filter and check fuel pumps. Dismantle carburettor (petrol) and atomisers (diesel), check fuel mixture (two-stroke). Clean floats (petrol and two-stroke), choke and intake. Check compression. Check exhaust system to ensure there is no blockage or build-up of carbon deposits.

Electrical system. Check starter motors and dynamo, thoroughly check all high tension leads for signs of cracking or wear, check low tension leads, terminals and connections; clean with sandpaper and cover with petroleum jelly where necessary. Check distributor (petrol) to ensure that rotor arm is not worn, that there is no play in the cam and that the points are clean and the gap correctly set to manufacturer's instructions. Check magneto (two-stroke) to ensure correct breaker gap, clean and reset where necessary. Check coil and condenser (petrol) and replace if faulty. Check spark plugs for contamination, deterioration, cracking of insulators and incorrect gap.

Replace where necessary. Check battery for specific gravity, check terminals for corrosion and clean where necessary.

Timing. Check the timing of the engine according to instructions in the maintenance manual. It is a good policy also to check engine oil level and pressure.

By following this routine—adapted for each individual engine requirement according to manufacturer's instructions — the average engine will respond with good performance and full power output. The frequency of tuning will not depend solely on the use of the motor and an engine which has lain idle for some months will need tuning as much as an engine which has worked consistently over the same period.

Once again it cannot be emphasised too strongly, that for each individual engine the manufacturer's specific instructions must be followed where plug and breaker gap measurement and similar factors are involved.

LAYING-UP A MARINE DIESEL ENGINE

In many parts of the world, yachts and power craft are "laid-up" for the winter. At other times it may be necessary to lay-up a vessel because her owner is away from home or unable to use the craft for some reason or other. Because of their need for regular periodic maintenance, boats and their equipment cannot be left unattended for long without deterioration setting in, and when force of circumstances make it necessary for the boat to be unattended for such a time, the routine of "laying-up" becomes of utmost importance.

The most important factor in this routine is the prevention of corrosion and other deterioration during the laying-up period. This is perhaps more important with the engine than any other part of the vessel, since the moving parts of the engine are designed to maintain their own lubrication and protection systems under working conditions, and are not designed to lie idle for long periods of time.

Prior to laying-up, diesel engines must undergo a thorough routine if they are to be correctly preserved

This is why, if possible, the best laying-up routine for any engine is one where, at periodic intervals, the engine can be turned over or—even better—run for a few minutes.

Unfortunately this is often not possible, and the engine must lie idle for a long time. In this case, the preparation for the laying-up period must be carefully undertaken in order to reduce the risk of deterioration.

The following routine is one advised generally by leading manufacturers of marine diesel engines. It would be difficult to cover all minor facets of individual engines in a broad coverage such as this, but the routine described below covers all major aspects of laying-up procedure where marine diesel engines are concerned.

Laying-up Routine

1. Thoroughly clean all external parts of the engine.

2. Run the engine until well warmed through. Stop the engine and drain lubricating oil from the sump.

3. Change the lubricating oil filter and refill the filter bowl with fresh oil of the correct grade.

4. Clean out the engine breather pipe.

5. Refill the oil sump to the correct level on the dipstick with fresh oil of the correct grade.

6. Drain the entire fuel system including tanks, pipes and filters. Put into the fuel tanks at least one gallon (more where the size of the tank makes it necessary) of what is known as *Oil for inhibiting fuel systems.* Manufacturers of this oil will be listed in the service manual together with application details, for these vary according to the temperature at which the engine is to be laid up.

7. Prime the system and start the engine. Allow it to run for fifteen to twenty minutes to ensure complete penetration of the entire system with the inhibiting oil. Stop the engine.

8. Seal off the air vent in tank or filler cap to reduce the risk of water condensation during lay-up.

Note: When draining fuel and lubricating systems it is important to prevent any oil from dripping on to electrical equipment and connections.

9. Thoroughly drain the water systems by opening all drain taps. To ensure complete drainage—and as a routine check of the taps—remove the taps altogether and examine them for growth or scale. Leave the taps open.

In the case of a closed circuit water cooling system, ethylene glycol may be used. This is an inhibitor and will stop rust.

10. Where a seawater system is used, involving the use of a pump with a neoprene impeller, the end plate of the pump should be removed and the pump packed with grease. If the pump cannot be dismantled easily, glycerine poured into the inlet pipe will have a similar protective effect.

11. Remove and clean the atomisers and spray directly into the cylinders about one-eighth pint of lubricating oil divided equally between the cylinders.

12. Replace the atomisers using new joint

washers, and slowly rotate the crankshaft one complete revolution.

13. Remove the air cleaner and any air intake pipe which may be fitted between cleaner and intake. Carefully seal off the intake hole with waterproofed adhesive tape, after inserting bag of Silica Gel to dry out the air passages.

14. Remove the exhaust pipe and similarly seal off the exhaust outlet hole.

15. Remove the cylinder head cover, lubricate the rocker assembly with engine oil and replace the cover.

16. Remove all driving belts and store away.

17. Remove batteries from the engine and top up with distilled water so that the top edges of the separators are just covered. Recharge the battery thoroughly from a separate source of supply.

18. Screw home the vent plugs and clean the exterior of the battery thoroughly, removing all dirt and dust and moisture. Smear vaseline or petroleum jelly on the terminals after cleaning them thoroughly.

High powered motors need particular care in laying-up as they are tuned to an extremely high pitch.
Photo courtesy Power Boat & Yachting

19. The batteries cannot be left unattended indefinitely, and arrangements must be made to see that they are stored in a cool dry place where there is no chance of them becoming frozen. They must be recharged once a month at the normal rate of charging.

20. Starters and generators should be cleaned externally and the terminals smeared lightly with petroleum jelly, unless removed altogether—which is far preferable—and stowed in a suitable spot.

21. Cover the engine if it is in any way exposed.

LAYING-UP A MARINE PETROL ENGINE

Basic principles apply to all forms of engines to be laid up for the winter or for any undue length of time, but there are important differences between diesel and petrol engines, and also between outboard and inboard motors. With outboards, however the principal problem is suitable stowage.

The marine petrol engine, unless of the outboard type, which is dealt with in the following pages, requires a little more care in laying up than does the marine diesel engine, because the electrical systems in petrol engines are extremely vulnerable to damp or humidity.

Like the diesel, petrol engines need to be laid up in a manner which reduces to a minimum the possibility of corrosion or other deterioration. As with the diesel, occasional turning over of the engine or—even better—an occasional short run, is the best protection of all. However, this is not always possible, and then the routine of laying-up must be followed carefully and in detail if the engine is to be kept in good condition.

Assuming that the engine is to be out of use for some months, and under conditions which could include extremely low temperatures, the following procedure should be adopted:

Laying-up Routine

1. Thoroughly clean all external parts of the engine.

2. Run the engine until warm, then stop engine and drain the lubricating oil from the sump.

3. Change the lubricating oil filter and refill the sump with clean oil—for extra protection refill with special rust preventative oil instead of normal lubricating oil. This is particularly recommended for old or worn engines.

Outboards are relatively easy to lay-up as they can be carried ashore for storage. Photo courtesy Power Boat & Yachting

4. Clean and renew air filter where fitted.

5. Drain the entire fuel system by disconnecting feed pipes and filter bowl, and, if necessary, the carburettor. It is important that no petrol be left in the tank, as gum will form during the lay-up.

6. Remove the exhaust pipe and plug the manifold opening, or, if this is not practicable, plug the exhaust pipe outside the boat.

7. Seal off the air bleeder pipe and any vents or filler pipes leading to the fuel tanks.

8. Open all taps to thoroughly drain the water cooling system. To ensure complete drainage—and as a routine check of taps—remove the taps altogether and examine them for growth or scale. When replaced, leave taps open. In the case of closed circuit water cooling systems, anti-freeze may be used, although it is better to drain these systems too.

9. Examine the water pump impeller and pack with grease, or pour glycerine into the intake. This prevents the impeller sticking to the side of the pump during the idle period. If the impeller is of rubber it is better removed altogether and stored in the workshop.

10. Remove all electrical equipment as follows:

(a) Remove the generator.
(b) Remove the starter motor.

(c) Remove the distributor and all wires connected to it.

(d) Remove the battery and provide for adequate storage and charging as described elsewhere in this section.

(e) Have the distributor checked before storing in a suitable place.

(f) Lubricate all linkage and pulley wheels after removing belts and stowing in a suitable spot.

(g) Ensure that all gauges and other electrical accessories are suitably prepared by cleaning terminals and covering with a layer of vaseline. Electrical equipment that cannot be removed can be suitably covered with plastic or similar dust-protecting material.

11. Remove the spark plugs and pour a small amount of lubricating oil or rust preventative oil into the cylinders. Turn the engine over by hand, and replace the plugs.

12. Drain the sump of rust preventative oil which has now had time to take effect. Drain gear box and refill with clean oil.

13. Cover the engine if it is any way exposed.

LAYING-UP AN OUTBOARD ENGINE

The basic procedure for laying-up an outboard engine can be summarised in a very few words —store in a clean, warm, dry spot!

But it is not as simple as all that, since an outboard engine, like any other type, suffers from lack of use, and unless it can be taken down at intervals during the laying-up and given a short run in a test tank, will deteriorate in performance. Fortunately, because of the convenience of storage, there is no necessity to strip the engine accessories or go to great lengths with the various systems. The following

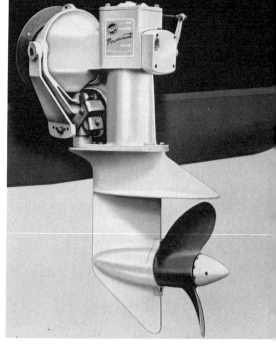

Greasing and coating all moving parts is essential if they are to be preserved during lay-up. Stern drives fall into this category. Photo courtesy Power Boat & Yachting

basic routine will keep an outboard in good condition provided it is stored correctly during the laying-up.

Laying-Up Routine

1. Flush out the cooling system with fresh water under pressure (hose), or run the engine briefly in a fresh water tank.

2. Drain the fuel tank and run the engine until the entire fuel system is emptied.

3. Remove the spark plugs and squirt a small amount of lubricating oil into the cylinders. Turn the flywheel by hand one complete revolution. Replace the plugs.

4. Clean the engine thoroughly with a spirit rag to remove all grease and dirt which may adhere to moving parts. Grease all working parts and spray the engine generally with a light lubricant spray.

5. Remove gearbox oil and replace with fresh oil of the correct grade. It is important to note that when dealing with outboard engines, only the fittings and lubricants recommended by the manufacturer must be used,

and where larger engines may often get away with substitute material it is most unwise to use anything but manufacturer's recommended materials.

6. Ensure that the cover fits tightly, and lubricate all joints, throttles, etc., as recommended in the manufacturer's handbook.

7. In the case of electric start motors, prepare the battery for storage as for other batteries mentioned in this section; remove terminal wires, clean and replace after coating thinly with vaseline or lubricant spray.

8. Store the engine in a dry, warm place, covered with a tarpaulin if necessary to prevent dust or dirt finding its way through the cover.

QUICK ROUTINE ENGINE CHECK

Quite apart from the complete winter overhaul all marine engines should be given frequent routine checks during the running season—once a month at least. But most weekend sailors will be wise if they do a quick routine check each Saturday morning before getting the family aboard. A rainy weekend is also a good time to give the engine the once-over, for nothing is more detrimental to any engine—and particularly to marine engines—than neglect.

Engines that are not run frequently should be checked regularly and turned over to keep

Easy access to the motor makes light work of maintenance chores

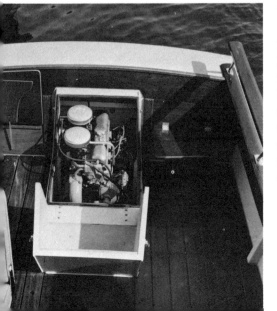

lubricating oils moving through working parts. To start an engine that has been lying idle for some weeks is to start bearings moving in their sockets before lubricating oil has time to move in, with resultant severe wear and tear. A routine check of the engine before starting can eliminate the risk of such damage.

The easy, weekend check-up can be done in less than an hour, before running the engine after a week's lay-up. Although few enthusiasts will want to go through such a check every week, they forget that the engine in the boat is much the same as the engine in the car, which goes through a routine check every time the petrol tank is filled, and a detailed lubricating routine at frequent intervals.

To simplify the check-up, it can be laid out as follows:

Battery: Check the battery for the level of the fluid—it should cover the plates. Use a hydrometer to check the charge. If the battery is getting weak or not holding a charge, take it to a garage for a check. The connections and terminals should be cleaned with sandpaper as mentioned elsewhere in this section, and covered with grease or vaseline. Weak connections should be removed and replaced.

Distributor: Clean with a rag saturated in carbon tetrachloride, making sure that the brass lead-ends are clean and not worn. If the rag does not clean the metal properly, rub with a light sandpaper until gleaming. Check the gap of the breaker points and clean by drawing a light sandpaper through them.

Plugs: When removing each plug, wipe or blow away dust or rusty powder that may have gathered near the base to prevent it from falling into the cylinder. The plugs must be removed with a proper plug spanner as an ordinary spanner can damage the plug. Clean the plugs with the carbon tetrachloride rag and insert a piece of fine sandpaper between the points to rub them clean. Check the gap with a feeler gauge and adjust if necessary.

If the plug is very dirty, it should be sent

Spark plugs trouble is usually quite readily seen on close examination

to a garage for cleaning and checking, for nothing is more detrimental to good engine work than fouled-up plugs. Check that the insulator is not crazed or cracked; if so replace with a new plug. Check that the lead terminals are clean and connect tightly to the plug.

While the plugs are out it is a good idea— if the engine has not been run for a while— to pour a small amount of engine oil into the cylinders and then crank the engine over once or twice. This lubricates the rings and ensures an easy movement of the pistons until the sump oil takes over. The plugs should not be oily, however, and should be wiped clean before re-inserting.

Once in position the plugs should be screwed down tight on their gaskets, sufficiently to prevent any leakage, but not so tight that the thread is stripped.

Ignition Coil: Clean all terminals with sandpaper and ensure they make good connection. Wipe down all wires with the carbon tetrachloride rag and check that the insulation is not cracked or damaged. Follow the wires through to the distributor and check the condenser.

Voltage Regulator: Unless there are signs of trouble, there is no need to uncover the voltage regulator, but merely check the connections and the wires to see that no damage has occurred. A wipe-down with the carbon tetrachloride rag is all that is needed to clean away dirt and grime.

Engine Oil: Check the level of the oil in the crankcase and gearbox. Replace if it is dirty or has run its recommended span, or top-up if it has fallen below the required level. Needless to say, *only* the correct grade of oil may be used, and the grade used for the engine may differ from that of the gearbox. Check the instruction manual for this.

The Fuel Tank: Many problems arise with fuel tanks in boats, mainly through dirt or condensation. Check that breather pipes are open and that taps and lines are clear. The best check is to break the line at the connection of the fuel filter (this will be opened for checking anyway) and allow fuel to gush through. The sudden rush may disperse any light clogging in the bends or taps along the line.

If there is water in the tank it must be drained off immediately. Add a quart of acetone to the petrol to absorb any water left.

Source of much motor trouble, the filter bowl must be checked and cleaned frequently

Skin fittings such as this water intake must be kept open and clean if the motor is to run properly. Photo courtesy Stuart Turner Ltd

the carburettor and clean out the bowl. The jets should be blown out and checked, by a garage if necessary. The seating of the needles should be free and all traces of dust or dirt removed. When replacing the carburettor, ensure that all gaskets are secure and leak-proof.

The Cooling System: If fresh water cooling is used, check the level of the water, and the connections to the tank. All hoses should be checked, especially those on outlets or intake, and taps freed if they are stiff or seized. The metal hose clips are inclined to corrode easily and should be checked thoroughly, for a broken clip on an intake or outlet can leave the skin fitting open to flood the boat. It is a wise precaution to have stop taps on all skin fittings for this very reason.

Providing the water pump is behaving properly, there is no need to dismantle it; a shot of grease in the cups will ensure continued good performance, however. The best check on the cooling system is a nice cool running engine that is pumping out plenty of water through the exhaust.

General: The eye is the best detector of troubles in an engine, and a quick check over nuts, belts, connections, etc., will soon reveal anything out of order. By keeping all parts clean, any cracking or corrosion can be spotted immediately, as can leakages or loose connections. The exhaust system sometimes is linked with the water outlet and this should be checked for signs of deterioration or corrosion of hose clips. Switches and electrical connections leading to the control panel should be clean and secure, with no signs of corrosion from salt air.

The linkage leading to throttles and/or choke should be checked out, particularly if they are in the form of cables, which can rust easily and jam unless kept lubricated and free-working. Likewise dials and gauges are susceptible to salt air corrosion and should be wiped clean underneath with vaseline or grease. Finally, a quick run round with the oilcan to ensure all bearings are free and well lubricated.

This will then be burnt off in the engine. If there is dirt in the tank it will have to be drained and cleaned.

The Fuel Filter: There are many different types of filters in use on marine motors, but whatever the make they should be checked for any signs of dirt or water. This can often be done visually, but a quick check by removing the bowl of the filter, or the filter itself, is the safest precaution. It will also indicate the condition of the fuel in the tank.

The sediment in the filter bowl should be removed and the bowl cleaned out. If necessary a new gauge may be fitted as also may the gasket if it is at all worn or warped. Check the nuts on the line from the filter to the carburettor to ensure that there are no leaking connections.

The Carburettor: Providing the carburettor is not giving trouble, there is no need to open it during the routine check. Often more damage can be done than by leaving it alone, especially as some carburettors are in difficult positions or have a rather complicated construction.

If the engine is not getting its correct fuel mixture, however, it will be necessary to open

199

CHAPTER THIRTEEN

Fitting a Marine Engine

INSTALLING THE ENGINE

PROVIDING CERTAIN basic factors are taken into account, installing a marine engine in a boat presents no great problem. Modern developments of couplings and mountings and sound-proofing techniques have made it possible for the average handyman to install an engine in his boat without the high degree of skill once required for this job.

Alignment was often the bugbear of engine mounting, and because of the considerable length of the shaft between the engine and the stern tube, this gave rise to a whole series of problems. Universal couplings have eased the problem considerably and alignment, though still important, is by no means the critical phase of the installation.

The compactness of modern motors make installation relatively easy

Similarly—particularly with engines adapted for marine work from automobiles or tractors—the installation angle and the possibility of the engine working on an angle came in for consideration. Bearings can quickly run dry when the engine is run at an angle which draws off lubrication oil from one end or one side of the crankcase. But modern engines designed for marine use are made to almost operate upside down, so well balanced is the lubricating system.

However, to obtain the maximum performance from any engine, a good, well-found and thought-out installation is of the utmost importance, and the extra time and patience involved in seating the engine correctly will pay handsome dividends in terms of running hours and reduced maintenance.

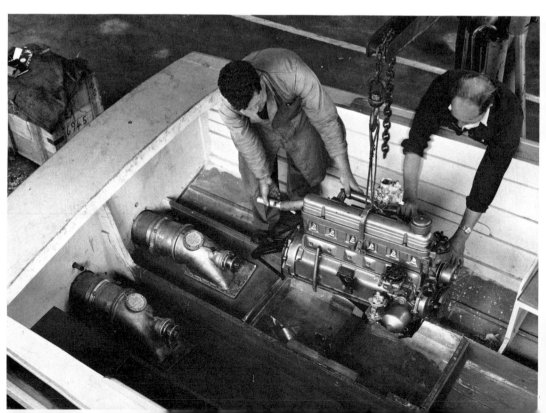

Solid engine beds and accurately mounted bearers are essential if the motor is to be held securely and not vibrate

INSTALLATION ANGLE

Because of the positioning of the propeller beneath the stern, most marine engines must be installed at an angle to the horizontal. As mentioned earlier, a well-designed marine engine is built to cope with such an installation; and an angle of some ten degrees from the horizontal will not affect most heavy inboard engines. This naturally varies from engine to engine, but the figure given here has been adopted by many of the principal manufacturers of marine engines.

In the case of high speed planing craft, the engine will be required to operate at a much higher angle of the engine from the horizontal, far above the original installation angle. This is where problems can arise. The amount of lift in the bow when at high speed must be known before the working angle of the engine can be calculated.

Some high speed engines are designed to operate at these high angles, but the incorporation of a "V"-drive is one solution. At slow speeds the engine is tilted slightly downwards towards the "V"-drive, but as the vessel comes up to planing position the engine is brought back to the horizontal or tipped at a slight backward angle.

Yachts sometimes require the engine to be run while beating to windward and this means that the engine is on its side. Once again, a well-designed marine engine will be capable

of safe performance at angles of twenty-five to thirty degrees, although naturally this aspect should be checked with the manufacturer beforehand.

MOUNTING THE ENGINE

Because of the considerable weight of large inboard marine engines, and the concentration of this weight in one zone of the boat's construction, some means must be found to distribute the weight throughout much of the boat's structural framework. This is done almost invariably by taking the weight of the engine on heavy beams or girders which are in turn supported by members of the ship's main structure.

In the case of steel, aluminium or fibreglass, the structural members may be welded or moulded in the material of which the hull is made. In the final girders used for the engine seating, however, timber is by far the most satisfactory. The engine "bed" as it is called, is usually made of two or more large baulks of timber designed to distribute the weight of the engine over a number of the ship's structural members.

There are two ways of mounting an engine on its bed: flexible and rigid. In the latter case the engine is bolted directly through the heavy timber beams, which in turn are bolted to the structural members of the boat. The bolts used in the engine bed must be taken as far through the bearers as possible and mounted with a steel pressure plate at each end. Coach-screws are not practical as the torque actions and vibration of the engine tend to work them loose, with resultant misalignment of engine and propeller shaft.

The main bearers should be braced at intervals with cross members to prevent any flexing because of engine vibration, and this may be done with timber beams or steel angle iron. The fitting of the beams will need to be carefully planned not to interfere with the fitting of the sump or other low-level attachments on the engine.

The top of the bearers may be reinforced by the use of angle iron between the engine mountings and the bearers, and bolting right through. In addition, coachbolts can be used to supplement the through main bolts to hold the iron in position.

The flexible system of mounting the engine is confined mainly to light craft with fairly small engines and incorporates flexible mountings used in conjunction with flexible couplings. The principal advantage is in reducing noise and vibration, although incorrect mounting or use of unbalanced mountings and couplings can produce greater vibration than rigid mounting.

Because of the great number of patent flexible mountings and couplings on the market, it is not proposed to enter into details of this type of installation. The instructions for installation of each individual type of mounting should be followed if the maximum results are to be obtained.

UNIVERSAL COUPLINGS

Because of the difficulty sometimes encountered in achieving correct alignment of engine and shaft, the use of a universal coupling may

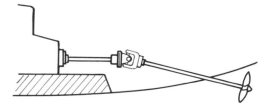

Illustration of a typical universal joint on a propeller shaft

allow the engine to be installed at an angle to the line of the propeller shaft. However, the use of universal couplings can lead to problems in the engine-shaft arrangement, particularly as the angle in the drive increases. All layouts using universal couplings should be referred to the manufacturer of the coupling or the engine before installation.

SKIN FITTINGS AND CONNECTIONS

Skin fittings, with strainers and seacocks, should be of equal size to the inlet pipe they supply. Strainers of the wire mesh or "cullender" type should be larger in area than the opening of the pipe they cover.

The sizes of pipes and fittings for any inboard engine will be specified in the manu-

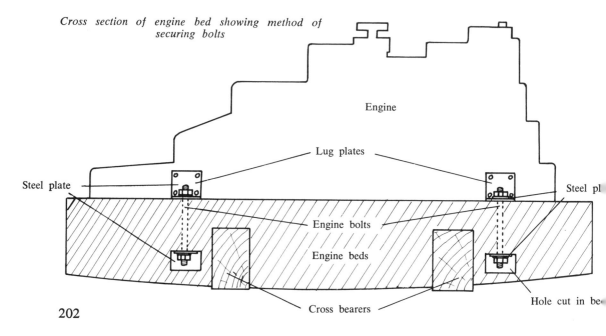

Cross section of engine bed showing method of securing bolts

Engine

Lug plates

Steel plate

Steel pl

Engine bolts

Engine beds

Hole cut in be

Cross bearers

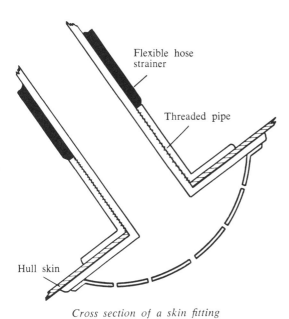

Cross section of a skin fitting

Flexible hose strainer

Threaded pipe

Hull skin

facturer's instructions, but it is important to note that only flexible pipes should be used where there is a danger that vibration may cause a fracture, and this is almost always the case with water cooling pipes.

Reinforced rubber or plastic hoses are suitable for flexible joins between copper pipes. A seacock should always be fitted at the skin fitting to prevent flooding in the event of the flexible tube breaking free or splitting. Galvanised metal hose clips should not be used, unless in a position readily accessible, for they tend to rust very easily and break away, freeing the flexible hose from the copper pipe.

Long lengths of rubber pipe should not be used on the suction side of the water pump, for if the intake strainer becomes partially blocked the suction can cause the pipe to collapse, with resultant loss of water delivery.

ENGINE EXHAUST SYSTEMS

There are two basic types of engine exhaust systems suitable for installation in boats. The dry exhaust system is used generally where the water cooling of the engine is carried out by a closed circuit unit, and the wet exhaust

system where the water cooling is non-recirculating and the cooling water is discharged after use. Although both systems are equally effective, the wet exhaust system is more widely used for two reasons:

1. reduced exhaust noise, and

2. elimination of the necessity for a water jacket or other heat insulation round the exhaust pipe.

The dry system can be muffled by use of patent mufflers, and this eliminates the first problem; but a red hot exhaust pipe running aft through the boat's structure is not to be contemplated, and a dry exhaust system needs efficient cooling—usually in the form of a water jacket round the exhaust pipe—to prevent the possibility of fire.

The wet exhaust system is simpler and is highly effective, both in relation to muffling noise and also to cooling the exhaust pipe. The cooling water is discharged into the exhaust pipe close to the engine, and this has such a cooling effect that most, if not all, of the remaining exhaust pipe can be of rubber hose, which in itself is a considerable advantage.

When the water is discharged directly into the exhaust pipe, precautions must be taken to ensure that this water cannot find its way back into the engine, particularly if the vessel

Air cooled exhaust systems can only be used under certain conditions and in certain craft

Wet exhaust system. Cooling water is injected into the exhaust through small diameter pipe. Note asbestos bandage prior to water injection

is rolling or the engine is stopped. Providing there is a good downgrade on the exhaust pipe from the point where the cooling water enters, there is little risk, although it is a fairly common practice to curve the exhaust pipe into a gooseneck which rises above sea water level.

fumes and salt water. Where possible, flexible hose should be used, and, as mentioned earlier, where the system is water cooled, rubber exhaust hose is better for this purpose. Flexible hose should also be used where the water cooling pipe leaves the engine, as a firm joint here may fracture with the vibration of the engine.

Dry exhaust systems, because of the need for elaborate cooling and insulation, should be short and discharge from the side of the vessel, unless the engine is mounted right aft. Wet exhaust systems, on the other hand, can be carried to any point for convenient discharge; the stern is the usual position, to allow fumes to be carried away from the vessel.

Exhaust systems should discharge at the water line, but not below it, for the water will enter the exhaust pipe and create back compression in the engine. An ideal system is to have the exhaust discharge at the waterline and a covering plate or "oyster shell" plate, carry the exhaust beneath the waterline. This offers the maximum silencing without the possibility of back pressure.

Illustration of cooling water injected into exhaust pipe

(labels: Water from cooling system; Injection joint; Exhaust pipe; Engine manifold; Flexible exhaust pipe)

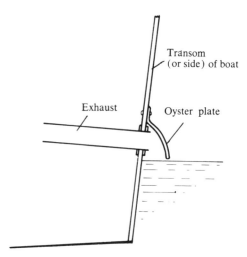

Cross section of baffle plate or "oyster shell" exhaust

(labels: Transom (or side) of boat; Exhaust; Oyster plate)

This prevents any possibility of water finding its way back up the exhaust pipe. In this system, the water enters the exhaust immediately abaft the gooseneck.

Pipes used for exhaust systems must be of iron, as copper and brass tend to deteriorate rapidly when in contact with both the exhaust

FUEL SYSTEMS

Fuel tanks should preferably be of stainless steel or black iron, although reinforced fibreglass is also suitable. Galvanised or non-ferrous tanks are not suitable for storing fuel as the metal tends to react with chemicals in the fuel.

Two systems may be adopted for fuel feed arrangements: gravitational and pump. The gravitational system is fairly common, particularly in small craft. It requires the fuel tank

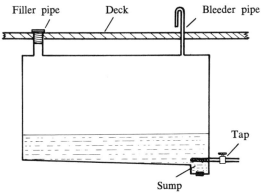

Typical fuel tank arrangement

to be situated higher than the engine so that the fuel is fed down by gravity through the system to the carburettor. Larger engines and almost all diesel engines use the pump system; here the tank may be situated at any point in the vessel and the fuel is fed to the engine by means of a pump.

Whatever the system, the tank should be located to make cleaning easy. Fuel systems in boats suffer from impurities, often condensed water or sludge, and for this reason a periodic clean out of the system, and the tank in particular, is recommended. A sump should be provided at the bottom of the tank for collection of water and sludge, and a tap fitted to allow easy drainage. The fuel line should never run off the bottom of the tank, but from the side, about half an inch above the top of the sump.

Copper or brass pipes, and in some cases polythene tubing, are best for fuel lines, providing they are tightly jointed to prevent air entering the lines or fuel leaking out.

Fuel filters come in all shapes and sizes. The two most popular are the filter bowl type and the cartridge type. Some patent filters incorporate features of both.

The filter bowl is perhaps the most widely used, as it enables dirt or water in the fuel to be spotted at a glance. The bowl is inserted in the fuel line before the carburettor and allows free flow of fuel into the glass "U"-shaped bowl. Any sediment or sludge settles immediately to the bottom of the bowl, allowing only clean fuel to be drawn off the top through a wire gauze screen which traps any floating matter. It is important when installing this type of filter to ensure that the correct inlet and outlet connections are made or the filter process will be reversed.

The cartridge filter system comprises a container — often plastic — inside which is a dispensible material filter which screens the fuel as it passes through, removing any foreign matter. It is not quite as successful in removing water from the fuel as is the bowl system, but its compact size makes it easy to fit and convenient to change at intervals. It is important to ensure that in fitting this type of filter, the flow of fuel is not restricted in any way, particularly with gravity fed systems.

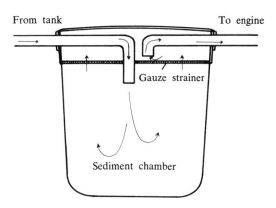

Cross section of fuel filter bowl

ELECTRICAL SYSTEMS

Starter batteries should be located as close as possible to the engine in order to avoid voltage drop through long leads. It is a wise practice to keep the starter battery separate from other electrical circuits, particularly where there may be heavy loads from instruments such as radio transmitters and where the boat is fitted with considerable electrical appliances or complicated lighting systems. Because of the high surge of power required for the starter motor, it is best run from a separate battery which can be kept topped up all the time and not be constantly drained by a mass of electrical installations.

A common fallacy exists among many boat owners that the bigger the battery, the better the installation. This is not so, and indeed the use of too large a battery can result in damage to the dynamo. Several batteries of the recommended size for the generator is a better system than larger batteries, particularly in multi-engined vessels, where one battery for each engine is the ideal system.

It is not proposed to discuss the installation of electrical equipment other than that relating to the engine in this chapter. A detailed description of an electrical layout for the entire ship may be found in Section V.

The actual installation of the engine electrical system is a highly technical process, and outside the elementary details discussed in this section, it is suggested that the job be turned over to a professional. Apart from the more obvious dangers in "amateur" wiring systems, radio interference from an incorrectly-screened system can render the navigational instruments on board useless.

ENGINE INSTRUMENTS

The installation of an engine must include the installation of a basic set of instruments. These are usually located on a panel in a convenient place such as the steering position or the switchboard. Instruments are supplied with a new engine. They must be matched, if bought separately, to suit the engine they are to service. Every engine has the pick-up points for the instruments, and installation becomes principally a question of cutting and fitting the

lengths of cable or capillary tube from the engine to the control panel.

The basic instruments required on the average marine engine are as follows:

TACHOMETER
WATER TEMPERATURE GAUGE
OIL PRESSURE GAUGE
AMMETER
STARTER SWITCH
THROTTLE AND GEAR CONTROLS

If the distance from the instrument panel to the engine is too great for mechanical connections (such as the tachometer cable) to be used, an electrical type must be utilised. Expert advice will be required for both the purchase and installation of these.

SOUNDPROOFING

A most important aspect of engine installation is the noise reduction. Various methods of muffling exhaust noises were described earlier in this section, but the final secret of a quiet engine lies in the soundproofing of the engine compartment.

A neatly arranged control panel with adequate engine instrument dials. Photo courtesy Coronet Boats

Naturally, much of the question of fitting insulating material will depend on the location and size of the engine compartment itself. The adaptation of one of the many proprietary brands of sound-insulating material to the individual installation should not be difficult.

Fibreglass panels, fibreglass matting, granulated cork etc., are a few of the many materials useful for this purpose. Large panels closely fitted to the surrounding bulkheads are the best proposition, but again this depends on the shape and size of the engine compartment.

BILGE PUMPS

Most engines incorporate a bilge pump or have a take-off to which a belt can be attached to drive an independent pump. The neoprene impeller type is by far the most popular, and is usually fitted low down on the engine.

In fitting pipes to the intake and discharge pipes of the pump, care must be taken to pre-

A good bilge pump system will have a key control to pump any part of the boat

vent acute angles which may cause a bend in the pipe and restrict the flow. The bilge end should be fitted with a large filter to prevent foreign matter clogging the pipe. The discharge may be directly through a skin fitting into the sea, or through the wet exhaust system.

WATER COOLING SYSTEMS

The two principal water cooling systems are the direct sea cooling system and the closed circuit fresh water system. In the case of the closed circuit system, the unit may vary from engine to engine and installation will depend on the individual manufacture. The completely enclosed system comprises a closed circuit fresh water system with an open circuit sea water system around it in the form of a heat exchanger. Another closed circuit system has the fresh water circuit running down through the bottom of the boat with cooling pipes running alongside the keel and re-entering the boat at another point. The heat exchange takes place outside the vessel. The open circuit sea water system merely draws water through a skin fitting, circulates it around the engine and discharges it, usually through the exhaust system.

In the case of the closed circuit system, installation must be made according to the manufacturer's directions. Probably an expert will need to be called in, particularly where the cooling pipes puncture the boat's hull. The open circuit, however, requires only a good diameter skin fitting, with a strainer covering the opening and a stopcock on the inboard side. The hose from the skin fitting to the engine should be flexible or fracturing will take place when the engine vibrates. The discharge of the cooling water is discussed earlier in this chapter.

Water pumps fitted to cooling systems are often of the neoprene impeller type and need little or no maintenance, as they are lubricated by the water they pump. Only when deprived of this water for some period of time can damage occur due to the impeller sticking to

Good cooling systems on heavy duty engines such as these are essential in the close confines of a boat's hull. Photo courtesy Chrysler Motors

the side of the pump. A small amount of glycerine poured into the pump will rectify this trouble.

Exterior cooling pipes form heat-exchange part of a closed cooling system

DRIP TRAYS

Because of the danger of fire on boats, great care must be taken during installation of the engine to ensure that fuel and lubricating oil

does not leak from joints or gasket. In the confines of the bilge, the fumes from these oils become highly explosive and need only a short circuit electrical spark to cause disaster.

Because of the vibration of the engine when running, there is considerable risk of slight leakage, even from well-made joints, and it is a wise precaution—to prevent these leaks from contaminating the bilges—to insert drip trays where necessary. One large metal tray, extending under the engine and gearbox, and smaller trays (or tins) under likely spots such as filter bowls, fuel tank connections, etc., reduce the hazard considerably.

Bilge water contaminated with engine or gearbox oil can also create a most unpleasant mess—and smell—inside the boat. Rolling in a seaway, the boat will swirl the bilge water up the side of the boat, leaving an oil slick on the timber. By gathering and containing the oil from engine leaks, the drip tray keeps the bilge water reasonably clean.

ALIGNING THE PROPELLER SHAFT

Because of vibration from the engine, it often happens, particularly with a newly-installed motor, that the propeller shaft works out of alignment with the engine shaft. This is of no consequence if it is only a small misalignment and the shaft is fitted with a universal coupling.

Where direct drive is employed, however, even slight misalignment can result in considerable wear and tear on bearings and the stern gland.

A check should be made at intervals to see that there is no working of the engine bolts. After they have been checked and tightened down where necessary, the fitting of the shaft should also be checked. This is best done with a feeler gauge used between the flanges coupling the engine shaft to the propeller shaft.

The coupling flanges must come together parallel, within about .002 inch. Since the propeller shaft is aligned in the stern tube and is very difficult to move, it is the engine which must be adjusted if any misalignment is present.

A feeler gauge of .002 inch setting should be inserted at four equidistant points around the circumference of the flanges, and the engine mountings loosened so that adjustment can take place. The gauge should be inserted at twelve o'clock, and the propeller shaft pulled forward into tight contact so that there is a drag feeling when the gauge is withdrawn.

The shaft should be held in this position and the feeler gauge re-inserted at the six o'clock position. A difference in the feel of these two positions indicates that the front or rear engine supports need shims. Similarly a difference in the feel between the three o'clock and the nine o'clock positions indicates that the engine should be moved to one side or another.

When a uniform feel is attained with the feeler gauge, the bolt holes of both flanges should be aligned and bolted. If the engine is in alignment, the bolts should fit easily into the holes. The engine should then be bolted down and a final check made to ensure that the feeler gauge fits perfectly in all four positions.

If this alignment is done on the slipway, another check should be made some time after the boat has re-entered the water. There is a tendency to slight distortion of the vessel when supported by a slipway cradle, or some form of unnatural support, and this distortion may result in poor alignment when the vessel is back in her natural element and resumes her normal shape.

FITTING ENGINE BEDS

The engine bed usually consists of two pieces of heavy timber bolted on each side of, and below the engine, to the transverse floors of the boat. Invariably the timber is hardwood, and must be shaped to take the specific engine contours, while holding it in correct alignment for the tail shaft to enter the sterngland exactly.

Because of the enormous strain on the engine bed when the thrust of the propeller is transferred to the boat's structure, the fastening of the engine beds is of utmost importance. The bearers forming the beds should be shaped to fit over at least two, and preferably three or more strengthened floors and bolted through with washers beneath the nuts. The shaping should be well carried out, as the tighter the fit of the bearers over the floors, the less room for movement and resultant vibration. The less "loose" fitting, and vibration, the less chance of nuts and fastenings being shaken loose. Hence all fittings in and around the engine bed should be well secured to a tight fit.

To ensure the correct alignment, considerable measurement must be undertaken before fitting the bearers over the floors. By stretching a wire from the centre of the tail shaft to a bulkhead further in the vessel so that the correct alignment of the shaft is obtained, the position for the bearers can be located. This gives the fore and aft alignment, and the thwartships alignment will depend on the shape and width of the engine.

Before the bearers are bolted down to the floors, they should be drilled and bolts inserted to take the engine mountings. Where possible these mountings should coincide with the join of floor and bearer, as this makes for more direct strain when the thrust is transmitted to the hull. The top of the bed should be faired off to fit snugly under the engine, allowing a small gap so that metal shims can be fitted to assist in the final alignment of the engine.

Depending on the size of the engine, a tackle may be necessary to lower it on to the beds, and this makes fitting very easy. Any adjustments to the seating of the engine can be carried out with the engine hauled up out of the way, whereas manhandling a heavy engine into position can cause damage to both the ship's structure and the accessories of the engine.

Once in position, the engine should be bolted down firmly, with steel pressure plates under the nuts. It is again important to tighten the whole engine arrangement into one firm body to reduce the possibility of vibration to an absolute minimum. It is not uncommon to mount the engine on rubber mountings, which must be placed over the mounting bolts before the engine is lowered into place. Rubber mountings tend to reduce vibration and noise, although they require maintenance to prevent decay or disintegration, and to keep the engine bolted down tight.

FITTING A FUEL TANK

The location of a fuel tank will depend to a great extent on the conditions under which it is to be fitted. It must be in a position where access is available for filling. It should also be located fairly well away from the engine and galley as a precaution against fire. It must be in such a position that it is accessible for cleaning. And if the engine is fuelled on the gravity system, then the tank must be higher than the engine, allowing for any heel or rolling movement which may cause an air lock in the fuel line.

Most fuel tanks fitted to power craft are situated well aft near the transom; in yachts usually under or behind the cockpit. This keeps them out of the way and allows any spillage or fumes when fuelling to be blown out into the open air and not be diffused into the cabin or bilges. Even if the tank is not situated aft, or

Poor fitting of a fuel tank can result in dislodgement in a seaway with disastrous results

near the sides of the vessel, the filling pipes should be run out so that their screw caps are on open deck. A fuel tank must never be filled from inside the boat.

The construction of the tank will also depend on the location, and it should be shaped to fit snugly into a corner without too much building work, for this all adds weight. The tank must be firmly secured with blocking pieces or metal straps to ensure that there is no possibility of it breaking loose in a seaway.

Fuel tanks should be of stainless steel if they are to hold petrol, and mild steel plate if they are to hold diesel. They should be fitted with baffles if the interior area is sufficient to cause considerable movement of fuel when the boat is moving in a seaway. Some stiffening of the sides is also necessary in fairly big tanks, although this can be added when securing the tank in position by using heavy wooden blocking pieces to both secure and strengthen the side of the tank.

Fuel tanks should be fitted with a screw-top lid big enough to allow cleaning, and with a sump fitted with a draining cock at the bottom to allow water or sludge to be drawn off. The tank should be fitted with a "breather" pipe at the top, and a cock at the outlet pipe which should be slightly above the bottom edge of the tank to prevent any water or sediment being drawn into the pipe. The height of the outlet above the bottom of the tank depends on the size of the sump which gathers the sediment.

The "breather" pipe is a device to allow trapped air to escape and there are several different types in use. The most common is a small diameter pipe which leads out to the open air in such a way that the water cannot be drawn back down it into the tank. It is important for the breather to end in the open air, or the expelled fumes from the tank will gather inside the boat; a very dangerous situation.

When the tank is secured into its position, the inlet and outlet lines can be connected up. These are usually of brass or copper, the inlet leading to a screw cap mouth on the deck, and the outlet leading through a cock and a filter bowl to the engine. Some vessels carry more than one tank, linked together, in which case a number of cocks will be required in order to control the movement of fuel from the desired tank.

Stability and trim of the boat must be borne in mind when fitting several tanks, or when fitting a large tank.

CHAPTER FOURTEEN

General Maintenance

CLEANING AN OUTBOARD AFTER IMMERSION

A COMMON trouble with outboards is dropping one in the drink—particularly small engines clamped on the transom of open boats. An all-too-sudden turn under high power can cause the engine to flip off its clamps, into the water. Incorrectly secured or tightened clamps can have the same effect, as also can a hundred other mishaps, not least of which is missing

Quick recovery of a dunked outboard can reduce the repair problems

one's footing as the engine is lowered into the boat.

Whatever the cause, the effect is the same; the engine has to be hauled up from the bottom completely saturated, not only externally, but probably throughout all its working parts. Everyone is familiar with the effect of water, particularly salt water, on metal parts and electrical systems, so it would seem that although the engine may not be a write-off after its ducking, it has certainly qualified for a long, expensive sojourn at the local repair depot.

This is not always the case, however. Indeed, often much of the damage done to the engine is the result of this attitude, where the engine is philosophically dumped into the boot of the car to be taken down to the repair depot when time allows. The time that elapses between the engine plunging into water and being opened up on the mechanic's bench is when the salt water gets to work. A few "first aid" efforts on the bench, or as soon as the motor is taken home, may well reduce the need for a mechanic's attention, and perhaps eliminate it altogether.

Two factors decide just how much damage the engine will suffer: the length of time the water remains in the engine, and the conditions under which it is immersed. If the engine is quickly brought to the surface, drained and treated, the chances are it will not suffer severe damage.

The following routine will reduce the possibilities of severe damage to the engine, although it should be emphasised that sometimes it is best not to attempt too much first aid, but to rush the engine straight to the nearest repair depot.

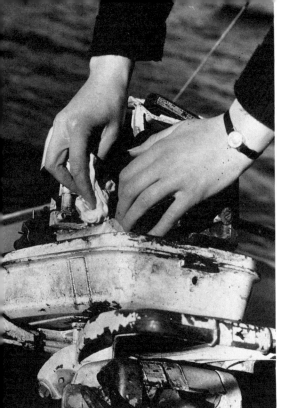

Wiping down all external parts will often indicate the extent of damage done by immersion.

should remove the remaining water and will quickly evaporate the chamber dry.

5. Remove the carburettor cover and blow out both the carburettor and fuel lines with fresh petrol. A mouthful of petrol is not pleasant, but it is not dangerous unless swallowed. Blowing petrol through the lines is a very efficient way of removing water.

6. Remove the plugs, clean and place out in the sunshine to dry. Shake out any water that may be in the cylinder. This is unlikely unless the engine was running when dropped as the valves will trap air in the cylinder head, and some time will elapse before the water can penetrate right inside. Squirt a small amount of light oil into the cylinder.

7. Very slowly and very carefully, turn the flywheel by hand. Listen carefully for any grating sounds indicating that dirt or sand

Liberal use of lubricant helps remove the water. Pressure pack oil can be driven right into vital spots

FIRST AID FOR AN IMMERSED ENGINE

1. Stand the engine upright to allow water to drain from exterior parts without running into exhaust ports.

2. Tip engine forward to drain internal water through air intake. At this stage the engine may be tipped in a number of directions to drain off any small pockets of water gathered in various parts of the engine.

3. When all water is out, mount the engine on a bracket (preferably out in the sunshine) and take off the cover. With a dry rag, wipe down all parts of the engine attainable, paying particular attention to electrical parts.

4. Remove the flywheel cover (or magneto cover) and with pipe cleaners attempt to dry out any water in the magneto chamber. Then pour in a large quantity of carbon tetrachloride, swirl around and pour out. This

has entered the cylinder or the bearings. If this is the case, this is the limit of first aid, and the engine must be taken to a repair depot for a complete strip-down. It should be pointed out, however, that the check on dirt or sand in the workings of the engine has been left to this stage since, even though the engine may still have to go in for repair, the various parts cleaned and treated earlier will be protected from further damage by the treatment received, and the repair bill will be considerably less.

8. In the lucky event that no dirt or sand has entered the engine, more oil and some carbon tetrachloride should be poured into the working areas to remove any last traces of water. This may take some time and patience, but it is well to remember that only one small spot of salt water can rust the cylinder wall and cause no end of trouble.

9. The engine is best left out in the sunshine to dry, even better, placed in front of heaters or heat lamps. Providing the heat is not sufficient to damage any insulation or rub-

The amateur should never strip down an outboard motor unless he is competent to do so

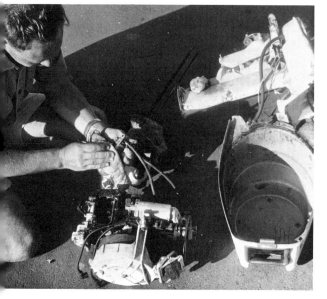

Prevention is better than cure, and a light chain will reduce many of the problems associated with losing an outboard over the side

ber or plastic parts, the engine can be left to dry out for some time.

10. Re-assembling the dismantled parts should be done with care to ensure that no dirt or water remains and that all working parts are well oiled. The magneto is the most likely spot to give trouble and a small piece of fine sandpaper inserted between the points may clean up any slight corrosion. At this point, with care and a great deal of luck, the engine may start again.

11. Depending on the make of engine, other points should be examined before putting the engine into use. Most gearboxes are sealed, since they are designed for immersion in water, but if the propeller was turning when it struck bottom, there is always a possibility of damage in this area. The water pump may have sucked up some sand or dirt and this, in many cases, puts them out of action. The method of hoisting the engine up from the bottom may damage light parts and this should also be taken into account.

In short, providing the engine has not taken in sand or dirt, and has not suffered any severe mechanical damage, by following the routine described there is every chance of getting the dunked outboard back into commission with a minimum of fuss and expense.

ANCILLARY EQUIPMENT

The Battery

In the course of normal use, a battery used with a marine engine should have a fairly long life. The amount of use it receives on board a boat is considerably less than when installed in a motor car, and since often the same type of battery is used for both, the marine battery should last considerably longer than its counterpart in a car.

However, despite less use, a marine battery can quickly deteriorate unless carefully maintained. This is mainly due to salty or damp atmospheres which causes corrosion on termi-

The battery should be located fairly close to the engine to avoid the use of long leads

nals and resultant deterioration of the battery capacity.

Once installed, every battery should receive routine maintenance at intervals of not more than a week, or about every twenty-five running hours of the engine, if the boat is used frequently. Such maintenance should follow the system described below, and if carried out at the intervals recommended, will afford the battery a long and useful life.

Routine Maintenance

1. Examine the battery for external damage in the form of cracks in the case, raised cells or leaks.

2. Inspect the battery carrier and any surrounding metal for signs of acid leakage.

3. Clean the top of the battery with clean warm water and baking soda. Scrub with a stiff brush, taking care not to scatter corrosion residue with the bristles. Wipe off with cloth moistened with ammonia.

4. Inspect the terminal posts, apply finger pressure to ensure that they are not deformed or broken. Clean terminals and cable ends with sandpaper. Replace cable clamps on terminals and screw down tight. Cover with a light film of vaseline or petroleum jelly.

5. Check the level of the electrolyte and top up with distilled water until the plates are covered.

6. Check the specific gravity of the electrolyte by means of the hydrometer. Ensure that the electrolyte is well mixed before checking the specific gravity, as this measures the quantity of sulphuric acid remaining in the electrolyte, and a reading immediately after topping up with distilled water can give a misleading result.

The hydrometer should be held vertically with the nozzle beneath the surface of the fluid, and the bulb squeezed firmly. Sufficient liquid to float the indicator is required and the reading should be taken with the eye level with the float. The hydrometer must NOT be tilted. The specific gravity should be 1.260 if the battery is fully charged.

7. If the specific gravity is abnormally low, or varies from cell to cell, the battery should be turned over to an electrician for examination or adjustment of the acid content.

THE STARTER MOTOR AND GENERATOR

Because of the wide range of starter motors and generating units, it is not possible in this book to deal with them in detail. In any case, the motors are sealed off and maintenance consists of nothing more than care of the exterior leads and connections and oiling where required of bearings and pulleys.

Servicing either the starter motor or generator is for a qualified technician. The amateur should not attempt to even open the housing. Irreparable damage can be done to delicate windings and wiring by dampness or careless handling once the housing is removed, and since invariably the interior of the motor requires technical know-how for even small repair jobs, no useful purpose can be served by opening or removing it.

When trouble strikes, a qualified electrician should be called in, or the motor unbolted from the engine and taken to an established workshop.

Routine maintenance, then, in terms of generators (which may be dynamos or alternators) and starter motors, consists of checking the tension of the driving belt (no more than half-inch movement each way when pressed halfway between pulleys) and oiling the bearings as recommended by the manufacturer.

The wiring attached to the motors requires attention, and this is dealt with later in this section under the general heading "Wiring".

THE IGNITION SYSTEM

The ignition system of a petrol engine consists, basically, of two circuits: a low voltage circuit and a high voltage circuit.

The current from the battery flows through the ammeter, ignition switch and primary winding of the ignition coil. Thence it travels through the distributor contacts to ground. When the contacts open a magnetic field is set up in the primary winding of the coil which induces a very high voltage into the secondary winding of the coil. This high voltage current is carried to the distributor rotor which makes contact in turn with each of the leads to the spark plugs, thus sending the high voltage current into the plugs and creating the ignition spark.

Because of the rapid firing of a petrol engine, this results in fast movement of the various components of the ignition system and close tuning so that the surge of high voltage is produced and delivered to the plugs at the correct instant and in the correct order. Maintenance of the ignition system is therefore of utmost importance if the engine is to function at peak performance.

The Wiring is important, since the production of current in the ignition system is allied to its distribution to the correct units at the correct time. High voltage and low voltage wiring is used; the high voltage wires are generally thicker and more heavily insulated than those of the low voltage system.

All wires should make good contact with the unit to which they are attached, and this is particularly important with the high tension wires. Wires that are loose or not inserted all the way into the connecting terminals will corrode and increase resistance as well as causing weaknesses at the terminals.

The spark plug nipples must be clean and close fitting: the push-on type should be firmly pressed down to make good contact, the screw type screwed on hard and covered with some form of insulation.

The insulation of coil and spark plug wires will deteriorate with use and a careful watch should be kept for cracked or damaged wires. Leakage from the cables will make for hard starting and poor engine performance.

Special resistance wires for suppression of

radio noise may be fitted to spark plugs. These are usually identified by the word RADIO marked on them. They should be replaced with wires of the same type.

All terminals should be carefully examined for signs of corrosion or for looseness in the fitting. Shorting out of the current is hard to track down in these areas, and only regular maintenance and checks will ensure trouble-free operation.

The Ignition Coil requires no maintenance other than that it be kept clean and dry. Condensation or oil film on the exterior of the coil and the high tension wires can cause leakage of the current, resulting in loss of power or irregular running of the engine.

The coil should be cleaned with a rag soaked in carbon tetrachloride to remove all traces of dirt or oil. If there is any sign of oil leaking from the tower, or the tower appears cracked, the coil should be taken out and tested.

The Distributor, for all its apparent complexity, can be easily taken out for testing or cleaning. However, unless there are signs of deterioration, the distributor can undergo general maintenance *in situ.*

The whole unit should be carefully cleaned externally with the carbon tetrachloride rag. Some schools of thought advocate warm soapy water as the best cleaner, but this must be used with caution as water in any of the tiny electrical crevices may short circuit the entire system.

The cap must be removed and cleaned carefully to remove any traces of dirt or oil. Signs of carbon tracking indicate a possible leakage and should be followed up with bench tests if necessary. The condenser should be examined and also the contact point which will need cleaning and possibly adjustment. This can be done with a feeler gauge adjusted to the maker's recommendation, but is more efficiently carried out with a special adjusting instrument.

Any cleaning or adjusting carried out in and around the contact points must be carefully done and a check made to see that no dirt or dust, or threads of cleaning rag, have found their way into the moving parts. The contacts should never be touched by fingers as burning will result in later use. Both the coil and the distributor can be affected by the heat of the engine, and indeed, because of its situation, the condenser is always vulnerable to heat damage.

The Ammeter shows the charge and discharge rate of the circuit and requires little or no maintenance other than an occasional check of the terminal connections. Usually the ammeter is installed on a switchboard or control panel and not in the vicinity of the engine where it can be damaged by heat and condensation.

The Spark Plugs come in for some of the harshest treatment afforded the whole ignition system, and thus are immediately suspect when trouble strikes. Routine maintenance will prevent spark plug failure in most cases, for the gradual deterioration of the plug is readily visible on inspection.

The plugs should be removed with a special plug spanner to prevent damage to the insulation. On removal, the gasket should be examined for deterioration and replaced if necessary. The plugs should always be kept clean and free of oil externally, as also should the immediate surrounding area. In this way, a deteriorating plug can often be detected early.

Spark plug points are subject to several forms of trouble. To ensure that plugs are maintained in fair condition, they should be taken out and cleaned and bench tested every 250 hours of running. Plugs that often appear sound, and may even give good service when the engine is idling, can fail at high speeds when they are most required.

Plug condition often indicates the condition of the engine. Forms of plug deterioration are listed below, together with the probable cause:

1. *Cold fouling* — dry carbon deposits around the mouth of the plug.

Can be caused by over-rich fuel-air mixture owing to faulty choke or carburettor. If only one or two plugs are fouled it could be caused by defective leads or sticking valves. Prolonged idling can also cause this condition.

2. *Wet fouling* — wet carbon deposits in mouth of plug.

Caused by excess oil, frequently the result of old or worn rings or excessive cylinder wear. This is often the sign that the engine is due for an overhaul.

3. *High Speed Glazing*—shiny deposits of yellow or tan colour.

Usually the result of a wrong-calibre plug for the type of engine. Mostly found in high speed engines; the correction may be a "colder" plug.

4. *Overheating* — white blistering of the centre insulator.

Usually the result of using the wrong type of plug for the engine. A "colder" plug may be the answer.

5. *Turbulence Burning*—burning away of electrodes on one side.

The result of turbulence patterns in the combustion chamber. This is relatively normal and can be ignored.

6. *Reversed Coil Polarity*—distinct "dishing" of the ground electrode.

Caused by reversed polarity at the coil, which can often be corrected by reversing the primary coil leads. Causes misfiring and rough idle.

THE FUEL SYSTEM

With the exception of the fuel lines and filters, the fuel system of both petrol and diesel engines are far too complicated and delicate to be handled at any length by the amateur.

The fuel filter bowl should be located where it can be easily observed and cleaned

In addition, the variety of carburettors and pump systems make it impossible to attempt to describe methods of maintaining and adjusting the involved workings. Generally speaking, adjustment of the carburettor or fuel pump is beyond normal routine maintenance and should be turned over to a technician.

For general maintenance, as with generators and starter motors, the boat owner should keep all units clean and free from dust or grease. The filter bowl should be examined frequently for sludge or water or other foreign matter, and cleaned and replaced when necessary. Likewise, fuel pipe connections should be checked for leaks or cracks and taps and joints tightened where necessary.

Air bleeder pipes must be kept free and filler pipes checked to see that they are secure and do not allow water to enter the tank. As mentioned earlier in this section, it is a wise precaution to install drip trays or tins beneath sections of the fuel system which may be liable to leak slightly. These should be emptied frequently and a careful check taken to see that any leakage is not excessive.

THE GEARBOX

A great variety of gearboxes is available for

marine engines. By and large, however, all types are relatively easy to maintain once correctly installed.

Because the gearbox is virtually a sealed unit, maintenance is confined simply to periodic changes of oil. This is done at intervals according to the use and number of running hours the engine has covered. Generally speaking 100 to 150 hours' running is sufficient for each lot of gearbox oil, although some manufacturers recommend longer periods between changes.

The correct grade of oil for the gearbox is most important, and the engine manufacturer's instructions in this regard should be followed to the letter. It is completely false to assume that the oil used for crankcase lubrication is also the correct grade for the gearbox.

Besides oil changes, maintenance of the gearbox consists simply of keeping it clean and all linkages oiled and free. This should be incorporated in the general maintenance schedule set down for the entire engine.

THE INSTRUMENT PANEL

The number, type and quality of the instruments on the instrument panel vary greatly from boat to boat and engine to engine. Generally speaking, the minimum requirements

Instrument panels which are open to the elements must be well waterproofed to protect their delicate mechanisms. Photo courtesy Coronet Boats

for satisfactory control of the engine from the panel are a tachometer, oil pressure gauge, temperature gauge and ammeter. Bigger or more complicated engines will have more involved instruments and, of course, twin engines will require a twin set of instruments. But basically, the four instruments mentioned above are sufficient to indicate the correct running of the motor under normal conditions.

Maintenance of the instruments is relatively simple, since the gauge itself is a high precision instrument and cannot be repaired or adjusted by an amateur. Any problems arising in the gauges necessitate removal and transfer to a qualified technician.

This reduces the maintenance to the transmission of the readings from engine to the gauge, and the methods are usually manual, pressure, or electrical. In the case of manual transmission, cables or linkages are involved and these require lubrication with light machine oil at intervals. Electrical wires need attention to terminal connections only, to keep them clean and tight and free from corrosion. Pressure pipes must be checked periodically to see that terminal connections do not come loose and allow escape of the pressure, or cracked from vibration of the engine. Blockages may also occur either in the pipe or in connecting valves, and these necessitate removal of the pipe for cleaning.

Also part of the instrument panel as a rule are the controls for throttle, choke, gearbox and steering. Unless they are of the hydraulic type, they will comprise mostly cables, rods and linkages. Their maintenance falls into the fifty-hour service schedule.

A light machine oil is best for sheathed cables, as when introduced at the top end of the covering, it gradually works down through the length of the cable. Where required, light grease can be used, particularly on pulleys in the steering system. Gearbox and similar heavy linkages are better lubricated with grease, although the boat owner should be guided by the manufacturer's recommendations in this regard.

219

Hydraulic systems are somewhat more involved than manual systems, and where hydraulic steering or gearbox or throttle systems are fitted, the maintenance should be followed according to the manufacturer's instructions, which usually require nothing more than the topping-up of the master cylinder and a periodic check against leaking pipes or joints.

PROPELLER SHAFT AND STERNGLAND

Most of the wear and tear in a propeller shaft is the result of incorrect alignment at the engine. Even when initially aligned correctly, vibration and thrust can alter the fine margin of alignment allowed between engine and shaft, and bring considerable strain on parts of both the thrust mechanism and the propeller shaft and sterngland.

The most likely result will be wear on the sterngland with subsequent damage to the stuffing box, and severe leaking around the shaft. Other effects come in the form of a badly vibrating shaft and subsequent wear and tear on sterngland and thrust mechanism.

Correct alignment of the shaft (see earlier this section) will eliminate many of the problems associated with shaft and sterngland, and should be on top priority for checking at regular intervals.

Other causes of wear and tear in the shaft and sterngland arise as a result of the whip of a long length of shaft, vibration damage, and physical damage owing to grounding, or some other form of damage to the propeller. Worn keys in the flanges can cause looseness and vibration and will subsequently splay out the edges of the spline groove into which they are placed. This necessitates a machine job to repair and replace the damaged spline.

Too long a length of shaft that is unsupported will set up a "whip" action, causing untold damage to the fittings at both ends of the shaft. Vibration can become a severe problem in this case also, and any signs of whip in a shaft should be rectified as soon as possible. The fitting of a plummer block is the only satisfactory solution, and more than one may have to be fitted. Once in position, light lubrication (usually through a grease cup) is all that is required for minimum friction.

The sterngland comprises the stern tube, making a watertight penetration of the hull, inside which is the stuffing box, which completes the watertight seal by packing around the propeller shaft some form of sealing material. The material itself varies from greased packing cotton, through forms of timber (lignum vitae) to more modern nylon seals It is held in position by a locking nut, usually on the inside of the stern tube, which can be tightened down on the packing as it wears loose, thus ensuring a tight seal at all times.

A small seepage of water through the gland is often unavoidable and, indeed, sometimes preferable as it offers good lubrication to the packing. But excess leaking will necessitate repacking the sterngland unless some damage has taken place, such as the whip vibration in the propeller shaft mentioned earlier. In this case the source of the damage must be rectified before the sterngland itself is repaired.

Damage to the propeller can set up severe vibration which will affect the sterngland. When the boat has been grounded or fouled some obstruction, the damaged blades are unbalanced and set up severe vibration in the immediate vicinity of the gland. In this case the propeller must be removed and re-shaped in order to prevent damage to the sterngland.

THE PROPELLER

Damage to a propeller falls into two categories: corrosion and physical damage. Since most propellers are of bronze or similar material, they are vulnerable to electrolytic corrosion, particularly if they are fitted to a steel hull or a propeller shaft of different metal. The question of corrosion is dealt with in detail in Section II and sufficient information is included in that section to cover the prevention and treatment of corrosion in propellers.

Physical damage to propellers can again be divided into two sections. actual damage caused by accident, and the fitting of an incorrect propeller.

Damage through accident—fouling a rope, grounding, striking a submerged object—results in a dented or chipped propeller blade. Where the damage is slight and the vessel is not used for racing, it may be possible to carefully file away the worst of the dent. However, as a rule the wisest move is to remove the propeller and have it taken to a workshop for re-shaping.

Most propellers are held in place by a large nut, through which a pin is driven to prevent the nut unwinding during the turning of the propeller. When removing the propeller, care should be taken to see that the spline key between the propeller and the shaft is not lost as these are often of a special shape.

One of the surprisingly common troubles is the use of the incorrect propeller for the engine or hull. Innumerable boat owners have been plagued with troubles ranging from lack of speed, through vibration trouble to actual damage to the engine as a result of not ensuring that the propeller matches both the boat and the engine. Particularly the engine.

A propeller is designed with a certain "pitch" which—when rotated at a given speed—offers a maximum thrust. When turned at higher speeds, the propeller loses its effectiveness and "slips"; that is, it cuts ineffective holes in the water without achieving forward thrust. Thus high-speed propellers are of a totally different shape and have a totally different pitch to propellers designed to be run at slower speeds. This can be seen easily by comparing the propeller shapes of slow-running diesel engines with those of a high-revving outboard motor.

Quite apart from loss of effective power—visually apparent when the boat "sits down" in the water, with her stern down and bow up, making a huge stern wash but getting nowhere fast—the use of the incorrect propeller can set up bad vibrations with resultant damage, and

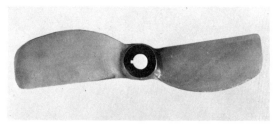

A typical two-bladed propeller—Note the spline key slot. Photo courtesy Stuart Turner Ltd

also place undue loads on thrust and stern bearings.

The question of correct propeller for the right motor is of utmost importance if performance is to be at a maximum, and wear and tear and resultant maintenance kept to a minimum. The manufacturer of the engine usually recommends the pitch and size of the propeller to be used with his engine, but failing that, the advice of a qualified marine engineer should be sought.

VENTILATING THE ENGINE COMPARTMENT

An engine requires air as much as it needs fuel, a factor often forgotten by amateurs installing an engine in a boat. In their anxiety to soundproof the engine and seal off the noise and fumes, the engine's need for air is often disregarded. Apart from the poor performance which will result, the fumes caused by the heat of the engine and possible leakages in the exhaust system must be carried out of the boat or dangerous toxic gases will gather in the cabin.

Without interfering greatly with soundproofing and insulation, good ventilation can be brought into the engine compartment through properly designed ventilators running either through the bilge, and drawing on the cabin ventilation system, or—even better—direct from the outside air. The latter system is particularly suited to power craft where the question of fumes in the accommodation can be acute. A scoop ventilator on the side of

Engine room ventilators can be neat and unobtrusive while carrying out their job effectively

the deck house funnelling air down into the engine compartment, and then a vortex-type exhaust ventilator near the after end of the vessel to draw off the fumes, are the ideal ventilating system. Needless to say, care must be taken with systems such as these, to ensure that the scoop ventilators scoop in air only, and not large quantities of water!

Forced draught ventilation is unnecessary on a boat. Ventilation—other than normal cabin ventilation—is required only when the engine is running and the vessel is under way. The passage of air at this time provides a ready-made forced draught, providing it is used to good effect.

The confines of the engine compartment on a yacht make it more difficult to achieve good soundproofing as well as good ventilation. However, the fact that the compartment is so confined makes it imperative to achieve good ventilation. Usually, an exhaust vortex ventilator is all that is required for the smaller yacht auxiliary, and this can be in the form of a small vent fitted on the deck above the engine, or just a small hatch which can be wedged open when the engine is working. Providing, of course, that weather permits.

In addition to exhaust fumes from the engine, there is always the possibility of petrol fumes from a leaking connection. Since these heavy fumes fall into the bilge, unless they are removed they will present a very real danger of explosion and fire. Good ventilation of the engine compartment will carry much of this danger away, and residue is taken care of by the normal ventilation of the vessel.

Typical layout of engine room ventilation on a motor yacht

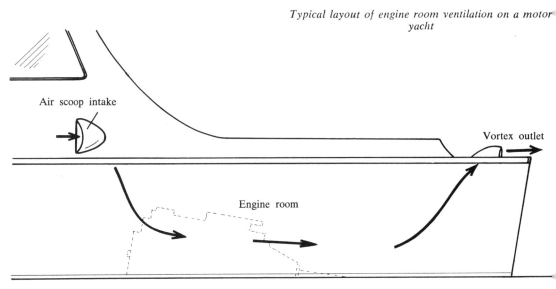

Air scoop intake

Vortex outlet

Engine room

SECTION V

General Maintenance and Repair Work

CHAPTER FIFTEEN

General Maintenance Work

SLIPPING THE BOAT

THERE ARE MANY WAYS in which a vessel can be pulled out of the water. Local conditions and the size of the boat govern which method is used. But by far the most common is the use of slipway and cradle. The advantages of this system lie in the ability to take the boat out of the water at any state of the tide, and to get right underneath her bottom when carrying out maintenance or repair work. The disadvantages lie only in the availability of slipways, which in some areas are few and far between. When this is the case one of the other methods of getting the boat out of the water must be adopted, and this again depends purely on local conditions.

A slipway consists of railway lines or some other form of track along which a cradle can be pulled. The track will run into the water. The angle of slope, and the depth of water into which it will run, depend on the local conditions. If the water is shallow and the cradle can only be lowered into a few feet of water, then slipping will be done only at the top of high tide, and the size of the vessel slipped will be limited by its draft. On the other hand, a well-designed efficient slipway will run out into deep water, enabling vessels of almost any draft to be slipped at any state of tide.

The type of cradle varies considerably, but basically comprises a solid base or platform on which the keel of the vessel can rest with-

The slipway cradle. Heavy beams on the base spread the weight and the adjustable arms hold the boat upright

out placing undue strain on any one point. To this platform are fitted adjustable arms which can be manipulated to hold the vessel in an upright position. Usually there are four arms on cradles for small boats, although this varies according to the length of the cradle.

The essential point is to ensure that excessive stress is not placed on any one part of the boat's structure. The keel must be supported equally along its entire length or distortion may occur. If the keel is supported in the centre and not at the ends, the ends of the boat will sag, giving rise to strains known as *hogging*. By contrast, if the boat is supported at the ends of the keel and not in the centre, she will be liable to *sagging* strains. Either can cause very bad distortion.

The most efficient cradles have a series of heavy beams on which the keel can be landed, and which are evenly spaced along the length of the cradle and laid level so as to bear an equal strain on each beam. A solid floor to the cradle is not suitable as the undersides of the keel must be available for maintenance and repair. Although the entire length of the keel, of course, is not available for maintenance, when the beams are spaced some work can be done underneath the keel on one slipping and the inaccessible spots left until a later slipping. It may also be possible to tilt the boat sufficiently to get a paint brush or scraper between the keel and the beams.

The adjustable arms may be manipulated by any mechanical means, and are usually padded where they are in contact with the hull. Some pressure must come to bear on these arms, when the weight of the boat leans to one side or another. Also in the initial slip-

(a)

(b)

(c)

The slipping sequence:
(a) The boat is floated into position with the cradle submerged
(b) Coming clear of the water a final check is made
(c) Everything bearing an even strain, the boat is pulled clean of the water

ping process, the vessel may move backwards and forwards until she settles into position. Either condition can damage the side of the boat if the arms are not suitably padded.

When the vessel is to be slipped, she is floated into the cradle and held roughly in position while the cradle is pulled carefully up the slipway for a few feet. As soon as the keel touches the cradle platform, the cradle is stopped. This is the point at which the boat must be correctly aligned in the cradle, for to raise her any further out of the water may cause her to topple over, or become subject to the strains mentioned earlier. Usually the slipway owner will know from experience where the arms should be placed in relation to the vessel he is slipping. If not it will be necessary to examine, under the water, the location of the keel in relation to the cradle platform. This is particularly necessary in the case of yachts with a short fin type of keel. Cruisers and yachts with long keels do not require such careful positioning as the long keel prevents the boat from tipping forward or aft.

Once the boat has been aligned on the platform, the cradle is pulled a few feet further up the slipway. The adjustable arms, which to this point have been manipulated near the sides of the vessel, are closed right in to hold her upright. Care must be taken at this point to ensure that she has no list. This part of the slipping procedure usually requires two people, one to operate the winch, the other to ensure that the boat lands squarely on the cradle. Once in position, without a list and with the arms secured tightly on either side, the cradle can be brought to the top of the slipway.

With vessels that have a long keel, the slipping process is straightforward, and no further attention will be necessary. Yachts with fin keels, however, may need some support under the bow and the stern to prevent them from tipping forward or aft. Sometimes the shape of the cradle arms will take care of this problem, but otherwise a chock must be placed under the forefoot of the stem and the transom, particularly if the slipway lies on a fairly steep slope. If, when the vessel has been pulled right up, some slight adjustments to her position are necessary, these can usually be done by driving wooden wedges under the keel until the required position is attained. Obviously, this adjustment can be only slight and any major adjustment must be done before the vessel is brought clear of the water.

CAREENING THE BOAT

This is the oldest method used for cleaning the ship's bottom; it dates back to the earliest days of sailing ships, when slipways or similar arrangements were rarely available. The boat, in order to be cleaned, had to be landed on

The longer the keel the easier the vessel rests on the cradle. Motor vessels are less trouble to slip than deep keel yachts

the bottom in shallow water and propped so that she was upright when the tide went out, with the bottom accessible for cleaning and painting.

This system is still in wide use today. In isolated fishing villages and rivers, particularly in the Northern Hemisphere, careening, or "landing on the hard" as it is called, is not only a common practice for maintenance and repair to the bottom of the boat, but is frequently an everyday occurrence in areas where the tide recedes to an extent that a vessel moored or tied to a jetty lands on the bottom.

Much the same precautions are required for careening a boat as for landing her on a slip way cradle. The ground on which she is to be landed must be level and able to support the keel evenly along its entire length. Sand is ideal, and mud, although somewhat unpleasant when working under the boat, is also good.

227

An efficient slipway allows the boats to be pulled well above high water mark

Rocky areas should be avoided unless they can be examined beforehand to see that the rocky shelf on which the boat is to be landed is completely level.

It is possible, if the boat is to be landed on sand or mud, to pre-arrange a landing bed for her. A few large beams or railway sleepers

Careening can be done on an improvised slipway where the boat is floated or pulled onto relatively dry ground

placed on the sand will ensure not only a level landing for her, but also raise the keel off the bottom and thus allow maintenance work to be done to at least a major part of the underside of the keel.

The vessel should be floated into position and secured with ropes either to the shore or to anchors, so that she will remain in position as the tide falls. At least two wooden props should be cut to a length slightly longer than the draft of the boat to shore her up as the keel touches bottom. In some areas where the vessels ground at every tide these props, or legs, are hung permanently over the side, and only taken inboard when the vessel is sailed off.

As the water drops and the vessel lands on the bottom, the props on either side hold her in an upright position on the beams. She should be supported with additional props, or some other means of shoring, as soon as the water has fallen away from her hull. Needless to say, when this method is used, any maintenance or repair work on the ship's bottom must be completed before the next tide.

The landing of the boat on the bottom is the most delicate part of careening, and particular care must be taken if the vessel is a yacht of the fin keel type, as shores or props will be needed under bow and stern, much as described in the section on slipping. Unless this is watched carefully, the vessel may tip forward or aft despite the props around her side, and serious damage can ensue. Since the props must be moved, one by one, in order to paint the hull, care must also be taken then to ensure that the vessel does not fall over.

Although adjustments may be made to the props under the hull one way or the other, to facilitate painting the underside, serious damage could result if she fell on her side. Apart from the damage, a vessel lying on her side, particularly a deep keel yacht, may fill with water before she can float off on the incoming tide.

Another method of careening the boat is to lie her alongside a jetty or wharf where the tide recedes completely, leaving the bottom dry. The vessel is securely tied to the wharf, and must be tended as the water falls, so that when she grounds on the bottom, she will be upright against the wharf, and with all lines tight. Neglect at this time may result in her falling away from the wharf, snapping the securing lines, and falling on her side. Although somewhat easier than the careening method described earlier, tying the boat up to a wharf has disadvantages. Working on the inside of the boat, between the wharf and the hull, is

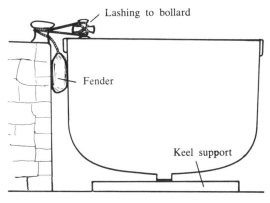

Careening alongside a jetty

somewhat difficult, and painting the hull where she lies against her fenders virtually impossible. It is possible to ease her away from the wharf, and suspend her by ropes, but this is fraught with dangers and should not be attempted unless absolutely necessary.

When slipped or careened the vessel can be moved slightly to facilitate maintenance and repair work. However, as mentioned earlier, great care must be taken, particularly when moving props, or the cradle arms, to ensure that the vessel does not fall on her side, her bow, or her stern. Like a seal the boat, so graceful and manoeuverable in the water, is heavy and cumbersome on land. Because of her bulk the slightest slip may result in severe damage, and all precautions should be taken to see that such a mishap cannot occur.

Two props are often sufficient to hold small boats in position provided the keel is evenly supported

THE UNDERWATER AREAS

Without doubt, the part of a vessel requiring most maintenance in the normal sequence of events is the underwater area. This is owing to several factors, one of which is the constant attack on any immersed surface by marine growth, and another the fact that treatments applied to hulls to combat this growth are of the "wasting" variety (i.e. they are continuously dissolving into the surrounding water) and thus need renewal periodically.

There is no known composition which will completely eliminate the problem of marine growth although there are many which will extend the normal "slipping" life of a boat to a year or more. Most, however, are based on a life of from four to six months under normal conditions if the hull is to be completely protected at all times. There is a common fallacy that fibreglass and aluminium hulls eliminate the need for maintenance, and perhaps where the topsides are concerned there may be some truth in this. But either of these materials, although worm-resistant, is as vulnerable to other marine growth as timber and must be slipped as frequently as a timber vessel.

The rate and type of marine growth vary

The result of neglected underwater areas. The weed on this boat's bottom was 3 feet long!

from place to place. Indeed, two boats moored at different spots in the same harbour will most probably show entirely different types of growth on their underwater surfaces. The factors affecting the type and virility of the growth vary from the brackishness of the water to the frequency with which a boat is used. Some forms of growth develop quickly in salt water but die in fresh, and vice versa. Therefore a vessel that is moving constantly between sea and fresh water runs less risk of fouling than does a vessel sailing in the same bay year in, year out. Similarly, if a vessel is used frequently, the movement of water past the hull makes it difficult for the growth to adhere, whereas a boat left lying on her mooring for months on end will soon establish an underwater "jungle".

Thus the research chemists, faced with the problem of combating marine growth on a vessel's bottom, have a wide and varied field to consider when attempting to formulate a treatment. They have, however, come up with a number of ideas; the most common and most widely used is anti-fouling paint. This is not really a paint, but a composition into which is incorporated a poison (usually a derivative of copper and mercury) which will prevent the growth from forming on the bottom of the hull at its embryonic stage.

In order to keep the poison fresh and thus ensure that no growth can establish a foothold, it would be necessary to repaint the bottom at frequent intervals—probably a week or less. Since this is completely impractical, the chemists came up with a composition which slowly dissolves away into the water, releasing new and fresh poisons as each successive layer dissolves. By governing the rate of "wasting" a layer of anti-fouling can maintain a supply of fresh poison across its surface for an extended period.

Once having gained a foothold, nothing short of scrubbing off can remove the growth which spreads rapidly across the hull as the effectiveness of the anti-fouling wears away. Thus the quality of an underwater anti-fouling paint depends firstly on its ability to prevent the marine growth from establishing itself and secondly on maintaining an even and lengthy "wasting" process which keeps the bottom covered with a toxic "skin".

Normal marine growth such as weed, barnacles, slime, etc., do not have a serious effect on the construction of the bottom or on any materials used in this construction. The marine borer, however, which is a kind of worm (often known as Teredo worm), needs only a fraction of an inch unprotected timber to begin its destructive work, and once into the timber can burrow through planks and plywood, underneath the skin of anti-fouling. It is not unknown for these worms to live in the hull of a vessel for years, slowly eating away the timber until it collapses completely. Few timbers are proof against the borer and few treatments completely effective. Only constant and adequate anti-fouling can assure freedom from this pest.

When a vessel is slipped for anti-fouling a sharp eye should always be kept for the tell-tale holes of the worm. They will be sometimes found in the seams where expanding caulking has pushed off the anti-fouling, or in rudder trunks or other spots difficult to coat with anti-fouling. A favourite place for them in centreboard dinghies is in the centreboard casing. Once in they are the very devil to get out, and often a new section of timber is the only cure, for there is no knowing what damage the affected timber may have sustained beneath the surface.

Other forms of marine growth are more a nuisance than a danger. The conglomeration of weeds and slime slow the boat down to the extent that she will hardly seem to move at all, even under full power. Even the almost invisible slime can slow a boat sufficiently to make a difference in a race, and hulls are frequently rubbed off to remove the slime just before a race.

To summarise: The only protection against worm and other marine growth is the consistent application of anti-fouling at intervals

A submerged waterline is soon attacked by marine growth. The antifouling waterline should be raised to prevent this

Typical weed fouling of a yacht hull. This picture was taken three months after new anti-fouling had been applied

which can be found by trial and error to be most satisfactory for the area in which the boat is moored. The type of anti-fouling used is again a matter of trial and error, for in some waters marine growth will react more vigorously than in others. Tropical waters are renowned for their virulent growth and special

Slime does not affect the hull of the boat to any extent, but will cause some drag

tropical anti-fouling paints are manufactured to combat it.

ANTI-FOULING (new surface)

Building up the underwater areas of a vessel from new material can commence in much the same way as for non-underwater areas. The procedure is to use the correct primer for the hull material, sand back and build up again as for any other type of painting, then apply a waterproof undercoat. Since finish is not as important here as on topsides and cabin, the sanding back need not be as vigorous, but merely to make a good surface for the adhesion of coats to follow. To a great extent, the treatment of the bottom will depend on whether or not the vessel is to be raced. If so, then attention must be paid to building up a finish almost as polished and smooth as the topsides. For cruising and general purposes, however, a slight unevenness in the bottom paint will do little to impair the boat's performance.

There is a school of thought which prefers not to use an undercoat beneath anti-fouling, but place it straight on the primer. The trend however, is to use the undercoat as a water-

232

proofing agent, as well as providing a firm base on which to apply the anti-fouling.

The anti-fouling composition should be applied quickly and without thinning. Because of its wasting properties it is thicker than most paints and thinning only reduces the effectiveness of the poisons. Full effectiveness depends on immersion in water soon after application, and the manufacturer's instructions should be followed concerning the re-entry of the boat into the water. Generally a minimum of six and maximum of twenty-four hours are permissible between painting and immersion.

Cutting in or boot-topping painting should be done beforehand so that the lower areas of the hull can be coated quickly and evenly. The paint will appear to dry almost immediately, and one coat is sufficient if applied according to manufacturer's instructions. The paint should be worked into all difficult corners and crevices as it is there that the eggs of the worm can be hatched. Particular attention should be paid to trunkways and beneath fittings such as the strainers over intake pipes, for the eggs can be drawn into these locations and will—if there is no anti-fouling to prevent it—breed rapidly. It is not uncommon for small engine intake pipes to become clogged with minute growth, with

Weed, even in small quantities, creates tremendous drag through the water

disastrous results for the water pump and—eventually—the engine itself.

As soon as the required time has elapsed after painting, the boat should be un-slipped to allow the toxic processes to get under way.

ANTI-FOULING (old surfaces)

After the initial treatment, the boat will need only a coat of anti-fouling each time she is slipped. The growth should be scraped off with a piece of flat timber or similar object and the hull thoroughly scrubbed off with a scrubbing brush and fresh water. Any repair work or adjustments should be made at this stage, and then the bottom completely rubbed back with wet and dry sandpaper.

If there has been any repair work, or if the old paint has been damaged and bare hull is showing beneath, primer and undercoat must be used to touch up these areas as for new surfaces mentioned earlier. A full coat of undercoat at each slipping is argued strongly in many circles and undoubtedly this has a binding effect on old paint and gives a good surface on which to build up the new anti-fouling. However, it is not necessary after the boat has been anti-fouled a few times and in fact can start to add too much paint to her hull. New anti-fouling should adhere quite readily to the old, providing the bottom has been well sanded back and cleaned off.

It is important that props or cradles supporting the hull be moved (one by one, of course!), so that the spot each covers can receive its coat of anti-fouling. It needs only a very small spot free of anti-fouling to start marine growth on its insidious way; and once started it is the very devil to stop.

Because of the thickness of the anti-fouling, the successive coats soon begin to mount up, and unless care is taken it will reach the flaking stage where a bump will take a chunk of anti-fouling right off, which may not be noticed for some time.

When it has reached the flaking stage, the anti-fouling should be burned off and the

Anti-fouling paint should be applied quickly and evenly. It is a thicker paint than most to allow for "wasting" processes

successive coats built up again from the primer to the final coat of new anti-fouling as for a new surface. Burning off is preferable to using paint removers, because the heat of the torch dries out any dampness there may be in the hull. Scraping off the paint also offers a fine opportunity to examine all those underwater fastenings such as keel bolts, skin fittings and so on. Previously covered with anti-fouling, they may well have started working or be in need of some other attention.

New anti-fouling, when painted over old, requires the same conditions regarding re-entry in the water. Six to twenty-four hours after painting should be right for most brands.

One final word: it is well worth the time and trouble to extend the anti-fouling well above the normal waterline. Not only does it improve the appearance of the boat but it ensures protection against growth in the event of the boat sitting lower in the water at a later stage—due, perhaps to re-arrangement of the ballast or stores—or taking a list while on the moorings. Only when one has experienced the insidiousness of marine growth and its ability to penetrate impossible areas does one treat it with the respect it commands, and raising

233

Most new boats are delivered with polythene covering on many items. These should be kept as useful covers for the winter lay-up period

the waterline is just one of many small precautions that help to ensure the boat will be free from attack by this pest.

LAYING UP

Winter is laying up time and laying up costs money. Whether it costs a few dollars or a few hundred will depend on the attitude of the boat owner. If he walks ashore with a shrug of the shoulders and instructions to the boat shed to "fix her up" for the winter, it is going to cost a few hundred. If he just leaves her sitting at the mooring where he tied up after the last autumn trip, it is going to cost many hundreds when spring comes and he tries to get the deteriorated gear going again.

But if he wants the cost to be only a few dollars, the wise boat owner will sit down after his last run, and start figuring out just how and where he can lay his boat up economically, both from the point of view of cash paid to the boatshed, and prevention of expensive deterioration of gear.

In some places, laying up means a complete wrap up in preparation for deep freeze conditions. In others, it is just a question of the

boat being out of commission for a few months. Either way, unless the right preventive action is taken, the winter lay up can be the most expensive time of the entire year.

For example, engines thrive on work, and deteriorate rapidly when out of use. Thus an engine which is, of necessity, laid up out of action, must be treated to prevent serious deterioration from setting in. If it cannot be turned over once in a while, then at least the necessary steps to prevent corrosion and deterioration will reduce the damage to an absolute minimum, if not avoid it altogether.

Sails, masts and spars, paintwork, all suffer the same problems as the engine during laying up and all need their own type of preventive treatment if they are to survive the winter period successfully.

The laying up routine begins at the wharf at the end of the last autumn trip. From the time the engine is shut off, a systematic procedure should begin which will ensure not only the saving of the many hundreds of dollars which deterioration can claim, but will also ensure a comfortable and happy ship (and owner) when the first run of the next season gets under way.

The following routine offers a good base for laying-up a boat.

Laying Up Routine

I. *To be stowed ashore*

1. Linen, blankets, clothing, wet weather gear, toiletries, carpets, curtains, etc.

2. Mattresses, cushions, covers, lifejackets, lee-cloths, etc.

3. Crockery, cutlery, gallery utensils, glassware, and all galley appurtenances, cleaners and detergents.

4. Food and drink normally stored aboard.

5. Charts and navigating instruments, binoculars, hand bearing compass, barometers, prisms, etc.

234

Small boats can be easily lifted out of the water and carried ashore for storage at the end of the summer season. Photo courtesy Fibremakers Ltd

6. Canvas covers, sails, awnings, wind-cloths, etc.

7. Gas cylinders.

8. Boat-hooks, anchors, rope, and all loose stowing gear.

9. Any electronic gear which can be satisfactorily removed such as radios, sounders, radar, etc.

10. Contents of all drawers and cupboards not already included in the previous check-list.

II. *Preparing the boat for the lay up*

1. Turn all ventilators on to the wind, open doors, hatches, windows, portholes and air her thoroughly.

2. Vacuum, clean, and if necessary scrub all lockers, cupboards, drawers, etc., with special attention given to galley areas.

3. Wash down with warm soapy water all brightwork and varnishwork inside and out. Wash off with clean fresh water and dry thoroughly.

4. Pour a detergent or de-greaser into the bilge, allow time to work, then pump over the side. Pour in fresh water, and pump out. Finally pour in salt water and slush around before pumping out. (leaving traces of fresh water induces dry rot).

5. Moisture-absorbing crystals should be placed in scattered containers throughout the boat.

III. *Preparing the engine*

Since this requires a very involved and detailed routine of its own, a special chapter has been devoted—in Section IV of this book —to preparing the engine for laying up.

IV. *Attention to moving parts*

1. Lubricate all moving parts of furniture and fittings, such as door locks and hinges, porthole hinges, winches, rudder stock, stern tube, etc.

2. Lubricate engine throttle cables or linkage, steering wheel cables and pulleys, rudder quadrant connections.

3. Dismantle, inspect and lubricate before replacing all sea-cocks, inlets, outlets, and pumps. Grease and check bilge pump and galley pumps, toilet valves and pumps, etc.

4. Inspect and clean all electrical terminals and wires, giving particular attention to the switchboard. Lightly grease with vaseline or petroleum.

V. *Masts, spars and rigging*

1. Remove all running rigging and stow ashore.

2. Lubricate all blocks and leads, jam cleats, levers, pulleys, etc.

3. Wash down the mast and spars with warm soapy water and if possible cover with canvas covers. Some owners prefer to remove masts and spars for the winter lay up; the best possible solution.

4. Grease all turnbuckles and mast fittings such as roller reefing gear, outhauls, halyard winches, etc.

5. Run standard rigging down with a rag thick with light grease.

6. Oil tracks and boom fittings and spinnaker pole parrot-beak, main sheet horse and boom-end swivel.

7. Check chain plates to see they are in fair condition and coat with light grease if they are not painted.

8. Check mast step for corrosion (aluminium) or rot (timber), check collar for watertightness.

VI. *Laying up the hull*

1. Pull the boat out of the water and land in laying-up cradle. (See description later this chapter.)

2. Scrub off bottom and attend to any damage or leaky seams.

3. Remove propeller/s and send for grinding if pitted or damaged. Grease shaft thread

and replace locking nut. Check condition of shaft and bearings.

4. Open and inspect all skin fittings to ensure they are free and clean.

5. Wash off topside paint and varnishwork with fresh water and wipe dry.

6. Open all possible ventilation systems and leave open all sea cocks.

7. Fit complete cover over the boat, ensuring that it is a tight fit overall. Lace down securely.

STORING THE BOAT ON DRY LAND

Where winters are particularly severe, it is preferable to store the boat on shore. Small boats are easily pulled up on to a trailer and run into the garage or shed. A few larger boats may get storage space inside a boatshed or similar shelter, but by and large, most of these when stowed ashore must be left out in the open with only their covers to protect them from wind and weather.

With an adequate cover, this is no problem, and providing they are secure in this respect and well landed on cradle or chocks, there is no doubt that boats will survive even the harshest winter.

Storing on shore is the best idea for laying up. The boat must be well chocked and supported to prevent hull strains

Covering the boat is a matter of common-sense. A good, all-round waterproof cover which can be lashed around the hull and prevent any sort of weather getting through to the boat is the only solution to outdoor storage, and money invested in the right nylon, terylene or dacron cover is money well spent.

Problems can arise, however, over cradling or supporting the boat. Out of the natural element, propped up on a cradle or on chocks, the hull of the boat can be subjected to stresses and strains which will cause considerable structural damage over the winter months, and involve considerable repair bills when the summer launching comes around again.

It is important, therefore, when storing the boat on dry land to ensure that she is correctly supported in such a way that no structural distortion can take place. This depends entirely on the way in which she is cradled or chocked. Attention should be paid to the following points.

1. When the vessel is cradled, it is important that the correct support is given to heavy ballast sections such as the keel, and to extensive overhangs of bow and stern. The illustration gives a typical cradle set-up for a keel yacht, showing the supports necessary, as well as to the normal bilge and hull areas.

2. The vessel, whether on chocks or cradle, should be trimmed slightly aft so that rainwater can run away easily.

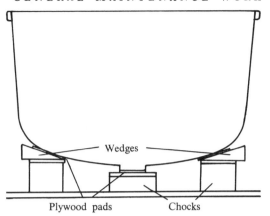

Supporting a launch hull

3. Where the hull is of shallow draft (such as power vessels), frame supports should be used to spread the weight of the hull and bilge supports inserted to prevent sagging.

4. Apart from the support mentioned above, care must be taken to ensure that the boat is wedged or otherwise supported fore and aft so that she will not tip on her nose or stern when someone clambers aboard.

Ventilation is important and a vessel, particularly if she is covered with an overall boat cover, must be provided with circulating fresh air throughout the inside of her hull, to prevent dry rot. If ventilators are covered, some form of air channel through the covers must be made. (See section on dry rot.)

Laying up a keel yacht

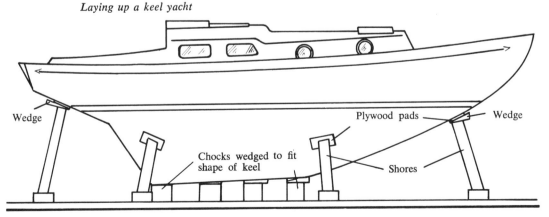

A thorough check of the anchor gear should include close scrutiny of the chain for any signs of a weak link

CARE OF ANCHORS

Several different types of anchors are available to the yachtsman, each with individual advantages. Which type is kept aboard will depend on the nature of the anchoring grounds in the vicinity, and the boat owner's personal preference. But regardless of the type of anchor, its care and maintenance is basically the same.

Made of iron and usually galvanised, the anchor requires little attention during its working life. Painting is of little advantage since the first time it is driven home in sand or rock, the paint will chip off. A small amount of rust is insignificant and can be ignored, as the next time the anchor is used all light rust will be scraped off. The only nuisance with rust spots on an anchor is the way they "bleed" on to the deck or locker sides; but these can be touched up with a rust killer and a coat of primer.

The anchor warp needs more attention than the anchor, for it comes under fairly heavy strain when in use. Since it may be used in an emergency, it is important to ensure that the warp is sound and not likely to part under heavy strain. With the advent of nylon and terylene ropes, maintenance of anchor warps is reduced considerably, and a close inspection of any part that may be chafed, and of the

shackle connecting the warp to the anchor chain, is usually all that is required. Fibre ropes need attention to prevent rot or chafing causing damage to them.

The chain is somewhat vulnerable and can be weakened in the links by rust, as a fairly light chain is used on anchors. Its purpose is to provide a spring effect which gives the warp some take-up and prevents any sudden shock jerking the anchor out of the bottom, and also prevents the chafe of the rope part of the warp where the anchor stock rubs along the bottom of the sea. Shackles connecting this chain to the anchor and the rope warp should be checked frequently for signs of rust or wear.

Stowing the warp in a locker where it cannot dry properly is the best way to introduce rot into the rope and also into the timbers of the locker area. Some system of drainage and ventilation in the locker is necessary, for some water is inevitable each time the anchor is used.

If the anchor is stowed on deck, it will be lodged in chocks; small wooden, shaped pieces screwed to the deck into which the blades of the anchor can be inserted to prevent it moving around in a seaway. The chocks must be well secured; bolting is preferable to screwing, as considerable strain may come on them when the boat is rolling hard, and an anchor which breaks loose in a seaway can do much damage before it is secured.

The forward bitts, or bollard, or samson post, as it may be called, should be examined periodically for signs of strain. It is on this fitting that the greatest strain comes when the boat is anchored, moored or under tow. The bollard should be through-fastened to a heavy beam beneath the deck, or if a beam is not available, then a prefabricated section made up so as to distribute the strain throughout the structure of the vessel, and not allow too much strain to be placed on the deck. Many a boat has had her bollard pulled out of the deck through neglect of this point, particularly when under such strain that may be met under tow.

238

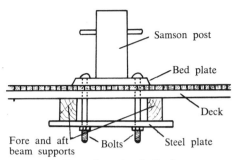

Fastening of a bollard

Hand or mechanically driven pumps are usually of brass and operate on a suction principle. Some employ large rubber diaphragms, others rubber or plastic wheels. Whatever the case, the bilge pump is a very vulnerable piece of equipment, for two main reasons—it is subjected to all types of corrosive liquids which may seep into the bilge, and it is liable to encounter large solid lumps of material which readily block either the access pipes or the pump itself.

Maintenance of bilge pumps, then, consists mainly of keeping all the parts clean and in working order. With this in mind, pumps generally are made with easy access, and easy means of dismantling and cleaning. A routine check on all working parts, and a check after pumping the bilge to ensure that no foreign matter is lodged in the pipe or the pump itself, will ensure that it will be in working condition in an emergency.

A strainer on the bilge end of the intake pipe is a must, and this should be as large as possible while keeping the gauge of the straining wire as small as possible. Thus if foreign matter clutters up one section of the strainer, the pump can continue to operate through another section. Too small a piece of gauze stuck in the end of the pipe will cause a blockage of the pump immediately foreign matter appears.

Another point often neglected is the attachment of the anchor warp to the bottom (or sides) of the anchor locker. This is important in case the warp is run out too fast and a turn cannot be made on the bollard. The warp should be secured to an eye bolt in the stem or some other heavy structural member in the locker, so that in such a case, the vessel can bring up on this fitting until such time as the warp can be transferred to the bollard. A relatively easy fitting to make, this eye bolt may prevent a lost anchor or running aground in an emergency.

The size and weight of an anchor vary according to the vessel and the location in which she may be anchoring frequently. As a rough guide, the C.Q.R. anchor, which is a good, all-purpose anchor, should be of about 10 lb weight for boats under 10 ft in length, 20 lb for boats of 30 ft, and 100 lb for a 50 ft length. This is a rough guide, and different types of anchors may need to be heavier or lighter for the respective lengths of the vessel.

BILGE PUMPS (hand operated)

Because of the enormous number and variety of bilge pumps on the market, it is impossible to deal in detail with the care and maintenance of this very important piece of equipment. Many pumps are hand driven, some are mechanically driven off the engine or by a separate motor, and some operate automatically, using the vortex principle to suck the water from the bilge. The latter variety is confined to small, fast boats as a rule.

A good location for the bilge pumps is beneath the cockpit thwarts. Here it is easily accessible for maintenance

The manufacturer's instructions concerning oiling, greasing and cleaning should be carefully followed. A bilge pump can be required in an emergency and mean the difference between saving or losing the boat. A neglected pump which is seized or blocked is not worth having in the boat.

Attention to the clips holding the hoses in position is also important, as these may be of light-gauge metal and rust quickly. The pump will not operate with one hose broken away.

Perhaps the most important point of all lies not with the pump but with the bilge. No pump can be expected to operate when the bilge is full of foreign matter or refuse, as it so often is. One paper tissue can block a bilge pump, so it is small wonder that no results are obtained when the bilge has everything from wood shavings to oily waste floating around in it. A clean bilge is not only a sign of a healthy ship, it is also a guarantee that in an emergency, the bilge pump will work adequately.

THE ELECTRICAL SYSTEM

Most modern yachts and power craft are fitted with an electrical system that is sufficiently sophisticated to allow the use of many modern electrical aids. The flashy, ultra super power craft may carry everything that modern electronics can offer, including radar, hot water systems, fully electric galleys, and so on. At the other end of the scale, the humble little fishing boat plodding out to the offshore reefs may carry nothing more startling than the legal lights and an electric engine start.

Whatever the size or shape of craft, and whatever its purpose, some form of electrical system will be fitted unless the boat is solely a day sailer, to be run on to a trailer and taken home each night. The system may be run on one of a number of voltages ranging from 6 volt to 240 volt, although almost invariably it will be run from a system of batteries.

To understand the highly involved technical aspects of the higher voltage systems and the sophisticated navigation aids such as radar, requires involved technical study far beyond the scope of this book. To know the basic layout of a low-voltage electrical system, to be able to maintain it in good condition, and to know where to look for faults is well within the capabilities of the average boat owner, and it is in this context that this section is written.

The batteries

Although there are several recently-developed batteries with features that make their use on board much more convenient and simple, the average boat's electrical system is based on the use of the familiar acid-cell battery, so well known in the form of the "car" battery. Developments of this type of battery for marine use have made it relatively easy to maintain, small and readily stowable, and most important of all, spill-proof.

Maintenance of this type of battery consists principally of keeping the plates charged. This also involves the maintenance of the generator and charging system, but these are dealt with separately in the section dealing with engines. As far as the battery is concerned, the main feature in keeping the battery well charged—providing that the battery itself is in good order

Old fashioned batteries are still widely used in boats and these must be well stowed to prevent acid spilling from them

Electric start outboards need good sized batteries and these must be kept in good order by frequent maintenance

—is maintaining the level of the correct electrolyte in the cells.

When a battery is charged for the first time it is filled with acid of the correct specific gravity. The resultant decrease in the amount of liquid in the cells is principally owing to evaporation, and therefore the battery should never be topped up with acid, but with distilled water to replace that lost by evaporation. As a near substitute to distilled water, rainwater may be used, but tap water should be avoided as it contains chemicals which may affect the liquid already in the cells. Salt water must never be used.

The caps can be removed and the level examined from the filler hole if an indicator gauge is not attached to the battery. The plates should always be covered by the electrolyte, and any sign of the top of the plates breaking the surface indicates the need for a refill. This can be done with a jug, or a small watering can with a long spout, such as is used to fill flower vases. A plastic can should be used as any acid splashing up on to a metal can will

promptly corrode it. Similarly, liquid spilled over the top of the battery should be wiped clean in case it contains acid which will attack leads and connections in the vicinity.

The condition of the battery terminals and their connecting leads is most important. These areas tend to corrode easily, and the efficiency of the battery can be reduced owing to corrosive material insulating the leads and robbing them of the full flow of current. The leads should be taken off the terminals and cleaned with a light sandpaper until the bright metal shines all over. A coating of grease (water pump grease will do) will protect them from further deterioration, and fastening the lead connections hard down on the terminals will ensure a good contact and full power.

The state of the battery can be tested by means of the hydrometer, an instrument which registers the specific gravity of the liquid in the cells. Some hydrometers are registered in figures, in which case a reading of 1250-1280 indicates a fully-charged battery and a reading of 1150 or lower a discharged battery. Other instruments have "colour zones" against which the level of the liquid is read. The colour zones vary according to manufacture of the

241

hydrometer, but usually a reading in the red zone indicates a flat battery.

A battery which is not in use will slowly discharge. This will be accelerated in warm climates and thus a stored battery should be kept in as cool a spot as possible. A discharged battery will freeze easily and must not be allowed to stand in low temperatures for too long.

Loss of power, particularly on the self-starter, may be the result of several factors, chief of which is a flat battery. If the battery is fully charged, the trouble may come from a collapsed cell or from bad connections at the terminals. Leads to the self-starter should be as short as possible and fairly heavy. Long, thin leads result in loss of current at the starter. Connections at all electrical points should be kept tight, as a loose connection has high electrical resistance and will prevent the current travelling easily.

Clean the outside case of the battery by mixing one pound of baking soda in one gallon of water, and rub the solution all over the exterior. Care must be taken, of course, that it does not get into the electrolyte.

A battery, once discharged, should never be left standing in this condition. It should never reach a state of complete discharge in the first place, and regular use of the hydrometer will ensure that the cells are recharged long before the battery is completely dead. If it is allowed to remain in a discharged condition, the plates deteriorate, making recharging slow and uncertain.

Leads and connections

Since the leads, or wires, carry the current from the battery to the outlet, they are next to the battery in importance. And the connections are all-important for they are the link between the leads and the battery or circuit.

Maintenance of leads and connections is an important job on board, since the metals most commonly used for these items are often susceptible to corrosion when in contact with salt water. In addition, unless they are in good condition and properly insulated, contact with salt water will cause short circuits and blow fuses or damage the battery.

Inside the boat the problems are relatively small. Well-insulated cables should be used at all times, and they should be secured with brass insulated clips driven into the timber of the cabin and hull. Spots where water contact may occur are always suspect and the wiring should be well covered or moved so that there is no possible contact with the water.

Connections should always be screwed up tight and periodically examined for corrosion. They should be dismantled and cleaned if signs of deterioration appear, then reconnected and smeared with water pump grease or some other water repellant. Where connections are of galvanised metal or material sold on the market as "waterproof and rustproof", a close examination should be made to see that rust spots have not occurred. If so, a light rust killer, preferably in the form of a lubricant spray, will take care of it. The oil in the spray will add a protective coating at the same time.

Where a lead pierces a deck or coaming, close attention must be paid to the possibility of friction rubbing away the insulation. Usually the hole will be made watertight by some method or other, and this can make it difficult to see any signs of deterioration in the wire. Fortunately most deck lights are limited to masthead and spreader lights and these can be taken down through the deck at one place, thus reducing the possibility of this kind of trouble spot.

When refitting or replacing a lead, it is important to use the right lead for the job. A wire that is too thin will result in loss of current. Studying the type and size of wire used in the previous leads or in leads in the other parts of the vessel is the best plan.

Lights

There is almost no limitation on the type and size of light used on board, other than the current available to light it. A variety of attractive lights and fittings is to be found in

any ship chandler's, or for that matter, a little
imagination with the accessory lights from
automobiles can provide ideal cabin lighting.
Fluorescent lights are available in low voltages,
although their harsh nature does not lend
itself to the cosy interior of a boat, other than
at the galley.

As with all boat fittings, lights and light
fittings are liable to rust and corrosion owing to
the salty content of the atmosphere, and a
constant check is necessary if they are to be
kept in good condition. In older boats where
there may be slight deckhead leakage or water
constantly swirling in the bilges, a light covering of vaseline or similar waterproofing is
recommended as the cabin atmosphere under
these conditions is often damp.

Connections need the attention described in
the earlier part of this section as also do
switches which can easily become gummed up
with corrosion or rust. The patent lubricating
sprays mentioned throughout this book are
undoubtedly the answer to corrosion prevention, providing they are used regularly.

The switchboard

The switchboard is the control panel of the
electrical system in the boat, and contains
switches to all instruments and lights as well
as fuses. It is usually designed in such a way
that the switches and fuses are readily visible
and attainable on the face of the switchboard,
which is hinged so that the wiring and connections behind the panel can be reached if
necessary.

A main lead from the battery provides the
power source, which is then divided up via
fuses and switches to the various parts of the
system. Navigation lights, cabin lights, instruments, power points and engine electrics each
have their own circuit and often a master
switch is inserted at the switch board so that

*Radar is also a heavy "juice" drain. Small generators
are often installed to cope with the heavy demand
from such instruments. Photo courtesy* Power Boat
& Yachting

*When a great deal of electrical equipment is fitted,
separate batteries are advisable so that their charge
can be kept under constant surveillance*

*Nothing drains a battery as heavily as a radio
transmitter. Batteries must be kept well charged or
transmission will suffer*

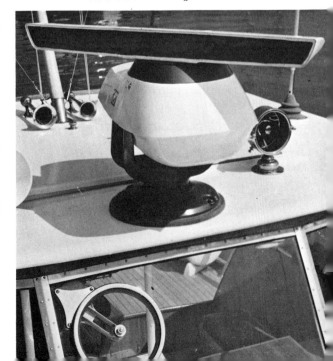

complete disconnection with all wiring can be achieved when the vessel is not in use.

Wiring an electrical circuit

The principal factor involved in wiring up an electrical circuit in a boat is the capacity of the batteries from which the circuit will be run, and the number and capacity of the units which will be incorporated in the circuit. Needless to say, the capacity of the batteries must be sufficient to cope with the circuit or the use of the power units will run the batteries down very quickly and constant re-charging will be necessary.

An assessment of how many lights, instruments and power accessories will be fitted in the boat should be made before wiring up the circuit begins. Not only do the size and capacity of the batteries depend on the answer to this, but also the size of the wiring to be used. Insufficient capacity in the batteries will only result in the inconvenience of constantly rundown batteries, but the effect of using too small a wire to carry the load can result in loss of power and also in overheating.

Modern vessels have many electrical accessories, including such luxuries as refrigerators, television and power cooking apparatus. Thus for a boat so fitted, the electrical source and wiring will need to be of a capacity to support the use of these fittings. It is a wise precaution at this stage to consult a qualified electrician regarding the size of wiring and number of batteries.

Where refrigerators and other electrical appliances are used, it is often a good idea to run separate circuits for lights and appliances, and even a third circuit for the electrical wiring of the engine. This simplifies the layout and allows for easy trouble-shooting in the event of electrical failure.

The circuit commences at the batteries and is carried by a fairly heavy gauge cable to the switch board. Here a master switch allows the circuit to be broken as a whole, a useful arrangement when shutting down before leaving the boat on the mooring. Only one lead is run to the master switch; the earth lead is taken directly to the switch board.

The switch board begins with a basic positive and negative terminal (the earth may be either) which is run to a series of dipole switches according to the number of lights to be wired up separately. Generally speaking the cabin lights are on one circuit, the navigation lights on a second, and spreader lights, deck lights, searchlights etc. on other circuits. One switch is provided for each circuit. Individual operation of lights is made by fitting switches to each individual light.

Immediately adjoining the switches on the switch board are fuses. The circuit then leads off around the boat via a cable of sufficient gauge to prevent any power loss through resistance. Positive and negative wires must be run to each light and the whole routed back to the fuses and switches on the switch board. In this way maximum power is obtained on all circuits even if they are all in use at the one time.

Wiring should be suitable copper wire, plastic-covered for insulation and stapled into place with insulated staples. The design and fitting of the switch board is a matter of personal preference, but, as mentioned earlier, ease of access, both to the switches and fuses, and also to the wiring is essential. Usually the switches and fuses are on one side of the board, the wiring on the other.

A properly-installed circuit should need little in the way of maintenance, providing the insulation of wiring and switches does not deteriorate or become corroded. The use of lubricant sprays will eliminate much of this problem, and prevention of chafing or contact with water should keep the circuits in first-class condition.

PAINTING DECKS

There are several different types of decks on modern craft, some of which do not require to be painted. Laid decks are rarely painted, and although some types of fibreglass decks

Decks of small yachts have little room for footholds and must offer a good grip. This is usually achieved by non-skid surfaces

Special deck paints incorporate a non-skid material which is laid as the deck is painted

require painting, most have an anti-skid pattern moulded into the fibreglass.

When paint is covered with water it becomes extremely slippery, and when such paint is on the deck of a lively boat, tossing in a seaway, the surface is not unlike a skating rink. To get a foothold is almost impossible and yet it is important, particularly under such conditions, that the deck is accessible to the crew for sail-changing, effecting a repair, or any other problem that may occur.

The traditional boatbuilders used ordinary paint (not gloss, or course) sprinkled with sand or some other coarse dust while still wet. This gave a surface like sandpaper which was hard on shoes and feet, but magnificent for gaining a foothold. Nowadays the paint can be purchased with the dust (usually pumice) incorporated in it. Apart from thorough stirring, it is applied in the same way as any normal paint.

It has one disadvantage, however, and this is the way in which, the special non-skid paint defeats its purpose. The paint applies the grit to the deck, but then covers it with a further skin of paint, thus reducing its effective gripping power.

To overcome this, the paint manufacturers have made the deck paint similar to antifouling in that it is a "wasting" paint. The skin of paint covering the top layer of non-skid grit quickly wears off and as the deck is subject to hard treatment and the grit is smoothed away or worn down, more comes to the surface as the paint surrounding it wastes away. In other words there is a constant wasting of the paint, bringing to the surface all the time the grit beneath and thus keeping the deck in a non-skid condition.

Many yachtsmen prefer to use a non-skid material such as sand or pumice grit, and sprinkle it on to ordinary paint, as was done in the olden days. There is nothing whatsoever wrong with this, and the result is often better

Strips of non-skid adhesive tape are ideal for use on such smooth surfaces as fibreglass

than the commercial product. There is, however, a slight lack in appearance unless the sand is either mixed with the paint or lightly painted over afterwards. It is very difficult to spread the sand evenly and the tendency is for it to be patchy unless treated in this way.

There are no hard and fast rules for deck paint and more or less any type can be used, provided it is non-skid. Naturally this is not as necessary on motor yachts and cruisers as on sail boats where frequent sail-changing entails the crew going forward and working on the fore deck, and also where the constant heel of the boat makes it difficult to gain a footing even at the best of times.

The non-skid paint can be applied to almost any surface, provided the proper preparation —as described in an earlier chapter—is carried out. The surface must be brought through the various stages of painting and sanding back to the undercoat stage before the deck paint can be applied. This work is done in a similar way to that used for any other part of the vessel's construction, although care must be taken when sanding back canvas decks or the weave of the material may be damaged. Canvas is a popular and effective medium for decks and is still widely used. It is painted in the same way as any other material with the added care mentioned here regarding damage to the weave of the material.

Once the final coat is in place, future painting can usually be done directly on to the old coat, providing it is given a light sanding down. The wasting process of the deck paint tends to reduce the build-up of coats, and burning off should not be necessary for some time.

Whether the paint used is manufactured as non-skid, or whether it is made up as described above, the essence of a clean, neat-looking deck is the evenness with which the non-skid particles are distributed. In the case of manufactured paint, this means constant stirring during painting; in the older method an efficient sugar shaker, a steady hand and a calm day is the answer.

CHAPTER SIXTEEN

Fitting Out

SIMPLE JOINERY

FITTING OUT THE INSIDE of a boat involves a considerable amount of carpentry work. Whether fitting simple cupboards or the more involved self-locking drawers and sliding chart tables, the handyman is confronted with difficult curves and shaping which do not usually occur when fitting out a house ashore.

As a result, more than just simple knowledge of tools is required, and, indeed, if a boat is to be really well fitted out, more than just simple carpentry. And since this volume is

Interior fittings can make or mar a vessel and yachts such as this can be as comfortable as a home when the fitting out is done wisely and well. Photo courtesy Power Boat & Yachting

intended to be a manual of repair and maintenance, it is beyond the scope of this text to deal with the complete fitting out of a vessel.

Sufficient at this stage to go briefly into aspects of elementary joinery and the way in which simple, but adequate fittings may be made. Armed with this knowledge the boat owner can, if he is so minded, follow up elsewhere the question of first class fitting out and apply it to his vessel.

The basic joints

The simplest form of joining two pieces of wood together is to nail, screw or glue them, one to the other. In the case of jointing, this means a simple butt joint in which the end of

one piece of timber is butted to the other to form a right angle.

The weaknesses in this form of jointing are obvious. Regardless of how well the joint is made, the stresses and strains which will fall upon it must eventually break the joint. Only if it were screwed, nailed and glued would it have any chance of standing up to hard wear and tear. Since joints in a vessel's construction or in her fittings are subject to the most violent, racking stresses when moving in a seaway, simple butt joints would last for only a very short time. Variations on the simple butt joint which offer greater strength are included later in this chapter.

There is an enormous number of joints, many designed for one special purpose. But in this section, only the basic methods will be described. With a little intelligent use, these can be adapted for most conditions, and a successful, if not high class, joint is the result.

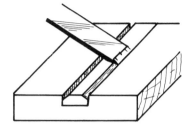

Chiseling sawing trench

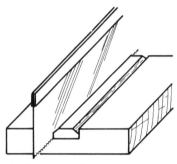

Sawing to required depth

Half lap joints

Widely used in all forms of joinery, the half lap joints are strong and easy to make. The basis of the joint is that half the thickness of one piece of timber is recessed into half the thickness on the other, thus making a successful joint from two halves while maintaining the original thickness of the whole.

Note the illustration. The procedure is as follows:

1. The pieces of timber to be lapped are carefully marked using a marking gauge where necessary to ensure correct alignment.

2. Along the face of the timber, the marking line is cut with a marking knife to lightly groove the timber.

3. Using a sharp chisel on the inside of the marking groove, a small "V" can be cut to the groove made with the marking knife. This leaves a neat "trench" in which the tenon saw can be started.

4. Using the saw square across the face of the timber, cut down the grooves to the marking line on the edge with the tenon saw.

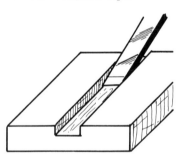

Chopping away waste with chisel (bevel down)

Cutting a housing for a lap joint

5. A sharp chisel should now be used to pare away the waste timber between the saw cuts, working on the basis (illustrated) of cutting towards the saw cuts on one side, then the other, then levelling the chisel to pare away the "hill" thus made.

6. Work down until the marks on the side are reached, and fair off the half lap thus cut. The accurate paring and sawing at this stage will decide the final accuracy and strength of the joint.

The Straight Half Lap

Closely resembling a scarf, this joint holds together the butt ends of two pieces of timber, making them virtually one long piece.

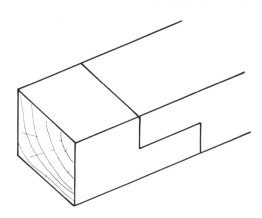

The Tee Half Lap

Again a common joint, this time for corners. Simpler than, but not as strong as, a dovetail joint, this provides the basic joint for gluing and screwing or dowelling.

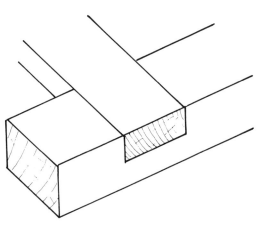

The Corner Half Lap

Commonly used in all types of joinery, this joint can be used for cupboards, drawer framework, etc.

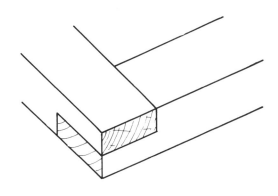

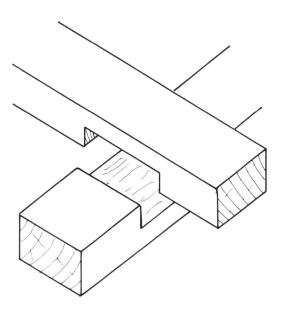

The Cross Half Lap

For strength in structural cross members this joint is ideal. Also used widely for construction of cupboards and other large interior fittings.

The Single Dovetail

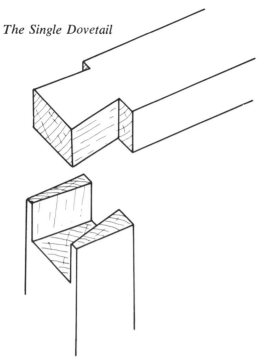

A more difficult but considerably stronger form of corner jointing. Where the edges are longer, double dovetails may be used. Drawers and strongly-constructed box formations may have many dovetails.

The Dovetail Tee Half Lap

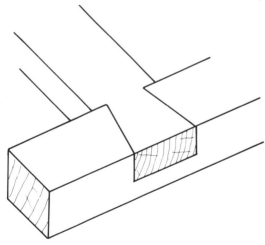

The wedge-action of the dovetail adds strength to the half lap. Used where strength is more important than appearance.

Mortice and Tenon Joint

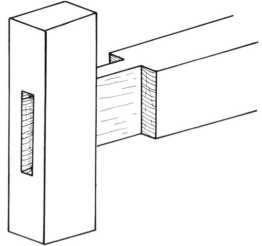

The strongest of all joints is the mortice and tenon where a large surface area suitable for gluing is combined with the interlocking of the pieces. However, this is a difficult joint to make and requires chisels of the correct size and good sharpness as well as a considerable amount of practice to ensure accurate cutting and thus accurate fitting.

In the common mortice and tenon joint, the tenon, at the end of the timber, fits into the centre of the other timber. A typical illustration is the centre rail of a chair.

The fitting of the tenon into the mortice is made approximately one third of the thickness of the wood. It may be wedged to ensure a snug fit after gluing. If the fit is too tight, the tenon should be pared rather than the inside of the mortice adjusted.

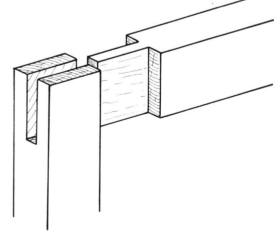

Open mortice and tenon, or bridle joint, is a corner joint, with the open mortice fitted over the tenon on the end of the other timber; a slightly easier joint than the common mortice and tenon, for all cutting may be done with a saw.

Although suitable for some purposes, as mentioned earlier, the butt joint is weak and will tend to distort under pressure. Gluing and screwing will improve the strength of the joint but since there are only two faces to glue, this is not a great improvement.

Mitre Joints

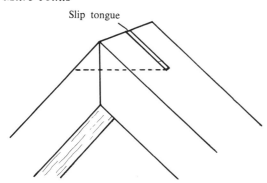

Slip tongue

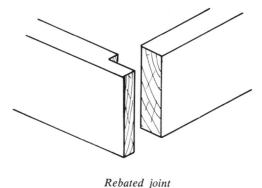

Rebated joint

A mitre joint is an angle joint whereby the end of each timber is cut to an angle half that of the finished angle of the joint. The two ends are then butted together and fastened and glued. The joint is weak owing to end grain gluing, and an inserted "feather" or "slip tongue" should be made to strengthen the joint.

The *Rebated Joint* is an improvement on the butt joint as it has more surfaces to which glue can be applied and can also be nailed from both sides. A rebate the full thickness of one member is made and the second member butted into it.

Box joints

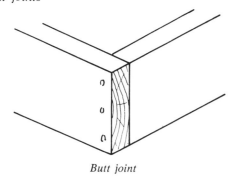

Butt joint

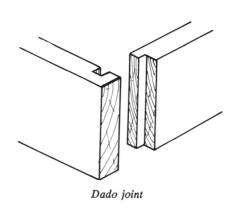

Dado joint

The simplest method of making a right-angled joint between two pieces of timber is the *Butt Joint,* where the butt of one piece is placed squarely on to the end of the other and then nailed or screwed.

The *Dado Joint* is the strongest of the box joints, as it is rebated to allow one member virtually to slip inside a trench on the other. It thus has more gluing and fastening surfaces. Its only weakness is in the short piece at the side of the trench, which, if short grained, may break away.

Fitting bulkheads

Bulkheads serve a twofold purpose in a boat; providing a strengthening piece to the hull, and dividing off compartments. Because of the former, bulkheads must be properly fitted and secured to the main body of the hull if they are to be effective, and only when their use is restricted to that of a partition are they made and fitted loosely.

The most useful timber for bulkheads is marine ply because of its ease of shaping and fitting, and also because of the strength imparted by the laminated construction. However, plywood in large sheets tends to buckle very easily and thus any bulkheads of size must have stiffeners attached to the ply when stresses and strains are encountered.

Before the bulkhead is shaped and cut, the area into which it is to be fitted should be examined and the location of all structural members noted. A structural member must *never* be cut to allow flush fitting of the bulkhead. Rather the bulkhead must be shaped to incorporate the structural member, or to go

Simple joinery is effective for most interior fitting work including galleys, cupboards and bulkheads

around it. Templates should be cut if a close fit is required.

A good base is necessary if the bulkhead is to give strength to the hull construction. It is not usually practicable to take the bulkhead down to the bilge, and a floor beam should be selected as the base. A fitting piece should be securely screwed to the beam to provide a stiffener on to which the bottom of the bulkhead can be fastened.

The best situation is where a frame runs up the side of the hull from the floor beam, so that the bulkhead can be made an integral part of the ship's construction. Similarly a deck beam, also adjacent to the location of the bulkhead, makes the fitting easy and very strong. Unfortunately, the position where the bulkhead is to be fitted is often between beams or frames, and in this case fitting pieces, or "dummy" frames and beams will need to be screwed to the side and deckhead of the hull respectively, to give a base to which the bulkhead can be fastened.

The stiffeners of the bulkhead should be of straight timber and at least three times the thickness of the bulkhead. Usually two stiffeners fitted vertically are sufficient, but if the

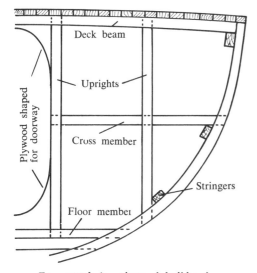

Framework for plywood bulkhead

bulkhead is wide, a horizontal stiffener may be necessary between the uprights. The stiffeners should be screwed to the bulkhead and the screws countersunk and stopped.

A doorway is usually required in full height bulkheads and in this case it should be cut between two of the upright stiffeners. Rounded edges to the doorway make for greater strength and less likelihood of splitting at the corners. A neat finish is obtained by running a light beading of silver ash or other attractive timber around the cut edges of the doorway. This may have to be steamed to be bent round the curves.

Needless to say, unless a double-skin bulkhead is fitted, all strengthening pieces and stiffeners should be kept on the side of the bulkhead that is not required to be part of an attractive decor.

Fitting an icebox

Many yachts and power craft have refrigerators fitted. Small units, designed to run on gas or low voltage electricity, are readily available on the market and are not over expensive.

However, often a refrigerator is either not suitable or not sufficient for a boat's needs. Most boat refrigerators are of necessity small

Icebox (left background) is a useful addition to a galley and is relatively easy to fit. Photo courtesy
Power Boat & Yachting

in capacity and only essential frozen food (and drink) is stored in them. Bulkier and less necessary items must either be stowed loose or placed in an insulated compartment such as an icebox.

An icebox can use up any spare space in the boat as, within reason, it can be fitted almost anywhere. Providing there is access to the top, an icebox is merely an insulated section of the ship's construction, and odd corners such as under bunks or cockpits are ideal.

The compartment should be made up, using a light marine plywood. It can be shaped

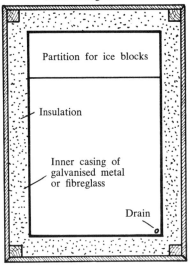

Plan view of an icebox

Whatever the insulating material, it should be shaped and glued or screwed into position so that the entire inside of the box contains a thick uniform layer of the insulation.

A drainage hole must be drilled at the bottom corner of the box, and this can be run off into a small plastic can or tank situated directly beneath it or—if circumstances permit—merely allowed to drip into the bilge. The latter is not the best system as there is a tendency for the water dripping from the icebox to contain small crumbs of food or other material which will rot in the bilge and make the atmosphere in the cabin very unpleasant. Preferably a small can or tank should be fitted, to be emptied when necessary.

The lid of the icebox should also be insulated, and should be made to form as tight a seal as possible. A rubber strip around the edge, such as described in the fitting of a hatch cover, is ideal, and the lid of the box can then be clamped down tight on the rubber to form a perfect seal.

To keep the food off the bottom of the icebox and allow free flow of the run-off water, a small grating should be fitted. This will also facilitate cleaning. Some people prefer to keep the ice in a separate compartment, in which case a similar wire grating can be used to one side and placed vertically. Failing this, the ice can be stowed with the contents of the icebox, providing they are wrapped in plastic or foil to prevent them becoming saturated as the ice melts.

Fitting a handrail

All too often a new boat lacks some of the useful or necessary fittings which only experience will reveal. Of these fittings, none is more common than the handrail. Many a boat owner has found, within a few weeks of taking delivery of his new boat, that a handrail is necessary at a certain point where there is nothing for a crew man to grip. Life rails around the outside of the boat offer some protection, but a means of gaining a firm grip

and screwed directly on to the structural members of the ship's construction, although where there are large gaps between members, stiffeners in the form of 2″ x 1″ timber must be run across the gap. In building the compartment, no special requirements are necessary, and parts of the ship's structure, such as the hull planking, can be used as one side of the icebox providing it is properly lined. The top must have a lid fitted with reasonably wide access so that large blocks of ice can be placed inside.

Once the compartment has been constructed, it must be insulated, and this can be done with one of a number of materials, ranging from the styrofoam-type products through fibreglass to any of the wood pulp boards such as Caneite. Providing it is a good insulating material there is no limit as to what may be used to line the sides of the icebox.

If one of the plastic styrofoam-type of products is used (and undoubtedly these are the most effective and the cheapest), there is little or no need to line the box again. If a soft, absorbent material such as cotton or cork is used, an inner lining in the form of a galvanised or stainless steel box must be provided as a receptacle for the ice and food containers.

Plan for handrails cut from one piece of timber

on the cabin top is essential when a boat is heeling hard.

Handrails are relatively easy to make and to fit. The simplest method is to cut out a rail shape with the bandsaw from a good thickness of timber; two-inch oregon is ideal. It should be shaped to follow the line of the cabin roof, for there is nothing worse than a boat with bits and pieces stuck all over it which do not blend in with the general appearance.

On power craft handrails are useful in many areas other than on the cabin roof; if the deck area alongside the deck house is narrow, a rail here and there adds to the security of the outside rails. Here again, the emphasis is on restrained, tasteful work which will blend with the shape of the cabin.

Once cut, the rails should be shaped with a plane and rounded off at the edges by sanding. They should then be drilled to take a reasonable sized bolt, and countersunk to a depth of at least quarter-inch. One drilling for each "leg" of the rail is ideal.

The rail on the cabin roof should be fas-

Simple but effective, these easily made handrails may well save a life

tened through a beam. This is often not possible, however, as the spacing of the beams would make the cutting and shaping of the handrail difficult. In this case, the bolts must be supported on the inside of the cabin by large washers, or even small chocks, if the roof is thin ply. Unless this is done, there will be a tendency for the bolts to pull through the roof when severe strain comes on to the rail.

When fastening through the side of the cabin, a stringer should be located, and the bolts drilled through this. However, if there is no suitable member at the required height, the procedure as described above must be carried out. Large washers, or a fitted chock must be placed under the nuts to take the strain.

The bolts should be coated in white lead or similar waterproofing to ensure that no trickling leaks result from piercing the cabin roof. The bolts should then be tightened up and the countersunk heads covered with a stopper, or dowel, if the rail is to be varnished.

Fitting a ventilator

Because of the great number of ventilators available and the various locations in which they may be fitted, the subject of fitting a ventilator is complex. Basically, the fitting of any type of ventilator boils down to a hole in

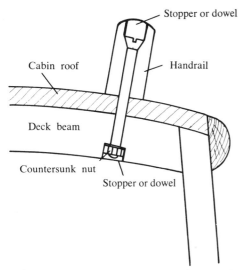

Cross section of handrail fastened through beam in cabin roof

255

the deck or cabin roof over which the patent ventilator must be fitted.

The hole can be cut with a keyhole saw after first drilling a "starting" hole with a large drill. It should be big enough to allow a good flow of air, but not so big that it extends to the limit of the ventilator itself. When fitted, the ventilator should more than cover the hole.

Mushroom, oyster shell, cowl or vortex ventilators are among the most popular. They all have the basic feature that they permit air to flow into the boat, but not water. This, of course, only applies to light water such as rain and spray, and there are few ventilators which are designed to be kept open when the boat is ploughing through heavy seas. Most ventilators close, or can be screwed down when putting to sea, and the object in having them on board is principally to ventilate the vessel while she is on the mooring and unattended.

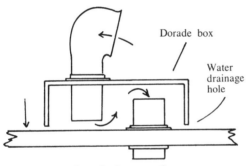

Dorade box ventilator

However, in the case of ocean racing yachts, or other boats intending to go to sea, some form of ventilation is necessary regardless of wind and sea. The most common of these is the cowl vent, which can be rotated into or away from the wind and which contains a water trap so that any water finding its way down the cowl can be immediately rejected back on to the deck.

The most suitable type of ventilator is called a dorade, and may have either a cowl or venturi type fitting. The air enters the cowl which is placed in a specially arranged structure, either as an integral part of the boat's con-

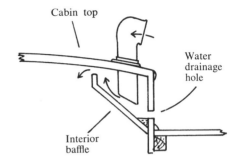

Dorade ventilator incorporated in cabin roof

struction — usually the cabin — or simply fastened to the deck in the form of a box. This box has an arrangement inside it in the form of a baffle which traps the water but allows the air to flow over the baffle and down into the accommodation. The water trapped by the baffle runs back out on deck through release holes in the end of the box. Short of filling up the entire box with water, it is impossible for anything but air to enter the cabin below.

A dorade box is simple enough to make and fit, and is adequate for all vessels, whether sail or power. To eliminate the need for the box-like structure on the deck, some patent cowls have inbuilt water traps, and can be mounted straight on to the deck. Because of the interior arrangement of the water traps, however, these vents are usually fairly large, and suitable only for larger craft.

With a little imagination, the dorade arrangement can be incorporated into the general construction of the cabin, thus avoiding the cumbersome arrangement of the box. An example is illustrated. In this case the cowl has been let into the cabin roof, and the dorade arrangement fitted on the inside. The baffle is on the inside of the cabin and angled to allow the run-off of water through a hole in the

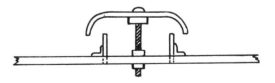

Mushroom ventilator

cabin side. If necessary, a valve may have to be fitted at this point to prevent the possibility of water flooding into the dorade arrangement through this release hole.

Mounting an outboard engine

The advent of the outboard motor hailed a revolution in the powering of small craft. Although designed primarily for use on the transom of small open boats, the outboard engine has proved itself the most versatile and useful form of marine power for a variety of craft far removed from the original concept.

Particularly is this the case with small yachts where the question of weight and space eliminate the use of conventional marine engines. The outboard—albeit only a modest auxiliary —was found to fill a long-felt need in providing small yachts with motive power, particularly since it could be easily removed when sailing, thus reducing the propeller drag so annoying with conventional marine engines.

From small yachts the popularity of the outboard spread to all shapes and sizes of craft, until nowadays it is no longer considered odd to see small outboard motors mounted on the strangest forms of craft from dugout canoes to floating caravans.

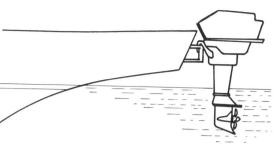

Outboard mounted on a stern bracket

Add to this versatility the fact that the engine can be taken off and run up to a workshop for repair instead of the arduous—and costly—business of towing the whole boat to the workshop or—equally costly—having an engineer brought out to repair the engine *in situ*. And the fact that the outboard can be switched from vessel to vessel—dinghy to yacht tender to yacht itself—and the popularity of this form of power is no longer hard to understand.

Since most outboards are designed to fit on to a transom by means of two or more clamps, adapting them for other shapes and sizes of craft involves some modification of the mounting system. This is never a very difficult problem and can be quickly overcome by most handymen.

Generally speaking, if the outboard cannot be clamped directly to the vessel, a bracket must be made and attached to the boat so that it presents a substitute "transom" to which the outboard can be clamped. Using the imagination is the best way of resolving each case, but any simple bracket strong enough to hold the engine will suffice.

In the case of yachts or power vessels where the outboard is to be used as an auxiliary mounted on the stern, a small plate, or timber baulk, suitable for mounting and clamping the engine, can be bolted through the vessel's stern planking on galvanised iron or stainless steel brackets. It is important to ensure that when the engine is in place on the bracket it is sufficiently deep in the water to give the propeller a good "bite". If mounted

Simple brackets allow the mounting of outboard engines anywhere they may be required

257

too high (apart from losing power) the cavitation of the propeller may upset the water intake system and the engine will overheat.

Some smaller yachts prefer to mount the engine through the bottom of the boat. This is a very efficient method, but requires care in preparation. In the case of moulded fibreglass a separately moulded "well" is inserted into the bottom of the cockpit and bonded to the cockpit floor and the hull of the boat. Providing adequate strengthening is maintained, this forms a very suitable mounting for the engine.

With timber, particularly plywood vessels, some difficulty is encountered since the "well" system, if mounted centrally, involves cutting through the keel—a most inadvisable procedure. In this case, a box-type well can be made up and let into the ship's hull offset to one side of the keel, and strengthened to prevent any weakness in the hull structure.

By and large, however, the "well" system is not as suitable as the bracket on the transom, as it involves the unpleasant process of cutting a hole in the boat's hull. Providing it is adequately and correctly fitted, an outboard mounted on a stern bracket is quite suitable for the auxiliary purpose for which it is intended.

Fitting ballast

Ballast can be added to a vessel either by placing it inside, in the bilges, or by bolting it on externally to the keel. In the former case, the ballast is simply placed in the required

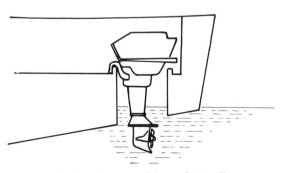

Outboard mounted in cockpit-well

position and secured against movement, either by screwing it down under battens, or laying it in box-like compartments screwed or bolted to the keel or the hull frames.

With external ballast, the only method is by through bolting, and the location and method used will depend on the shape of the underwater area of the vessel. Shallow-keeled boats, such as power craft, can carry the ballast on either side of the keel, although in these vessels it is usually preferable to have the ballast inside the hull. Yachts may carry the ballast either bolted to the keel on either side, or as a built-on section of the bottom of the keel.

Lead ballast is undoubtedly the best, but other materials such as cast iron, mild steel, or concrete are often used. These materials must be treated against rust and corrosion whether stowed inside or outside the hull, and a good anti-corrosive, followed by primer coats, is the most effective. This should also be applied to iron bolts used for securing the ballast, and further care must be taken to ensure that the bolts are watertight and do not allow seepage into the hull. White lead in the bolt holes, and leather or cotton grommets beneath the washers should take care of this.

It is obviously necessary to secure any external ballast through a main structural member in order to distribute the weight throughout the boat and not place any undue strain on any section of planking, and for this reason external ballast is invariably bolted to the keel.

Fitting a self-draining cockpit

A self-draining cockpit has several uses, the most obvious of which is to drain out seawater which may come aboard in heavy seas. Another use is to run off rainwater or condensation which may fall in the cockpit and which, if not removed quickly, will provide a breeding ground for dry rot.

All vessels, whether power or sail, find a self-draining cockpit handy, particularly if they are liable to encounter heavy weather at sea. Very little is involved in the fitting of this type

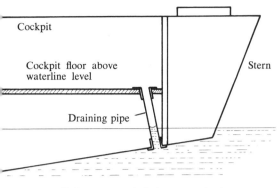

Cockpit

Cockpit floor above
waterline level

Stern

Draining pipe

Self-draining cockpit (cross section)

of freeing cockpit and it is surprising that it is not a standard fitting on all ocean-going boats.

The only limitation to fitting a self-draining cockpit is the height of the cockpit deck above the waterline. If it is more than a few inches above the waterline, the fitting is easy. If it is below or close to the waterline, the deck will have to be raised before self-draining can be fitted. Since the self-draining works on the principle of gravity, a self-draining cockpit below the waterline will be unable to spill water upwards, and in fact will have the reverse—and drastic—effect; the cockpit will fill.

Most self-draining arrangements consist of one or two drainage holes at the lower end of the cockpit which run directly out through the bottom of the boat. A drainage hole of about two inches diameter is all that is necessary unless the boat is liable to have a lot of water in the cockpit, in which case a larger hole is required.

The vessel will have to be slipped so that the holes can be bored in the bottom and skin fittings attached to the hull and to the cockpit deck. Inside the boat, between cockpit and hull, a tight fitting hose connects the upper and lower fittings. The hose may be of any material—plastic is ideal—and should be secured firmly around the skin fittings with stainless screw collars.

A wise precaution is to attach a stopcock to the lower skin fitting before attaching the hose, as this allows the skin fitting to be sealed off in the event of the hose bursting or work-

ing loose from the fitting. Few boats have such stopcocks on their self-draining equipment, but a few minutes' thought about what would happen if a hose came loose, leaving the underwater skin fitting open to the inside of the hull should convince any sceptic. All skin fittings in a boat should be fitted with a stopcock.

There are several variations on the way in which self-draining gear can be fitted. Some people prefer only one drainage hole; others drain both holes through the one hull fitting by joining the pipes beneath the cockpit deck. These are all suitable ideas, and providing the basic principle described above is followed, adaptations are permissible.

If the cockpit floor is near or below the waterline, the deck section will have to be raised before the self-draining can be fitted. The procedure will depend on the individual case, but should not be a very difficult process

Cockpits remain clean and dry when fitted with self-draining equipment. Photo courtesy Power Boat & Yachting

and providing the finished deck is watertight and above water level, the normal process for fitting the self-drainer should be followed.

Self-locking drawers

One of the most essential parts of a boat's joinery work is ensuring that the doors and drawers do not fly open or slide around when the boat is rolling in a seaway. Nothing is more frustrating than to spend all day picking up the spilled—and broken—contents of drawers that have flown loose with the motion of the boat.

There are several simple remedies, most of which involve the use of hooks or bolts and catches, and any handyman can fit these. But they do not always look the best; a cabin cluttered with hooks and gadgets is not going to please any eye. Also human nature is fallible, and someone some day (perhaps a lot of people on a lot of days) will forget to put the hook on or draw the catch, and the result will be disastrous.

The most efficient and safest way, and one which cannot offend the eye, is the self-locking drawer. This to outward appearance is an ordinary drawer which by some magic does not fly out when the boat heels. The magic lies in a small recess in the bottom of the drawer immediately behind the front face. When the drawer is pushed home this recess lets the drawer drop down over the bottom sill and lock into position.

To open the drawer it has merely to be lifted as it is pulled, so that the recess is lifted up over the sill, and the drawer can slide out normally.

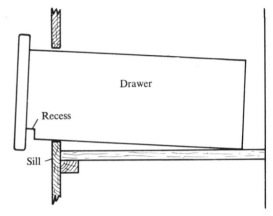

Self-locking drawer

CHAPTER SEVENTEEN

General Repair Work

Repairs to carvel planking

CARVEL PLANKING is more difficult to repair or replace than clinker, mainly because of the necessity to ensure a good fit between old and new planks. A damaged plank, or section of a plank is relatively easy to take off, as the fastenings need only to be removed from the frames and the butts, and the plank will come out. When cutting out a new section, however, it should be cut cleanly vertical, and no attempt should be made to scarf it, even if the planks of the original construction are scarfed together.

If the fastenings are screws, they should be easy to remove, although there is a tendency for brass screws to become brittle and snap off at the head, particularly if they are beneath the waterline. Copper rivets will need to have their heads cut off before they can be drawn, whereas clinched nails can usually be prised

Extensive repair of carvel planking is a shipwrights job if the new seams are to be fitted flush and watertight

open quite easily. The same holes can be used in the timbers to refasten the new section of plank, but a slightly larger fastening will be required to take up the slackness in the hole.

If the damage is considerable and several planks have to be removed, the new butts must be staggered well away from each other or there will be a weakness. Adjacent strakes should be butted at least two frame spaces apart, and the old timber cut out so that the butts are between frames, never on them. A pattern arrangement such as illustrated can be developed so that the butts are staggered and well away from each other in each successive strake.

New planks or sections of planks must be very carefully shaped to fit tightly together and between the old planking. It is possible that, particularly with small sections, the curve in the hull will be difficult to follow, and steaming or clamping might be necessary to get the plank to fit. Because of this difficulty, a section to

be renewed should be no less than about three frames in length, and where the timbers are well spaced, intermediate frames may be inserted to help fasten the new plank section into the right shape. This will be a case of trial and error.

The new planks must be grooved at the edges and at the butt ends so that when in position, they have a "V" shaped groove between them for caulking. The size of this groove will depend on the thickness of the planks, but a maximum of quarter-inch is a good size for a caulking groove in any hull. Butt blocks should be placed behind each butt and these should overlap adjoining strakes by about half the width of the plank. It is better to screw butt joints than clinch nail them.

A description of caulking is given elsewhere in this section, but it is worth mentioning that in the event of difficulty with the exact fitting of the planks, and a rather large caulking gap resulting, a batten should be secured behind such a gap in order to prevent the caulking from being driven right through; also, this will prevent a leak if the caulking is poorly finished.

Refastening the planks to the timbers can be done by means of screws or roved copper nails; the latter are better. As mentioned before, if the old holes in the timber are to be used, a slightly larger fastening than the old will be needed.

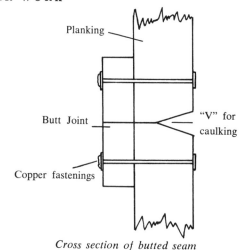

Cross section of butted seam

Repairs to clinker planking

Clinker planking is very popular for smaller boats. Although it is fairly liable to damage because the overlaps stick out from the hull, it requires no caulking and is therefore more durable than carvel planking. However, it is liable to movement and is also fairly vulnerable to strain, causing leaks at the joins, due either to excessive strain during use, a heavy bump, or shrinkage or warping of the timber.

It is particularly popular in small dinghies and skiffs, and yachts up to thirty feet are sometimes clinker planked. It gives additional longitudinal strength to the boat, as well as avoiding the problem of leaky seams and re-caulking jobs during maintenance. However, it is becoming less popular as the years go by,

Staggering butt ends in planking repair

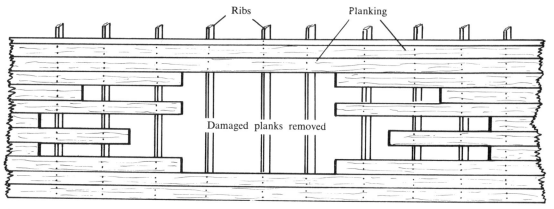

particularly with the advent of moulded craft, possibly because of more difficult maintenance.

Although basically sounder than carvel planking, clinker is more difficult to repair. If any damage occurs it is usually in the vicinity of the overlap and since it cannot be simply re-caulked, as with carvel, the section of the plank, sometimes the whole plank, must be removed and replaced. Again a difficulty arises when a plank has to be removed for repair or replacement, and that is the problem of removing it without inflicting further damage or unsettling the planks around it.

If a plank has to be removed, it must first have all its fastenings drawn. This is achieved by nipping off the riveted or clinched ends of the copper nails with pincers and driving them out with a small punch. In order not to enlarge the hole, the punch should only be used to drive the nail head clear of the timber, and then the pincers brought in to finish the job, using a small piece of wood as a fulcrum.

The fastenings both in the planking and the timbers (ribs) will have to be removed and although it is best to nip off the roved end— since it protrudes above the timber more than the head—if this is in a difficult position the head can be nipped off and the fastening driven back the opposite way. Clinched nails may need to be prised up before the pincers can gain a firm grip.

If the section to be removed is fastened with screws (as is often the case near bow and stern) then the screws must be removed after the roved nails have been cut and punched out. Needless to say, some vessels will have fastenings in a place of difficult access, but unless the plank to be removed is a complete write-off and can be torn out, then the effort to remove the fastenings carefully must be made, however difficult the location.

One of the great advantages of removing the old timber without breaking it up is its use as a pattern in cutting a replacement timber. Often clinker timbers are of a difficult shape, and must be very carefully cut if they are to take the curve of the hull and still make

a good land (overlap) on adjoining planks. By clamping the old plank to the new with G clamps, an exact replacement can be marked and cut, thus ensuring a good watertight fit.

When the plank has been cut and the ends shaped to fit the rebate in the stem or stern, it may have to be steamed in order to bend it sufficiently to fit the hull. A description of steaming a plank is given in this section.

Apart from its attractive appearance, clinker planking adds strength to the boat's construction

The bent plank, whether steamed or not, can be very easily fitted into position. Providing it has been correctly shaped, it should slip under the plank above it and stay in place without any trouble. If this proves too difficult, G clamps will have to be used to hold it in position until the fastenings are secured.

With the plank in position, new fastening holes can be drilled through the new plank by using the old holes in adjacent planks as a guide. The holes should be as small as possible to take the fastening, and care taken not to enlarge the old holes or leaking will occur. If the old holes have been enlarged during removal of the old fastenings it is safer to plug them (see later this section) and drill new holes for the new fastenings. Loose fastenings

263

make for leaks and are very difficult not only to cure, but also to find.

Drilling too many new holes can, of course, weaken the timber, and thus the old holes should be used as much as possible. A larger size fastening will help to avoid looseness, and a liberal amount of glue or loose putty between the planks will help to reduce the chances of leaking. The new fastenings should be drawn up tight and the glue compressed into position and squeezed into the fastening holes. The shape, size, and composition of fastenings is described in Section I.

Fixing leaks in clinker planking

As mentioned earlier, there are several causes of leaking through clinker planking. In the normal course of events straining, working or loose fastenings can cause leaking. Grounding and collision damage can cause severe leaking even if the timbers are not badly damaged. If the leaking is severe along the length of the plank it will have to be removed and replaced or refastened as described earlier. If the leaking is restricted to a few isolated spots, it can often be cured by tightening up the existing fastenings, or putting in a few new ones, strategically spaced to cover the leaking area.

If the leak is severe, but the timber is sound and does not justify replacement, the trouble can be cured by sealing the clinker join. Almost invariably the timber has warped or some form of grit has worked between the planks and even new fastenings cannot draw the planks up tight. Therefore the join must be sealed by securing a fillet of timber below the plank concerned.

The fillet must be carefully cut to shape and bent around the planks concerned. It should be fitted carefully and marked for drilling and then taken away and drilled. At this point the planks of the hull where the fillet is to be fitted must be scraped off and cleaned down to bare timber, to allow the use of a marine glue. The fillet is replaced and the drilled holes drilled out again so that screws can be driven up into the overlapping plank.

With a good bedding of marine glue, and a sound fastening screwed upwards into this plank, the overlap should be well sealed.

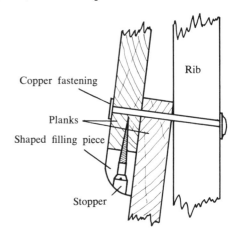

Securing a fillet on a clinker land

Cracks in clinker planking are more common than with carvel owing to the method and frequency of fastening. Longitudinal cracks between nails and fastenings are a great source of trouble and invariably leak when below the water level. Puttying will often prove effective with these cracks, providing a hole is drilled at the end of the crack to prevent it splitting further, and the correct type of putty is used. An elastic type of putty, of which there are many brands, is best suited to this purpose. Epoxy putties are also good, although for these the timber must be bone dry or the resin will not take.

Fibreglass can be used if the crack is sufficiently large, although this can give rise to problems unless the timber is extremely well dried (see section on patching with fibreglass).

Copper tingles can be used to patch leaks in clinker planking, but owing to the irregular surface of the clinker, they are not over successful.

Plugging holes in timber hulls

Holes in timber hulls occur frequently for a variety of reasons, ranging from a loose fastening which has to be removed, through gaping holes caused by grounding on rocks, to the aperture left by removing an exhaust outlet or similar skin fitting. In all cases the result is the same, albeit in varying degrees: a hole in the hull—often below the waterline—which will cause the boat to take water unless plugged.

If the hole is very large, as in the case of grounding, major repairs will be necessary and these are dealt with elsewhere in this section. if the hole is relatively small, however, several different methods can be employed to plug it satisfactorily.

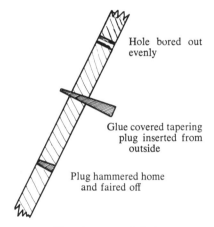

Hole bored out evenly

Glue covered tapering plug inserted from outside

Plug hammered home and faired off

Plugging a small hole

A small hole, such as is caused by losing a fastening, can be easily plugged by shaping a small piece of timber to fit. The timber should be in the form of a cone, with the point small enough to fit into the hole. The cone can then be driven home from *outside* the hull until it is securely jammed into position, when it is sawn off flush with the hull. A touch of marine glue around the cone will give added grip.

Larger holes can be dealt with in much the same way. A hole caused by removal of an exhaust outlet, for example, only requires a larger plug than the fastening hole. However, if the plug is of considerable diameter, it is wise to ensure that it does not work loose by covering it with a copper patch or similar medium and not rely entirely on the marine

Seepage such as this is often caused by small holes which can be easily plugged and sealed

glue to hold it in position. The patch should always be on the outside of the hull.

Repairs to double planking

There are different ways of laying up double planking. The most common is known as *double diagonal,* mostly found in motor cruisers. It is very effective, although it gives rise to problems when repair work is involved. Double diagonal planking consists of two layers of planking laid, as the name denotes, diagonally across one another, with a layer of waterproof fabric between.

The difficulty in repair work arises when both the skins are damaged, or when the inner skin has to be repaired. The outer skin is relatively easy to repair, providing the damage is superficial. It can be stripped off to remove damaged areas by taking out the copper fastenings which are invariably used, and removing the planking carefully so as not to disturb the layer of fabric between the skins.

If the nails are roved, they will have to be removed by cutting, as drawing them with pincers will damage the inner skin and waterproof fabric. The roves should be sheared off with a hacksaw and the nails drawn from the outside. If the nails are clinched they should be easy to remove.

New planks can then be placed into position, after first coating the exposed fabric with white lead, glue or a thick paint. The nails can be

265

replaced in the same holes, remembering that if this is done a larger-size fastening must be used.

If the inner skin is damaged, either by rot or some internal damage, or both skins are damaged as a result of collision, the repair becomes more difficult. Even a small section of damage to the inner skin will result—because of the diagonal nature of the planking—in removal of a larger area of outer planking. This can be done by the amateur, but it is an extensive and difficult job, often involving the use of steamed planks, and should be turned over to a professional if a first-class job is required.

If the damage is through both skins and not too severe, it can often be patched up in the way described for plywood; i.e., hammering the skins back into position and securing by means of a third skin laid inside the hull for strength. The damage to the individual planks can then be repaired by gluing in fitted pieces

Double diagonal planking may be used for yacht construction where lightness of weight and good strength are required

of timber or, if small, by plugging with a filler, then sanding the whole back, flush with the original skin.

Since double diagonal planking is a very strong form of hull construction, there are usually far fewer frames and other structural members than with normal planking. Most structural members are sawn, rather than shaped, and this in itself makes for easier repair work, for a member can be readily removed and replaced after the repair has been effected.

Repairs to Plywood

Plywood tends to be more difficult to repair than normal planking, particularly over a large surface such as the hull of a boat, where the plywood is fastened only on the edges and the frames. When a repair has to be made, and a piece of planking replaced, the chances are that there will be no frame behind it to which it can be fastened, or if there is a frame or other structural member, it is the only one in the area. As a result, most repairs to plywood require stiffening pieces to counter the lack of structural members.

In addition, the large sheets of plywood used in boat construction can rarely be removed and replaced as a whole, unless the extent of the damage warrants such expense. More often a small piece must be taken out and replaced with a similar section from a sheet of plywood of the same thickness. Fitting the new section in so that it lies flush with the surrounding area and is sufficiently strong to withstand the stresses which may come upon it, makes this a difficult task and one which requires considerable care in the execution.

Plywood is very resilient, and if the damage is slight and the surface of the timber dented rather than holed, it is often possible to repair the damage by carefully hammering out the dent, in much the same way as for metal, until it is almost flush with the surrounding surface. A backing piece screwed on the inside of the hull will provide necessary strength. The splintering of the veneer which will have occurred as a result of the damage, must be sanded off to give a smooth surface, and any cavities thus left may be filled with putty or epoxy filler and sanded down to match the surrounding area. If the plywood is broken right through its thickness, this method is not satisfactory, as leaks may occur after the repair. However, by using marine glues and putties slight damage can be repaired quite effectively in this way without impairing the strength or the water-tightness of the original plywood.

To repair a hole in plywood the hole must first be cut out to a regular—preferably rec-tangular—shape. This can be done with a straightforward cut, but if possible the cut should be made with angled edges, with the greater circumference on the outside. When a new piece is fitted, this angling gives greater strength to resist outside pressure, and also provides the greatest surface area for glue used in the repair. Needless to say more care will be required in the cutting and shaping of the fitted piece when the edges are recessed in this way. However, since the finished job will be far superior to a straight-cut fitting, this method should be adopted where possible, particularly on a hull where the strains are almost all from the outside.

A strengthening piece of the same thickness material, cut to a size larger than the hole, should then be glued and screwed into position on the inside of the hull covering the hole itself. The strengthening piece may have to be shaped or cut to fit around any members in the vicinity. The fitting piece can then be placed in position, the edges of both the original hull timber and the new piece having been glued. Screws are the most suitable fastenings, and the newly-fitted piece should be screwed through to any members behind it, or to the strengthening piece mentioned earlier.

Once screwed and glued into position the repair can be finished off by filling any joints with putty or epoxy filler, and sanding back to match the surrounding surface. Properly

Large areas of plywood are more easily repaired than small sections due to the number of beams or frames available for fastening

finished, a patch of this type should not be visible under a coat of paint.

Scarfing a join in plywood

Scarfing a join in plywood is a job best handed to a carpenter, as it stretches the limits of the amateur, particularly if the timber is later to come under strain or is to be immersed in water. However, if it must be undertaken, the scarf joint must be very carefully pre-pared and laid up.

When cutting the angle for the scarf joint, the slope of the edges should not be less than the following: For sheets less than half-inch thick, 1 in 10; sheets over half-inch, 1 in 8.

Repairing a hole in plywood

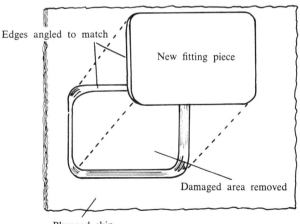

Edges angled to match

New fitting piece

Damaged area removed

Plywood skin

If the angle is any less than these recommendations the joint will be weak and possibly give under pressure, particularly if it is part of a curved section.

The sheets of plywood to be scarfed should be of uniform thickness and finished to a smooth surface. The edges must be cut square and smoothed off so that they are clean and free from uneven patches. A marine glue similar to the type used for the original bonding of the plywood should be used if possible. Failing this a first-class marine glue must be employed, and a check made to see that it is suitable for conditions the scarf joint is to be subjected to at a later date.

After gluing, the scarf joint should be clamped up tight and laid on a level surface so that it can bond firmly and not be subject to bending stresses which may cause uneven setting of the two surfaces.

Deterioration of plywood surfaces

The deterioration of top veneers of plywood can be caused by several factors. Wet rot and dry rot both cause definite deterioration of the veneers, often penetrating well below the surface. When this occurs replacement of the section, or even the whole area, may be necessary as patching will not prevent the spread of the rot.

Deterioration of the glues, or the use of improperly seasoned timber can also cause separation of the layers. This is particularly the case when the plywood is not made for marine use. The glues used for normal plywood differ from those used in marine plywood by virtue of their waterproof qualities. Without this type of glue the plywood veneers separate and buckle when in contact with water, and here again the only cure is replacement by new marine plywood.

Probably the most common of other factors is weathering. Very hot sun can cause expansion and contraction of plywood decks to the extent that the glue will begin to lose its bonding power and buckles will occur. Constant use in all kinds of weather can cause deterioration of a few fibres in an otherwise sound top veneer. With continued use, the damage spreads, and the deck can become pockmarked as small sections of veneer flake away.

Always the best cure for damaged plywood is replacement, as its construction does not favour a great deal of rubbing down and building up with fillers and putties. However, where only a small area is affected on a fairly heavy piece of plywood, such as a deck, temporary repairs can be made by sanding back the paint and the loose fibres until the plywood has been scoured down to a new surface (not necessarily down to the next veneer). By using the correct primers, undercoats and paints, it can then be built up again, with the paint forming a new bonding surface to hold the veneer together.

Very often neglected paint can cause damage to top veneers of plywood, and attention to the painted surface can extend its life.

Separating of the veneers causes plywood to become fragile and break up

Because of its ease of use, plywood is widely used in the construction of small, home-built craft

The edges of plywood are particularly vulnerable to damage and, again because of the nature of plywood, can rarely be treated successfully other than by planing back to firm timber. This, of course, reduces the size of the timber and is not always a good solution.

Once the edges have deteriorated they cannot be built up again, and the only alternative to sanding or planing back is the replacement of the entire area. Once again, correct attention when building, and subsequent maintenance is the best preventative of the problem.

If the damage is a dent, or hole, or other damage not affecting the veneer as a layer, its treatment is similar to that described for repairs to plywood in the previous paragraphs.

Repairs to chines

Because of its location, forming a "corner" in the section of the hull, the chine is somewhat vulnerable to damage. Grounding, bumping alongside a wharf, collision or incorrect slipping can cause damage to the chine. Often the edge of the planking is unprotected and this can be easily splintered, particularly in the case of plywood. Leaky chines are not uncommon since the chine itself is a structural member of the boat and is therefore liable to work under the stresses and strains of a seaway.

The edges of the planking should always be covered by a strip of timber or some form of "rubbing strake", to protect the vulnerable areas, particularly if they are formed from light veneers as in the case of plywood. Superficial damage to the edge of the planking should be planed or sanded back and the rubbing strake fitted to a good bed of marine glue and screwed into place. The shape of the strake is not important, although it should suit the appearance of the boat, and not produce any drag.

Fast motor launches often use this covering strip to form a "spray rail" which at speed lifts the bow up out of the water. When this is the case a strong piece of timber will be necessary, and secure fastenings used to ensure that it can withstand the impact of hitting a wave at speed. In the case of very large or very high speed launches, some strengthening of the hull will be necessary to distribute the strain coming on the spray rails throughout the boat or the chine will be torn open when the boat crashes down on a big sea.

A leaking chine can often be fixed by this method, the glue and the covering strake providing a watertight seal at the turn of the chine. If the leak is not in the join of the planks at the chine itself, other methods may have to be adopted. Leaking fastenings should be tightened or replaced or joins or cracks caulked. If the leaking is general, copper tingles or a copper strip set in putty or composite will often be effective.

Weakness in the chine itself, giving rise to working, and subsequent leaking, is usually the result of bad workmanship in the building of the boat or the result of overall strains from collision or damage on a heavy sea. To strengthen the chine, new gussets should be fitted, either over the top of the old gussets or in place of them. The gussets should be sawn from thick plywood and shaped to fit the frames at the turn of the chine. They should be fastened by screwing into place, on top of a coating of good marine glue.

Since chine gussets are strengthening pieces at a corner section of the hull, they are similar in construction to beam knees and provide much the same sort of strengthening.

Fast speed boats made from plywood are very vulnerable to damage on chines and other corners. Note protective beading on this boat

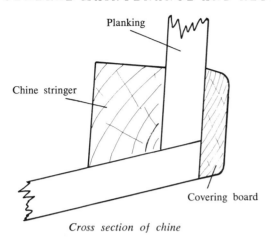

Cross section of chine

Making a butt joint in planking

Carvel planking is laid up on frames with a butt join to run one plank into another. This method of joining planks is also used in other parts of a boat's construction, particularly where a sound, smooth finish is required.

Making a butt joint can be carried out in one of two ways. In both cases the planking is fitted together, glued and fastened, and then covered with a strengthening piece on the inside. In one method careful positioning of the butts allows the frames to be used as the backing piece, as illustrated.

In the first method, the butt joint is made at any point along the planking and not necessarily on a frame. The two planks are scarfed together with a scarf join that has a length between plank ends of not less than four times the thickness of the planking. In some cases a straight butt end joint is made, but unless

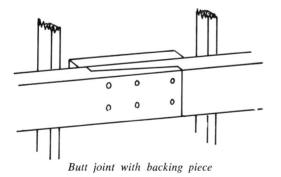

Butt joint with backing piece

this is carefully carried out and strengthened, a weakness can occur. Scarfing the planks makes for a more secure job.

A butt strap is then placed in the inside of the hull to cover the join. This is fastened through the two planks and also through the strake above and below the join.

The second method of making a butt joint is by the use again of the scarf join, but this time in such a position that a frame lies directly behind the join, and the scarf can be through fastened to this frame. Glues are necessary, as with any scarf join, and the through fastening to the frame pulls the butt join up tight and secures it to the main structural part of the vessel, thus eliminating any possibility of a weakness at the join.

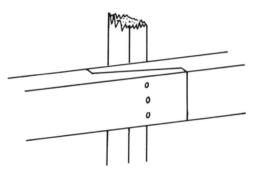

Butt joint on frame

Butts must be well spaced and staggered from strake to strake in order not to create a line of weakness. Where more than one butt join is being made or repaired, other joins should not come within five feet of the first on any adjacent strake. Similarly, no butt should be in a vertical line with another unless at least three unbroken strakes separate them.

Patching up planking and stopping leaks

Patches are never really satisfactory on hull planking, unless the damage is very light. In the case of rotted or split areas, a patch will only cover up damage temporarily: the trouble will continue, spreading underneath the patch. Some areas may be small enough to chisel out and plug with a dowel or similar peg, and some may get by with a "tingle". But such repairs can only be used on very small leaks or damaged spots.

Where the damage is slightly more but still does not justify removal and replacement of the plank, the surface damage or rot can be chiselled out to a depth of about two-thirds of the thickness of the planking and a small "plate" of fine-grained wood tacked into the recess, with a good marine glue to hold it in place. This can only be done where the hull is constructed of fairly heavy timber.

Putty or epoxy fillers can be used for scratches or small holes, and this is often the most effective, for in addition to filling the holes they also are sufficiently pliable to fill awkward angles which cannot be reached from the outside. The surface should be sanded off when hard and painted over with undercoat and two top coats.

Leaking between seams or through cracks or small holes is always a problem, and depends principally on the location of the trouble as to the method used to cure it. Patching with fibreglass is effective if the timber can be dried out sufficiently, and this is described elsewhere. Thick tar compositions are also effective and can be squeezed in directly from the tube although many of these tend to wash out gradually if they are left open to the underwater wash. Used beneath a tingle they are effective, and this also applies to the looser caulking putties.

Other hull leaks may come from loose fastenings, which will entail refastening or tightening of the existing fastenings, or splits in the timber caused by working or badly driven fastenings. Here again the tingle or epoxy filler is the best solution.

The tingle

This is perhaps one of the oldest and most traditional repair jobs handed down through the years. It is still very effective, although does not look the best, and can be easily damaged by a boat coming alongside a wharf.

Neglecting a boat invites all kinds of repair problems. Regular maintenance is the only way to avoid unnecessary work and expense

The tingle comprises a copper patch beneath which canvas and glues or tars provide the waterproofing.

The surface surrounding the damaged area should be roughed with sandpaper and thickly coated with glue, paint or tar composite. A patch of sail canvas is then tacked tightly over the area, using copper tacks to hold it in place. A sheet of thin copper must then be prepared to cover the entire patch, with the edges of the copper turned under to form a "hem", and starting holes punched at close intervals through this hem.

The patch is coated again with glue or paint and the copper placed over it. If the area to be patched is large, the patch should be tacked in place with one or two nails through the centre, and the copper then nailed through the edge, starting at one side and working slowly around the edge, beating it into shape with a hammer before securing it with copper nails. In this way the patch can be made to fit flush over the entire area and be almost invisible when painted over.

The nails should be long enough to be driven well into the timber planking but not through

271

it, and where a sharp curve has to be taken, the copper may have to be annealed by heating it to red heat and plunging it into cold water. If canvas shows around the edges of the copper, it can be cut away with a sharp knife.

Caulking

Most leaks in the hull come from poorly caulked seams. Caulking deteriorates with age, and any working of the ship's structural members or planking, can cause the caulking to be gradually worked out of the seam or at least worked loose, and thus allow the water to seep in. There is only one effective cure for poor seams, and that is complete renewal of the affected area.

There are many methods of caulking, and many materials used; the oldest (and cheapest) is pitch and tar. This is still used quite extensively, particularly on decks or underwater areas, but cannot be used where the seams are to be painted over. In this case putty is used, applied either with a knife or a putty gun.

The seam is first cleaned of all old putty and oakum, by using a knife blade or special cleaning tool and scraping back to the "V"-shaped timbers between the planks. New oakum or caulking cotton is then forced into the seam by means of a special caulking tool. The cotton is purchased in the form of a ball, in which there are strands of varying thicknesses. The seams will vary in size from place to place around the boat and the most suitable size

of cotton for each seam should be selected before commencing to caulk. Oakum comes in bulk and is made up into strands in much the way that tobacco is rolled.

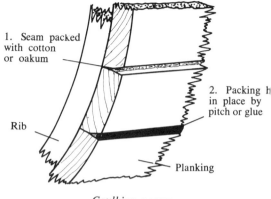

1. Seam packed with cotton or oakum

2. Packing h in place by pitch or glue

Rib

Planking

Caulking a seam

Before commencing to caulk, the seam is painted with a white lead paint, applied liberally, and the caulking should commence before the paint has time to dry completely. The tackiness of the paint will help to hold the caulking in place. The cotton (or oakum) is then fed into the seam and piled up in a series of small loops and driven home loop upon loop, by using the special caulking iron and mallet. The caulking is driven hard down into the "V" of the seam and in doing so the caulking iron forces open the timber slightly, then releases it to grip firmly on the cotton.

The caulking is driven home to within a short distance of the surface of the planking

The Tingle

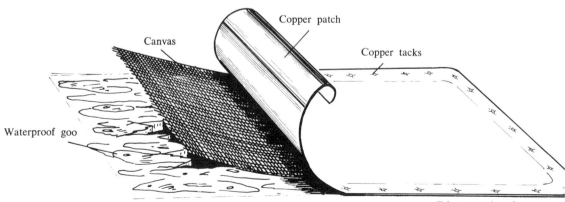

Canvas

Copper patch

Copper tacks

Waterproof goo

Edge turned under

so that when finished, the seam should be almost filled to the top with a thick, hard layer of caulking. The method of working is not really important provided satisfactory results are achieved and the caulking is driven home firmly throughout the length of the seam and not left in uneven patches.

The finishing, or "paying" as it is professionally termed, is then poured or laid over the caulking. Putty is often used for hull surfaces, but a harder composition such as tar or marine glues can also be used. They are simply applied directly to the remaining space in the seam, over the caulking, to seal it off, and when dry can be sanded back flush with the surrounding surfaces. It is a good idea, particularly when caulking decks, to leave the paying protruding from the seams for a week or so in which time it will become trodden into the caulking and provide an even more secure binding.

Caulking can only be done satisfactorily when the boat is on the slipway. A check of the seams should be made each time she is slipped

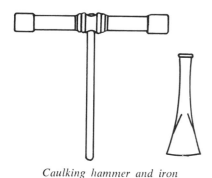

Caulking hammer and iron

Hull splining

Although caulking is a very effective way of making hull seams watertight, there is a tendency with age, or with hard working, for the caulking to become loose and allow leakage. Also, particularly in hot climates where the topsides are in strong sunlight all day, the timbers above the waterline can dry out, rapidly causing shrinkage and subsequent loosening of the caulking.

Naturally, both these problems can be easily resolved by renewing the caulking, but this is a tiresome and expensive job if done too frequently, and allows water to seep constantly into the timber. The modern system of gluing up the seams is more efficient and more durable. It is called splining because splines of timber are used instead of caulking, and they are glued in place instead of the usual packing action with caulking materials.

Old boats which have succumbed to leaky seams can be effectively treated in this way, although it is important to note that before they are splined the timbers must be quite dry. In the case of old vessels where years of saturation have made the planks almost sponge-like, this drying out process must be very carefully carried out. The boat should be brought out of the water and allowed to stand for some weeks to ensure that all moisture has left the planks.

Splining is carried out by first cleaning out all the superfluous caulking in the seams, and then shaping the plank edges with a special saw. This must be done carefully to ensure that the angle of the plank edge coincides with that of the spline, or a good surface contact cannot be achieved. Special tools can be obtained for this job and should be used if the best results are required. Failing this, careful

273

alignment of the spline batten with the plank edges and shaping with a chisel to remove blemishes will assist in obtaining good surface contact.

When the seam has been thoroughly cleaned and shaped the spline batten should be cut, usually in lengths of about four feet for convenience of handling. A "test run" with the dry spline is advisable to check that it fits the seam well and allows a small amount of the spline to protrude. Then the glue can be applied to both the plank edges and the spline

however, pins may have to be driven in or some other securing method employed to keep the glued surfaces in close contact.

When the glue has thoroughly hardened, and the securing pins are removed, the protruding edges of the spline can be cut away and planed and sanded back flush with the hull planking. Usually splining is done when the hull has been burned or stripped of paint so that the new work can be blended with the surrounding surfaces under completely new coats of paint.

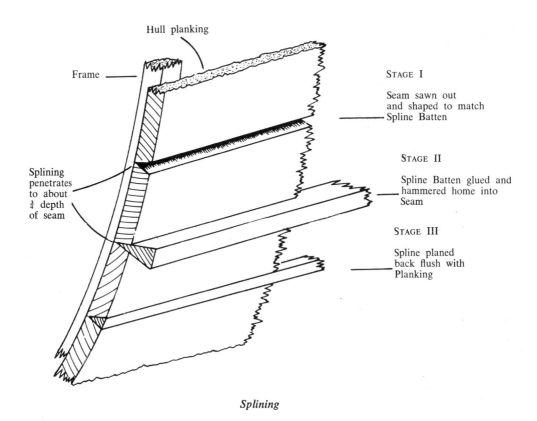

Hull planking

Frame

STAGE I

Seam sawn out
and shaped to match
Spline Batten

Splining
penetrates
to about
¾ depth
of seam

STAGE II

Spline Batten glued and
hammered home into
Seam

STAGE III

Spline planed
back flush with
Planking

Splining

batten and the spline replaced and tapped home with a hammer. For this job a good waterproof glue—such as a resorcinal resin glue—must be used.

Once hammered home, the wedge-shape of the spline should hold it firmly in position until the glue dries. If there is any sign of movement,

Repairing split timbers

Two factors govern the repair of split timber—the extent of the split and its location. If the split is considerable, it will have to be removed or securely repaired, no matter where it arises. Likewise, if the split is in a main structural member, then it will be necessary

274

to remove or repair it efficiently, no matter how small the split.

Outside these two conditions, the split may be simply stopped up, using a filler of the epoxy-based type, or plain putty. (Not plastic wood as it tends to harden and come away from the side of the split after movement.) Often fine splits are merely the result of incorrectly seasoned timber and do not affect the body strength of the member. In this case, stopping up, sanding down and painting will cover the job efficiently and well.

Where the damage is in a prominent structural member, however, this is not sufficient. The repair must be effected in a more lasting way, and one in which the weakened strength of the member will be regained. Often glueing, with a few screws to draw the edges of the split together, can be most effective. This is a particularly suitable method with deck beams or other accessible parts when the split has been caught at an early stage. Rivets can be used instead of screws for a tighter join.

If the split is large, however, the member will be weakened considerably and the only cure is its removal and replacement. The cause of the split should be noted and, if necessary, the thickness of the member increased to withstand any abnormal strains. More often than not, the split begins its life as a careless slip on

the part of the shipwright and is enlarged by the movement and strains of the vessel in a seaway. Careful drilling of fastening holes can prevent this occurring, as also can attention to the size and fixing of the fastening itself.

Where splitting occurs in masts and spars it is usually the result of loading stresses owing to poor staying. This is dealt with in the section on masts and spars.

Splitting owing to unseasoned timber can be ignored to a certain extent. Just what that extent is will depend entirely on the amount of splitting and its location. It is found more often in larger sections of timber, particularly the hardwoods, and therefore is more liable to be found in the keel and frames of a boat than in the coach-house. These splits are usually smaller and more frequent than splits caused by damage or stress, and are often accompanied by buckling of the timber. The extent of the damage will govern the repair to be effected.

Laid decks can split relatively easily owing to exposure to the weather, but these can usually be treated quite effectively by stopping or putty. Splitting of surface veneers of plywood is dealt with separately in this section, as this can result not only from deterioration or damage to the timber, but also deterioration of the bonding glues.

Badly split timber may need to be replaced. Small splits can often be filled or patched

Repairing a damaged rib

Because they form the shape of the hull,

the timbers, or ribs as they may be called, come in for a great deal of stress and strain, particularly when the boat is in unnatural conditions and the strains are concentrated in one area, such as when grounded or in collision. When this happens, apart from the effect of direct blows, the stresses are transmitted to the structural members of the boat, principal of which are the ribs. Any severe upwards strain on the keel (such as when grounded), or "squashing" stresses around the deck line (such as bumping up against a wharf), can fracture and break the nearby timbers.

There are several ways of making ribs, principal of which are bending by steaming, and laminating. In the former case, solid timbers are bent to shape in a steaming tube, and in the latter strips of timber are built up around a suitably shaped frame and glued together. In some smaller craft the timbers may be cut to shape from a single sheet of ply or timber, but this is not often seen in boats above dinghy size.

When a vessel is in for annual overhaul, her entire structure should be checked out for signs of damage or deterioration

When a rib is fractured, it creates a weakness in the hull which, unless corrected, will cause working of the planks with resultant leaking and spewing of the caulking. A broken rib can be replaced altogether, or in part, or "doubled" by having a new timber or part timber fixed alongside the broken one. In either case, when a broken rib is to be repaired, the first step is to take away any hull linings or fittings so that the damaged area can be examined and the extent of the damage assessed.

Where only one rib is fractured, and the ribs on either side are sound, there may be need for little repair other than a strengthening piece screwed alongside the damaged timber. Indeed, in a large vessel with numerous ribs, one fractured rib may be almost left alone, providing the area is examined for possible leaks and fastenings are tightened up. Where more than one timber is damaged the procedure for repairing is as follows:

With the hull linings stripped away and the extent of the damage assessed, it must be decided whether the ribs are to be doubled or renewed. The latter will only be necessary in extreme cases as it involves the possibility of damage to the hull, or some distortion of the shape of the hull. Such damage will necessitate a shipwright being called in.

Doubling the rib can be done in two ways. If the old rib is severely broken and there is a possibility of hull distortion unless it is renewed, then the doubling will have to take place for the entire length of the rib. If the fracture is of the "green stick" type, the area adjoining the fracture, and for about six or seven planks above and below it, is all that needs to be strengthened.

Doubling the entire length of the rib means making up an entirely new rib, either by steaming or laminating. A pattern of the hull shape must be made with cartridge paper or cardboard and the dimensions measured from the old timber. By laying this template on the floor of a shed or garage a mould can be made in which a laminated rib can be built up to the exact shape required. If the rib is to be bent by steaming, it should be soaked in water for some days before steaming, then when steamed to the right elasticity, should be placed quickly into position and fastened before it hardens. Full descriptions of laminating and steaming are given elsewhere in this section.

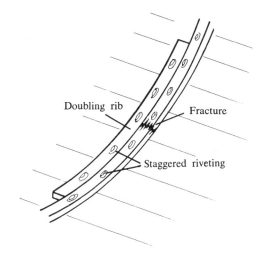

Doubling a damaged rib

When fastening a rib into place, the hull should have been previously bored out so that the steamed rib can be fastened quickly into place. A nail or fastening driven through these holes will pass through the steamed rib without splitting it, providing it has not hardened. In this case drilling will be necessary. The laminated rib can be simply placed into position in the hull and fastening holes drilled right through rib and hull in one operation.

If only a small section of the rib is to be strengthened, there is usually no need for steaming or laminating. The relatively short section of the hull is unlikely to involve severe bending of the timber, and even if it does, the new timber can be shaped to fit with a plane or band saw. The fastening process is then the same as described above, with the holes drilled through timber and skin in one operation.

It is possible to remove the old rib and replace it with the new and, of course, this gives a much neater finish. However the diffi-

culties involved in removing the old timber from beneath deck stringers and keelsons can be considerable, and since a doubling timber does not have to be fitted right into these difficult corners the amount of work involved in doubling is considerably less than in removing the old rib, and the result equally effective. Naturally, if fastenings have been badly pulled or damaged and are leaking severely, some remedy for this will have to be effected, but whether this can be done by simply stopping the leaks, or whether the rib must be removed and the area treated before replacing the new rib, will be a matter of decision for each individual case.

If the rib to be renewed or doubled is in a very difficult position and it is impossible to fasten a steamed rib into place before it starts to harden, the rib can be steamed and shaped in a mould similar to that described for laminating the timber. But it should be borne in mind that when the timber is taken out of the mould, it will tend to straighten a little, particularly where long lengths are involved. This can mostly be rectified by fastening into place in the hull, but if an exact shape is required, the curve of the mould may have to be made slightly sharper than the template to allow for straightening.

Steaming will take care of most bends but where reverse bends occur, or where there is a very acute bend that no amount of steaming will allow, lamination is the better method.

Usually a doubled timber is placed on the hull skin alongside the damaged timber. However, if there are numerous stringers or other skin fittings which make this difficult, the new timber can be placed over the old and fastened into place by means of filler blocks at intervals.

Repairing damaged stringers

The stringer is the heavy piece of timber which runs the length of the vessel on either side immediately below the deck line. There are usually other stringers spaced at intervals down the side of the vessel, according to her size. These are the longitudinal supports and

277

serve to strengthen the ship longitudinally just as the timbers and beams strengthen her athwartships. For the same reason these members come in for severe stresses when the vessel is not in her normal environment, particularly when she is aground.

However, stringers are usually of such large proportions that broken or fractured stringers are more the result of a direct blow (collision) than of grounding. And because of their size, repair to stringers is more difficult than to smaller members. When a break occurs often the best procedure is simply to straighten the damaged section and double it with a similar piece of timber. Because of its awkward position this is not easy. The new timber should be bolted on to the stringer and since the stringer may lie over the top of the ribs, it will require considerable dexterity to get a nut up between the stringer and the skin planking and hold it in place while the boat is pushed through from the reinforcing piece.

This is the only really satisfactory way of fastening a doubled stringer, however, as it is impossible to rivet it in such a difficult spot, and screws or coach bolts are not sufficient. The damaged section should be pushed back into place if possible, and planed down to its original smooth surface. The new fitting piece should be measured to cover the damaged section and continued for some distance each side. It may be held in position by nailing while the bolt holes are bored through. Galvanised iron or bronze bolts may be used,

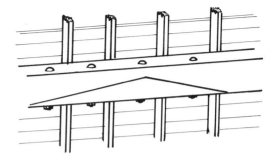

Scarfing a new section in damaged stringer

providing there is no possibility of electrolytic action taking place with other metals.

It sometimes happens that a section of the stringer has been too badly damaged for doubling, or else rot or worm has got into it. When this is the case a section must be cut from the stringer and a new piece scarfed in. This requires judgment and accuracy as the scarf must fit perfectly if it is to renew the original strength of the stringer throughout its length. Any gap in the fitting will allow working and subsequent leakage, to say the least. Severe structural distortion may come about if the stringer is not properly repaired.

The type of scarf employed for this repair is illustrated. A roughly triangular section is cut out to remove the damaged area and replaced with a new piece which is fitted and glued into place. Fastenings are then driven down through the scarf to secure it to the old stringer. In the case of a stringer under the deck line, through fastenings will be difficult to obtain and heavy screws can be used from the underside.

Note that where possible the stringer should not be cut through completely, but if this is necessary then the new timber must be scarfed into place with even greater care and also fastened through to the ribs behind.

Repairing a damaged stem

Repairs to a damaged stem will depend entirely on the type of damage. Mostly a stem is damaged by collision with another boat or object, and quite often the stem will have to

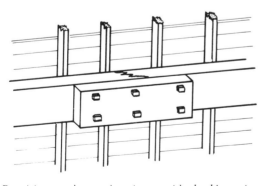

Repairing a damaged stringer with backing piece

278

be replaced completely, or at least as far down as the scarf at the curve of the stem piece. This is a difficult job as the stringers must be unfastened. In all probability they will have been glued. When the damage is inspected the fastenings of the stem to the keel must be examined as also must the stringers for some distance back from the stem itself, for the force of the collision may well have started the fastenings in the ribs and planks.

Usually, the stem cannot be repaired by a doubling piece. Because of the stresses that fall on this part of a boat's construction, it is better, unless the damage is light, to remove and replace the entire stem piece, a job which will stretch the ability of the amateur, and is probably safer left to an expert. If the damage is superficial it can be filled and treated as described for hull repairs in other parts of this section.

Bending timber by steaming

Most timbers can be bent by steaming, although softwoods lend themselves to the process better than do the harder woods.

Repair work to light timber boats of this nature is relatively easy if one is handy with tools

Bending by steaming is essential when a solid piece of timber has to fit a curved section of hull. In repair work, this comes about quite frequently since the replacement of almost any structural member or planking involves the use of bent timber.

There are several ways of steaming the timber, and naturally the more elaborate, professional ones are the best. But for amateur repair work, satisfactory results can be gained by almost any method that will keep the timber in a hot steam bath for a period of about an hour per inch of thickness. For small pieces, soaking in a scalding hot bath of water will often suffice, particularly if the bend is not too severe. Another method for slight bends is to wrap the timber in cloths and continuously pour boiling water over it, testing it at intervals to examine its pliability.

But since the steaming apparatus is a very simple arrangement, and is used frequently if much repair or building work is done, then it is as well to either make or purchase a good steaming box and save a lot of time and trouble. The simplest arrangement is a small boiler from which steam is piped into a long tube (a drainpipe is ideal). The boiler keeps

the steam passing into the tube and the timber to be bent can be laid inside and the end plugged (although not entirely or the thing will blow up!) to compress the steam and force it into the fibres of the wood.

Any timber which is to be steamed for bending must be dressed (planed) before the steaming process. Rough sawn timber is not suitable because the indents of the saw marks

timber out of the steaming box with a rag and bending it in the mould already prepared. It should, after little more than half an hour (depending on the thickness and type of timber) bend readily without whipping back to the straightened shape.

A mould is constructed by first making a template from odds and ends of timber cut to shape and nailed or screwed to the floor.

An efficient steaming apparatus

could create a weakness which, in the bending process, will cause the timber to split.

The wood should be soaked for some time before steaming, preferably for a couple of days. It will then need only a short steaming, probably half an hour to an hour. The pliability can be tested frequently by pulling the

By using shaped timber blocks, or plywood, the outline of the template can be formed so that when the steamed timber is placed in position, it locks around the shaped blocks.

It is as well to remember that when the steamed timber hardens, it will tend to straighten out slightly and allowance must be

Thin timbers can be steamed in this way

made for this when setting up the mould. It is better to have a slightly over-rated bend than under, since the timber can be straightened again more readily than it can be bent.

Bending timber by laminating

Laminated timber requires a little more effort than timber bent by steaming, but the result is very effective and stronger than steamed timber. Although easier to bend, and with far less risk of fracturing, laminating takes more time than steam bending, and is more costly.

Laminating is the laying up of timber in a series of layers of about one-eighth inch thickness, glued together in the manner of plywood. Thicker strips will probably need steaming to bend them to shape before laminating. Indeed, plywood can be said to be a form of laminated sheet. The strips are thin and can thus be bent into shape without risk of breaking and the resultant "sandwich" of layers is very strong indeed. A good marine glue must be used, to ensure that the finished product is waterproof and will not disintegrate under stress.

A mould similar to that used for bending steamed timber can be used, with the shape marked on the floor of a garage or shed, or a mould set up on a framework to enable the work to be carried out at bench level. The curves of the shape must be correctly measured as, unlike steamed timber, there is no

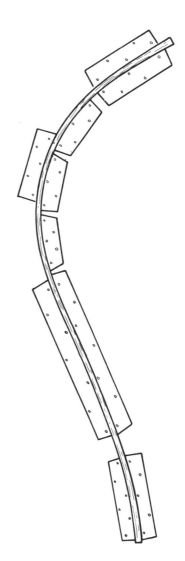

The joys of summer sailing are easy to take, but they must always be followed by the demanding winter maintenance

Plan view of mould nailed to floor in which steamed timber can be bent to shape

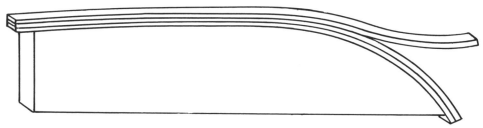

Laminating timber over a mould

likelihood of the shape straightening at all when removed from the mould. Quite the reverse, in fact; it would be difficult to bend the laminated material once it has set.

The strips should be of the correct thickness, with all the grain running along the length, and the first thin layer placed into the mould and held in position. A thin layer of glue is spread across its surface and the strip placed on to it. This is repeated with each layer until the thickness is sufficient for the job. Each layer must be given time to harden before the next is applied and each strip of timber must be held firmly in place by small nails or clamps until the glue has set. When the final layer is in position the whole piece should be clamped up tight and allowed good time to cure properly. Then the clamps can be removed and the piece sawn or shaped for the job in question.

Laminated timber, apart from the ease with which it can be shaped, and the enormous strength of the finished product, can be most attractively finished as a decorative piece. Beams, knees, fashion pieces, and even tillers, look most attractive when sanded back and varnished. The layered appearance of the timber and glue can enhance any brightwork in the boat considerably. Many shipwrights consider it a sin to paint over a neatly laminated piece of timber.

Repairs to Knees and Beams

Knees and beams provide the structural thwartships strength in a boat. They complete, as it were, the top of the box formed by the rest of the hull. As such they are extremely

282

important as some of the worst stresses in the boat's structure fall across the ship, particularly when she is in a seaway. "Racking" strains, which tend to push the boat out of shape, come into play as she rights herself from a roll and there is a tremendous strain across the beams, which prevent the sides of the hull from collapsing inwards. Even more strain comes on the knees which prevent the entire structure from collapsing like a squashed matchbox.

As a rule, beams and knees are of such strength that they are rarely damaged in the normal course of events. However, when

Laminated sections are very strong and have an attractive appearance

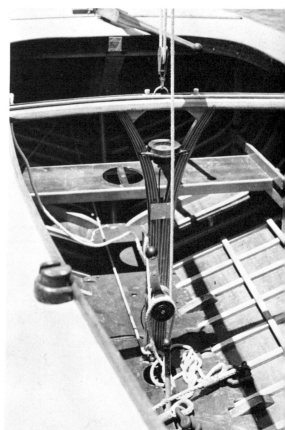

damage occurs, say from collision or rot, the members must be repaired effectively if the boat is to regain her structural strength.

Damage to beams can generally be treated as described in the section on damage to stringers. Beams are the thwartships stringers, as it were, and are of much the same construction as the stringers. Knees, however, are individual, and made for a specific purpose—to prevent the wracking of the boat when she is moving in a seaway. They are roughly triangular in shape to fill the weak corner between beam and rib. Repairing a knee means almost invariably replacing or doubling it. Because of its position it is as difficult to replace a knee as a rib and, where a weakness has occurred, doubling is the usual answer.

Knees are made in many forms. The best and most effective is the grown knee in which a piece of grown hardwood, with the grain following the shape of the fitting, is cut to fit into the corner between beam and rib. Unfortunately, grown knees are sometimes hard to obtain and in order to be fully effective will require the old knee to be removed so that the edges of the new knee can be fitted flush with the beam and the rib strength is to be maintained. However, if a grown knee *can* be used then it is by far the best.

Fabricated knees can be cut from plywood or timber. The former is ideal, as it has the strength of the grain running in transverse directions. Often two fabricated knees are used for a repair job; one is placed on each side of the damaged knee. Next to replacing the damaged knee with a new one of grown timber, this is probably the best repair job that can be effected.

The ply should be of marine quality and of sufficient thickness to give good support to the beam adjoining the damaged knee. It should be cut to shape from a template made with a piece of cardboard fitted tight up under the deck and *overlapping* the beam and the rib. When in position, both prefabricated knees can then be screwed not only into the old

Even the smallest boats must be structurally well built if they are to stand up to the rigors of a season's sailing

knee but also into the beam and the rib for some distance along their lengths.

Correctly fitted and fastened, this type of knee will provide an effective and strong repair without the need to remove the old knee.

Needless to say, knees can be fashioned from a number of materials and imagination can be used to effect the repair of any individual knee, according to its location. A strong steel bracket, shaped on a forge, will also make an effective knee when placed over the old. Steel can be used instead of plywood for the prefabricated

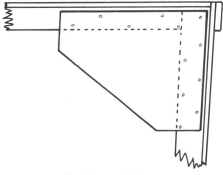

Prefabricated knee

knee mentioned in the previous section. If the knee is in a visible part of the cabin it can be prettied up by using fancy laminations or finishing off with a fitting piece to match other knees in the cabin. Providing the basic strength is incorporated in the double knee, there is no limit to shape, size or material.

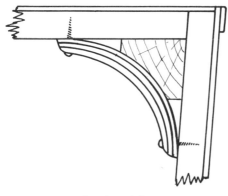

Laminated knee

Gussets and Floors

By and large, the treatment for damaged or rotted gussets and floors is the same as for knees. Here again the strength of the fitting lies in the "filling" arrangement whereby the gusset holds together two structural members where they meet at an angle. Fabricated gussets and floors are usually of heavy plywood or timber and fitted in the same way as knees. Fastenings may have to be driven through the hull in the case of floor repairs in order to achieve maximum strength.

Laminated sections can often be used in floors, since the shape lends itself to their use.

Repairing a laid deck

Damage to a laid deck is usually caused by rot. Accidents can add their quota, of course, but a laid deck is usually fairly thick and well supported by deck beams, and a considerable force is required to cause serious damage. Whatever the cause when a section of decking is damaged it must be replaced.

The old decking is first removed, taking

care not to aggravate the size of the fastening holes in the beams. These must be used again for new fastenings and too large a hole will result in a weak fastening. The damaged planks should be cut away, and this must be done so that either a whole plank is removed or the plank is cut directly over a beam. The new section of plank must butt on to the old on a beam, or it cannot be securely fastened.

With the old section of plank will come most of the caulking and any that remains should be scraped away from the adjoining planks so that new caulking can be laid.

The new timber must be shaped exactly to fit the space where the old plank was removed. If this section involves bent planks, the new section will have to be steamed in order to bend it. Bending edgewise is very difficult, especially with a short section of plank and it may prove impossible to bend the plank sufficiently accurately to fill the gap. In this case, the new section must be cut from a plank and shaped with saw and plane until it makes an exact fit.

The sections to be replaced should be kept as short as possible. If the damage is extensive, then the planks should be replaced as a whole. Leaking will occur unless a very good fit is achieved and fitting long sections of planking can be very difficult without distorting or warping them. Short sections will usually be watertight as they can be shaped more accurately and fitted to ensure watertightness.

If the rot extends over a great proportion of the deck then either the deck will have to be completely relaid or another surface laid over the existing deck. Needless to say, if the trouble is dry rot, the old deck will have to be removed altogether or the rot will spread beneath the new surface, but often decks deteriorate with age and, in this case, a covering is suitable.

Laying a plywood/fibreglass deck

Some boat owners, wishing to keep their deck surfaces in timber, simply lay a new, thinner timber deck over the old. This can be

Laid decks are attractive in appearance but require a lot of maintenance work to keep them that way

achieved quite simply by laying either strips of thin timber or plywood sheets over the old deck, first gluing and then screwing the new deck in place. However, if the deck is of a leaky nature—and many laid decks are—a solution lies in continuing the covering process by fibreglassing on top of the newly-laid timber.

Fibreglass will not take readily to old timber and a new surface must be laid before the glassing is begun. Plywood is ideal as it can be laid in large sheets, is easily fastened through to the old deck and the deck beams beneath, and can be easily shaped to fit around cabins, skylights, hatches, and other awkward fittings.

The plywood is shaped (using marine plywood only, of course), to fit the deck space to be covered, carrying it right out to the bulwarks. A good thick coat of marine glue or white lead paint is laid over the old deck and the plywood screwed into place. Although generally the fastenings can be made in the old decking, if it is badly deteriorated it is as well to ensure that as many fastenings as possible are secured right through to the deck beams, to prevent any chance of the new deck lifting.

Before there is any chance of the plywood surface becoming damp, the fibreglass should be laid. The resin is made up in small quan-

tities (about half a gallon at first) and painted on the plywood with a stiff brush. The amount of hardener should be varied so that the resin does not dry too rapidly; a tacky feel is the right consistency for laying the glass mat.

The glass mat or chopped strand should be pre-cut to shape and ready to lay when the initial covering of resin is down. It should be cut to fit around any obstructions, although the actual shape of the glass is not critical and it can be "pulled" quite considerably when the final layer of resin goes on. Providing it fits fairly close to all borders it will suffice in this case.

Any form of glass mat is suitable, although the stranded mat is better for decks as the finished result is irregular and gives a good footing in difficult seas. Non-skid paint added to this surface gives the best footing possible.

With the mat laid, the second coat of resin must be put on, again with a fairly stiff brush. It must be well worked into the cloth to ensure that there are no air bubbles trapped in the resin as these can cause separation from the timber beneath. By covering the entire mat with a fairly thick layer of resin, an even surface is ensured as, like any liquid, the resin will flow through the mat in an attempt to find its own level. It is of too thick a consistency to run away and will settle down to an even surface provided it does not start curing too soon.

A final check should be made to ensure that the resin is completely covering the mat and no isolated patches of "hairy" glass are sticking up. Likewise, a check to ensure there are no bubbles beneath the resin should be made as these will now show up more distinctly as the colour of the glass becomes clear.

The fibreglass should harden within an hour or two but should be left for at least a day to cure. Then the sander can be brought into action and all bumps and uneven patches sanded down to achieve a level, watertight surface. Correctly laid, on virgin timber, this type of decking should outlast the life of the boat. It can be painted to any colour, as described in the chapter on painting.

Laying a canvas deck

Canvas decks were in use before fibreglass was even a gleam in its inventor's eye and to this day there are many adherents of the cult of canvas-covered decks. Indeed, the final result of a well-laid canvas deck is often vastly superior to either timber or fibreglass and there is great use for it to this day, particularly in covering deckhouses and cabin roofs.

Although canvas has the advantage over fibreglass that it can be laid on any surface, even an old timber deck, it is debatable whether it is easier to lay. The secret of a good, watertight canvas-covered cabin or deck is the way in which it is laid initially. This also applies to its appearance, for a few wrinkles in the wrong place can make a cabin roof look a mess.

Launches and motor yachts have less deck problems than do sailing boats which are subjected to stresses when heeling

The type of canvas for use varies slightly with the type and size of vessel on which it is used, but as a general guide canvas weighing about 20 ounces to the square yard is good for most decks and a slightly lighter calibre should be used for cabin tops and areas which will not get so much wear and tear. The canvas should not be laid in one piece but cut into convenient sections to fit around deck houses, skylights and other obstructions.

When first purchased, the canvas should be stretched for at least forty-eight hours in each direction and washed in hot water if it is covered with size or other surface preparation. At the same time the deck to be covered should be given at least two coats of paint so that when the canvas is ready, the paint will be dry but not over-cured. If possible the canvas should be laid the day after the deck is painted. Some people prefer to set the canvas in white or red lead and this is quite a good practice but takes a long time to dry.

Laying should be started from the centre of the canvas and each section worked aft and stretched then worked athwartships and again stretched, before securing in position. The edges, where the canvas curves over the edge of the deck or the cabin top, can be tacked with copper nails before securing in place with a strip batten to cover the edges.

The seams must be folded carefully and tacked with copper tacks. Two rows will be required to hammer the seam in place. Some shipwrights prefer their seams to be sewn and undoubtedly this makes a neater job, but to do this, all the various sections, cut and fitted beforehand, must be sewn together into one large piece before laying—a very difficult job when it comes to fitting round skylights and obstructions.

As each seam is tacked into place and the laying continued, the emphasis is on the stretching. One person is not enough to stretch the canvas sufficiently and as many hands as possible should be called in for the job. The copper tacks should be driven home hard; usually five-eighth inch tacks at about half-

Well laid canvas decks are as effective and attractive as any other

inch centres is sufficient, although they will be closer where the fitting round deckhouses and obstructions becomes more difficult.

When the laying is completed and a satisfactory surface is obtained, the tacked areas, other than the seams, can be covered with battens or quartering pieces which have been painted on the underside. The canvas can then be painted with primer or red lead in the normal way, followed by a few coats of undercoat and a top coat of anti-skid.

Stopping deck leaks

One of the most annoying of all leaks in a boat is the deck leak. This is partly because it is always above one's head when down below and it invariably finds one's neck, also because the deck leak is one of the most difficult to locate and stop. Because of the sheer of the boat the water may run undetected for some feet from the actual source before becoming a visible drip.

Laid decks, for all their beauty, are notorious for leaks and, for this reason alone, they are slipping in popularity among modern boat builders. No matter how new the deck and how well laid the planks, it will be only a short while before some insidious trickle gets through and into the cabin below.

Obviously, the first problem is to locate the source of the leak and no book on earth could describe how to go about that. It will be a matter of patience and diligence and, most of all, back-bending work. Caulking will have to be pulled out and replugged, cracks and knot holes checked, and fastenings and their plugging given a thorough examination. A small watering can or hose may be used to test each possible spot, although some leaks need a gallon of water before showing even a single drop under the deck-head.

Because of the great number of seams in a laid deck, leakage is a major problem. Good caulking is the only solution

If the leak is in a seam, the caulking will have to be taken out and renewed, probably for some feet on either side of the leak. The pitch used for caulking decks is often suspect as it tends to be brittle and crack without showing visible signs. If the pitching is fairly old or looks worn, it may be as well to re-pitch the entire deck. The seams are the most vulnerable part of the deck and a new pitch coat, or its replacement with a marine seam glue, may solve the problem quite easily.

If the leak arises from a defect in the plank itself, such as a knot that has worked loose, or a patch of timber that has deteriorated or rotted, then the affected area should be cut out and replaced. If just a small section, it can be chiselled out and a fitting piece glued in its place. If a large area, then a plank, or a few planks, may have to be taken up and replaced. This is described in detail elsewhere in this section.

If the deck has deteriorated generally, which is sometimes the case in very old boats, then either the deck will have to be relaid or covered. Since re-laying brings back all the old problems, covering an old deck with plywood or canvas—although not as attractive as the laid planks—is more effective. If it is essential to relay the deck, then it should be laid on plywood, using only the best grade of marine plywood and covering it with a layer of white lead before starting to lay the planks. The process is otherwise the same as for laying the deck directly on to the beams, and the fastenings should be made through the beams as before.

This method retains the beauty of the laid deck and eliminates the problem of leaking. But too much emphasis cannot be placed on the need for using the right grade of *marine* plywood that has been treated against rot, since in its location beneath the laid planks, it will be very liable to patches of rot that will not be visible to the eye.

If the deck is to be covered then a choice of three methods is available. Covering with plywood, covering with canvas, and covering with fibreglass. Since fibreglass does not always take too well to wood that has been long weathered and is particularly difficult to lay on uneven surfaces, then it should always be used in conjunction with plywood, i.e. the plywood should first be laid and the fibreglass placed over it. This is the best method by far of sealing a deck, though it might be somewhat expensive. Best quality marine plywood must be used. The method is described in this chapter.

Canvas covering is also an attractive and waterproof finish for a deck, providing it is carried out in the proper manner. Full details on laying canvas are also described in this chapter.

Some deck leaks are caused because inferior timber has been used, which after some years in the sun and weather, begins to warp or split. The leaks can be treated by stopping with an epoxy-based filler; but the warps can only be removed by planing back the timber, which may be a lengthy job. If the warping is too severe for planing the planks will have to be removed and either relaid, or the deck replaced with some other form of decking.

Warping causes leaks through seams, fastening, and splits in the timber itself, hence the

need for the best quality timber in laid decks.

Covering a warped deck with some other material is not sufficient, unless the warping can be planed back. Plywood placed over a warped deck will form an uneven surface and the face of the ply will not make good contact, thus leaving small pockets of air between the old and new decking. Water will gather in these pockets and set up severe rot in next to no time.

Canvas cannot be used over warped decks for much the same reason. The unevenness of the deck will prevent the canvas making a good, even contact, and pockets will result under which water will gather or which will be depressed and stretch the canvas when walked upon. Also, raised sections of the warped deck will cut through the canvas as it comes into use.

Over and above the standard deck coverings described here, many patent materials are available to the boat owner that are effective. Some are in the form of rubberised or plasticised material, others in the form of pastes that are spread on to leaking decks and allowed to harden. Undoubtedly some of the patent products are satisfactory, particularly on covered decks such as the well deck of a cabin cruiser. However, experience has shown that very few of the patent materials can withstand

Composition decks provide reasonably attractive surfaces and are generally watertight if laid correctly

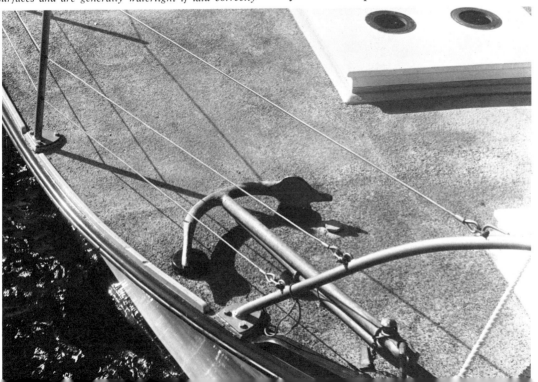

the full effects of sun and weather on exposed decks for any length of time. The question arises of whether to use these relatively easy methods of covering a deck and replace them at intervals, or of making a solid, lasting job of the repair which is going to mean a lot of hard work initially.

Repair of rotten plank ends (transom)

One of the most vulnerable parts of a boat's planking is the area where the planks butt on to the transom. Movement caused by insufficient fastening or the working of a boat in a seaway, causes cracking of the covering paint and lets water into the joins. Because these ends are not usually caulked, the water tends to seep into the butt end of the planks and, over a period of time, causes deterioration of the wood. Since this is an area which bears a great deal of the working strains of the boat, the deterioration of the wood causes loosening of the fastenings, which in turn magnifies the cracking and leaking, and a vicious circle of events sets up, resulting in complete rotting of the ends of the planks.

If the damage is not severe, it can be corrected by building a new stern frame inside the transom and refastening the planks ends to this frame. The fastenings will be a few inches farther up the plank and should have good timber on which to bite. However, this is only a temporary repair and before too many seasons have passed the entire transom

Dry rot—scourge of the timber boat—can attack anywhere and at any time

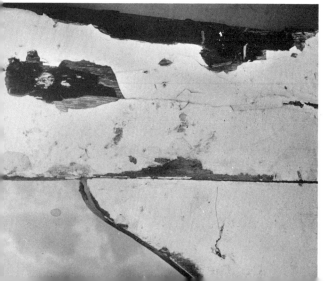

will have to be removed and a few inches sawn off the ends of the planks before re-fitting the transom again. This, of course, is a job beyond the scope of the amateur. When contemplating purchase of a boat, be it a yacht or a power vessel, close attention should be paid to this section of the boat's construction.

Plugging rusty fastenings

The obvious and only really satisfactory cure for rusted fastenings is complete removal and replacement with non-rusting fastenings. If the fastenings have rusted down their length, then this is the only possible cure. However, more often than not the rust has attacked only the exposed head of the fastening and the main body has not deteriorated at all. If this is the case, it may be left in position and the head treated to prevent further rusting and also to improve its appearance.

The old stopper, if it has already broken up and fallen out, will leave the head exposed and this will need only to be cleaned off with a wire brush before treatment. If the stopper is still in place it must be prised out with a knife in order to get at the rusty head beneath. Usually, at this stage, the bristles of a wire brush worked into the cavity will remove surplus rust. However, if the rust has formed scale over the head of the fastening it may be necessary to chip it out with a pointed knife or a screwdriver.

When the flaky rust has been removed, a patent rust killer should be dropped into the cavity and allowed to act on the remaining rust. The rust killer should be given plenty of time to operate and it may even be necessary to repeat the dose. When it is dry a coat of primer should be worked into the cavity.

It is important at this stage to ensure that not only the head of the fastening is treated but also surrounding areas as the rust may have diffused into the surrounding timber where it will cause deterioration and discolouration if not treated. When the primer is dry, which should take about twenty-four hours, the cavity may be filled with a patent filler, preferably one of the epoxy types.

When the filler has hardened it can be sanded back to match the surrounding areas. The area must be cleaned off and the undercoat and succeeding top coat should be applied to cover not only the repair area but also a considerable amount of the surrounding timber. Providing this treatment is done correctly the head of the fastening should be completely sealed from the salt air and thus prevent any further rusting from taking place.

This type of treatment for rusted fastenings is very effective, no matter in what part of the hull they are located. It is particularly effective in difficult spots and corners where removal of the offending fastening is impossible. Providing the flaking rust can be pricked away and the rust killer dropped into the area a reasonably sure form of protection can be guaranteed.

It should be remembered, however, that although patent rust killers can effectively kill rust on both the offending objects and the surrounding areas, it is not sufficient to leave the rust killer exposed to the air. When it has acted upon the loose rust and formed a sealer over the metal, it must then be covered with paint in order to protect it from further attacks by moist salt air. It is equally important that the rust be reduced to mere surface rust and all heavily rusted areas chipped clean. Rust killers are only effective on light surface rust. If these conditions are followed the treatment described here for curing rusted fastenings can be applied to almost any affected area, providing it is not too large. For large areas of rust the treatment described in the section on treatment of rust should be followed.

Repairing rust-damaged canvas

Where metal fastenings or fittings are used near or under canvas, the rust which forms on such fittings may deteriorate the canvas work for some area around it. Particularly is this the case when metal screws or other fastenings

Removal and replacement of fastenings calls for a high degree of workmanship if the result is to be completely watertight

rust underneath a canvas deck. The rust penetrates the canvas and sets up an area of deterioration which not only looks unsightly but also causes the canvas to disintegrate. The best repair, of course, is to remove the canvas deck covering and the offending fittings beneath. But if the area of rust is very small this makes for unnecessary work and expense. Providing the canvas has only disintegrated in small patches, these can usually be successfully treated without the need to completely replace the canvas cover.

Using a sharp-pointed knife the damaged patch of canvas should be cut out, together with any immediate areas which may be affected. The rusted fastenings can then be removed. The area must be treated with a rust killer in order to remove any powdered rust which may still be in the vicinity. Providing the area is clean and dry the patch may now be covered with a coating of marine glue or, preferably, one of the epoxy fillers. Whatever substance is used, it must be spread over the patch taken out of the canvas and into the adjoining area in order to glue down the loose edges of the canvas. When the filler is dry it can be carefully sanded back and painted.

291

This method of patching rust spots is only suitable for small areas such as those mentioned where a fastening or nail has been removed. If too large an area of canvas has been removed it will tend to break away from the filler when subjected to hard use. In this case a canvas patch must be used. The procedure is as follows:

The damaged area is cut out with a sharp-pointed knife and a patch of new canvas, with an overlap of about one inch, prepared. When the surface to be patched has been correctly treated and given a coat of primer or undercoat, the patch may be placed over the repaired work and its four sides folded under. This will necessitate some cutting at the corners but it is essential that the folded-under edges are even and do not build up any bulky areas. When placed over the repaired section the new patch, with edges folded under, should overlap the edges of the cut-away canvas by about a quarter to half an inch. Small copper tacks may then be used to tack the new patch into position. The new canvas is treated and painted to match the surrounding areas.

This is not the most satisfactory method

Modern fibreglass decks frequently have a non-skid surface moulded-in, thus eliminating many of the problems associated with other decks

of patching a deck or cabin top canvas, as it leaves the patch superimposed on the old canvas. However, it is a suitable alternative if the damaged area is too large to be filled by stoppers or glue, or if the canvas deck covering cannot be taken off and the patch stitched neatly into it.

Repairing or replacing a covering board

The covering board is the edge board around the deck which provides the join of the deck to the hull and into which the planks of a laid deck are set. Where the decks are of ply, the covering board does not exist as a separate piece of timber, for it is one with the whole deck covering.

The covering board is often called the "scuppers" since it carries the run-off of water from the deck. For this reason it is an important piece of timber as it prevents leaks through the join between laid deck and hull planking. It is formed by shaped pieces of timber sawn and scarfed together and rabbetted to take the edges of the deck planking.

Any damage to this piece of timber can be fairly easily rectified by removing the section that has been damaged and scarfing in a new section to replace it. The old section can be used as a template for the new providing it

is not too badly damaged, and the new fastenings placed in the holes made by the old, providing they are still sound. For a clean finish the fastenings should be screws countersunk and dowelled.

Needless to say, the fitting of the edge of the timber, where it meets the sheer strake, is of considerable importance. Leaks at this point may set up rot in the structural timbers, underneath which it is difficult to see and get at when the planking is in place. A watertight packing of white lead, or gluing of the edges of the timber is advisable to ensure a good join.

Securing a hatch cover

One of the biggest problems with hatches is to make them watertight. Since they must be able to open, either by means of hinges or by sliding, they cannot be screwed down on a bed of watertight glue, as are most watertight sections of a boat. They must be so designed and secured as to make them watertight in their own right.

The design of a hatch cover is usually such that, providing it is held securely in position, little or no water can enter. However, with wear or damage the hinges or securing devices of the hatch often allow the watertightness to open somewhat and some water seeps in. The best remedy may be to replace the damaged or worn sections, but this may not always be satisfactory, in which case a rubber seal is recommended.

The rubber should be glued in a strip about three-eighths inch thick all round the top of the coaming. An even better job is to recess it into the coaming itself and then glue in position with the edge of the rubber sticking about three-eighths inch above the coaming. If the present fastenings are sufficient to pull the hatch down tight on this seal, it will be all that is necessary, but if the seal proves too thick or the fastenings too weak, a strongback beneath the hatch coaming is the answer.

This is the safest and easiest form of hatch fastening, albeit not the most glamorous. A long bolt, of three-eighths inch or half-inch diameter, is pushed down through a tightly drilled hole in the centre of the hatch cover. The head may be countersunk in the top of the cover, or a low convex head used and flattened hard down to the surface of the cover. The bolt must be long enough to pass through a strongback placed across the underside of the hatch coaming and should have a butterfly nut and washer attached.

The strongback can be of any hardwood, about one and a half inches minimum thickness, by about two inches width. It should be long enough to seat securely on either side of the hatch opening against the deckhead, and shaped to a pleasant appearance so that it does not clash with the general scheme of the internal fittings.

The centre bolt in the hatch should pass through a loosely drilled hole in the centre of the strongback, and the butterfly nut used to screw it up tight. Where a particularly large hatch is involved, two bolts may be necessary to screw down the hatch tightly. With this method of securing the hatch and the rubber seal described earlier, a watertight cover is ensured.

Where sliding hatches are involved the watertightness is gained by the fitting of the slide guides. Either timber or metal slides may be used and these are fitted in "U" form to provide reasonable watertightness along the entire length of the slide. A typical cross section of a hatch slide is illustrated.

Needless to say, the watertight fitting of a hatch is only as watertight as the hatch itself and any signs of leaking should be promptly dealt with either by means of a filler or glue or a covering such as canvas, fibreglass, etc.

Cockpit repairs

Generally speaking, any repairs to be effected to the cockpit area are of similar nature to repairs elsewhere on the boat. However, there are a few features of the cockpit which can give rise to more specialised repair work.

The coaming around the cockpit, if high,

comes in for considerable strain, particularly on a yacht where, in addition to the weight of the crew leaning on it when it heels at an acute angle, the coaming often has to withstand the stress of jib sheets and winches taking the full strain of a taut sail. This causes the coaming to work and loosen its fastenings in the structural members supporting it. The coaming itself may split or come away from the decking, leaving a crack which will cause considerable leaking when a sea boards the boat, or heavy rain falls.

Repairing a split coaming will depend on the extent of the splitting. Severe splitting will necessitate the removal and replacement of

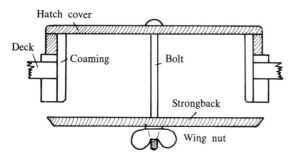

Securing a hatch cover with a strongback

the coaming itself and this should be done by cutting the new coaming from a pattern of the old to ensure a good fit. Steaming is rarely necessary as the coaming is not usually bent in a severe curve but clamping when gluing

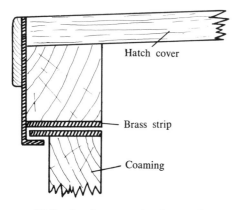

Sliding hatch cover using brass strip

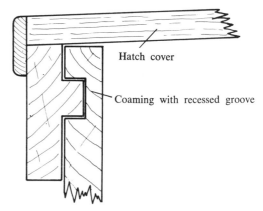

Sliding hatch cover using rebated timber

and screwing will most certainly be necessary if there is any curve at all.

If the splitting is not severe, it can be simply filled with some form of stopper and sanded back to give a smooth surface. Where the splits are in the timber grain this is usually fastenings, glue should be used as a filler and the cracks clamped together if possible. This is only a temporary repair and the splits will widen as the vessel continues to work, until replacement of the coaming is necessary.

Where the coaming has come away from the deck a crack will form and dirt will get into the gap between the timbers, making it very hard to draw them together again. If the use of large clamps does not achieve this it may be better to cut one's losses and simply hold the coaming in its present position and merely prevent the gap from becoming any wider. This can be done by inserting bolts and screwing them up tight. The gap can then be stopped with filler or putty to make it watertight, and painted over.

Occasionally a coaming is of a type that does not pierce the deck but is fitted above it. In this case any damage is most effectively repaired by replacing the coaming, a relatively simple operation.

External damage to the keel

Because of its location, the keel is vulnerable to damage, particularly in a vessel which is grounded frequently or which rests on the bottom when the tide goes out. The full weight of the boat comes onto the keel at these times and, since it is mostly of wooden construction, it can suffer damage in several ways. A great deal will depend on the type and shape of the keel. Obviously, a fin-type yacht keel will be liable to far more strain than the long low keel of a cruiser which can distribute the weight over its entire length.

Another factor is the material used in the keel. Timber is the most common, but cast-iron or lead may be used for yacht keels. In addition, the keel may be copper sheathed or have a metal bearer running along its length. All these factors, plus the shape and size of the keel, make for considerable variations in the type and severity of damage which may be sustained.

A well maintained cockpit enhances the appearance of the whole boat. Note the neatly coiled ropes

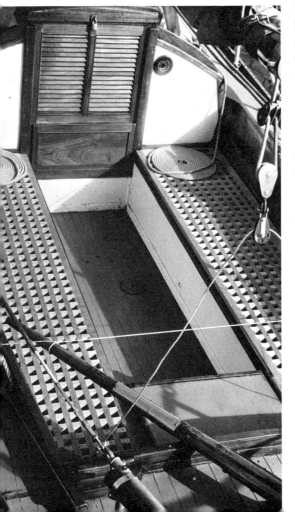

Fin keels

These are used only in yachts and are mostly of cast-iron or timber and lead construction. They differ from other yacht keels in that they are not an integral part of the boat's construction but are an accessory bolted to the outside of the keel proper—i.e. the heavy timber "backbone" of the boat.

They have numerous advantages over the normal deep keel but such advantages are not of interest in this volume. More to the point is the weakness of this type of keel, particularly when subject to the enormous strain put on a small section of the boat when the vessel is grounded. Unless she is supported by a cradle, or props, as described in the section on slipping, the entire weight of the vessel will come on to the bolts holding the keel in place, often with damaging results.

The keel bolts holding the fin keel in place are usually bolted through heavy floor members in the bottom of the boat, and through the hog keel itself. Iron bolts are the most satisfactory, although stainless steel and monel can be used. The latter is ideal, but very costly; stainless steel bolts are excellent but must be carefully watched because of the tendency for the metal to crystallise and break with work.

Strain on the keel bolts may bend them or, worse, they may break off. If there are signs of damage after grounding, the boat should be slipped and the keel bolts drawn. This is a simple process involving only the removal of putty or other composite filling the recessed holes about the head of the bolts, and the unbolting of the nuts on the boat floors. The bolts can be gently tapped outwards, using a piece of timber to protect the thread from the hammer, and drawn, one by one, for examination.

Replacement of each bolt requires careful packing of the hole with white lead and tallow or some other protective coating before the bolt is driven home and screwed up tight. If damage has been sustained to the bolt, the

A fin keel. Note the bulge of ballast at the bottom of the fin

chances are the hole will be enlarged and in this case a larger bolt must be used.

Damage to the keel will usually be negligible if the entire fin is of cast-iron. At worst the keel will be cracked, in which case it must be replaced by another casting, but normally the cast-iron keels stand up to the shock of grounding well and transfer the strain to the bolts. If the fin is of timber and lead construction, however, considerable damage may have been sustained, particularly to the timber areas.

In this type of construction, the keel bolts run down through the timber to the bottom of the fin and are thus more vulnerable when the vessel runs aground with severe impact. The lead is bolted on the bottom of the timber sufficient but where the splits occur around and can readily break off or bend the bolts. If the timber area is made up of a series of

timber sections bolted together, the keel may split and break up, with the wood and lead being torn away and the bolts being bent severely.

In all cases, considerable repair work will result and the keel may have to be dismantled and rebuilt. The bolts must certainly be drawn and examined, even if the damage to the timber is superficial, since strain on these bolts could cause fracturing in the hidden section between head and bolt. Because of their length, the bolts are very vulnerable to damage and should be suspect immediately if the vessel is grounded hard.

Deep keels

The normal keel fitting, especially in larger yachts, is an integral keel which is part and parcel of the hull construction. The planking of the skin is carried down past the turn of the bilge to form the keel shape and usually ends with iron or lead ballast at its foot, forming the weighted section of the keel. The timbers or ribs of the hull are also carried down through the floors thus giving a strongly constructed keel shape which is an integral part of the boat, not bolted on as an attachment. From a repair point of view, this type

Enormous strain comes on the bolts holding a fin keel in position when the boat is heeled and the righting moment of the ballast in operation

A conventional deep keel. The ballast becomes an integral part of the keel and may be either external or internal

of keel is easier to get at from both inside and out, particularly for periodic examination and maintenance. The disadvantage is that any severe damage sustained by the keel will be damage to part of the boat's construction as a whole and may involve repair work to structural members other than the keel.

A vessel which is grounded heavily, for example, may well strain or loosen frames well up to her topsides since the initial shock will be placed on the bottom ends of those frames where they form the keel. Similarly, where a severe blow to a fin keel may require only the immediate area to be repaired, the same damage to a deep keel may require planks to be replaced for some distance above and below the damage, as well as for many frames fore and aft.

The outside ballast of a deep keel is usually bolted through in much the same way as a fin keel. Heavy blocks of timber are used to shape the keel, particularly where it draws in to a narrow section, and forward and aft where the underwater shape is of importance. Repair to these sections are as for the same fittings in the section on fin keels, and they will be liable to much the same stresses and strains.

The built section of the keel, however, is virtually a part of the normal hull and any repairs to this area will be carried out as described in the various sections on hull repairs. It is important to note at this point that, because of the very sharp bend in the timbers at the point where they curve downwards from the bilge to the keel, there is a weak spot liable to damage. The timbers at this point need little strain to bend them past the fracturing point and it is very common to examine a vessel and find these timbers, in the turn of the bilge, splintered and fractured. Indeed, some vessels incur splintering of these frames when they are built but, providing the damage is not serious, they are left in place.

However, splintered ribs at the turn of the bilge is not to be recommended, for this section of the hull is liable to many stresses and strains, particularly when grounding or slipping. Fractured or splintered ribs should be doubled, as described earlier in this chapter. Because of the severe curve in the timber at this point and the likelihood of further splitting, the doubling pieces should be laminated rather than steamed.

Flat keels

Most power craft and motor sailers have flat, level keels running from stem to stern

297

Twin bilge keels are an adaption of the fin keel to reduce draft and allow the boat to remain upright when grounded

virtually parallel with the deck line. Obviously, this makes for far less strain and damage in the event of the boat stranding, as she can settle evenly on the short, flat keel without undue strain on the keel bolts and with the weight distributed fairly evenly throughout her length. The disadvantage is that since the keel is so shallow, the bottom of the hull is more liable to be damaged when grounding hard, particularly on an uneven bottom.

Most keels of this nature have a "grounding strip" of iron or similar metal running the length of the keel on the underside. This distributes the shock across a wider area when taking the ground. Thus grounding on a flat keel, providing it has a grounding strip (also known as a "shoe") and providing the bottom of the hull is not damaged, rarely incurs anything worse than a strained bolt or splintered timber. The shape of the grounding strip when examined after grounding will usually indicate

the extent of the damage. If it is severely dented or buckled, the chances are the bolts holding it in place will have been strained and they should be drawn and examined.

Structural damage is rare unless the boat has been grounded very hard indeed and her back broken. Isolated damage such as strained timbers at the keel or loosened fastenings in the same area may be encountered, but the keel is designed to take the shock and the weight of the vessel stranding and (again depending on the severity of impact) should absorb most of the punishment. Damage to nearby planking on the bottom, of course, is far more liable. Repairs to this area are dealt with in the section on hull planking.

Copper sheathing

Copper sheathing was at one time very popular with boat builders, particularly in tropical areas where toredo worm is very virile, and where coral reefs make short work of timber planking. However, with the advent of modern anti-fouling compositions and fibre glass, copper sheathing is now confined almost entirely to older vessels.

Its advantages cannot be denied since it is very effective against the worm, and also provides some protection for the timber planking when grounding. Unfortunately, because of its light gauge, copper sheathing is liable to damage and, once damaged, can defeat its own purpose by allowing the marine borer or worm to work unnoticed behind its covering sheets. A small damaged section can give the worm an opening and, once behind the copper sheathing, it grows rapidly, and is not noticed until suddenly there are ornamental fountains in the cabin!

The essential thing with copper sheathing, then, is to keep it in good condition and repair any damage immediately. Because of its light gauge, bent or broken sheets can be repaired

Copper sheathing requires close attention as the slightest damage can tear it from the hull, allowing access to marine worm

easily. The old damaged sheet can be cut away or pulled off as a whole and a new sheet tacked into place, fitting it carefully to correspond with the original pattern of the sheets, with small copper nails. The sheet is easily shaped to the curve of the hull and should be tacked from the centre of one side, working outwards along the edge and hammering the plate into shape as the nails are driven home.

The underside of the keel is usually covered with sheets of a thicker gauge than the hull, for obvious reasons, and should have a grounding strip of steel bolted in place over it. The most vulnerable areas of copper sheathing are in difficult corners such as the join of the keel to the hull and the area around the propeller shaft gland, and these should be examined frequently to see that the copper has not opened up or come away, allowing access for the toredo worm.

Moulding a lead keel or lead ballast

It often happens that, because a boat is unbalanced, ballast must be added to her keel or her hull. In the case of a yacht, this is done either in the form of internal ballast in the bilges, or external ballast in the form of lead shapes or a lead keel bolted to the keel proper. Motor vessels usually ballast inside, although it is not unknown for exterior ballast to be bolted to each side of a cruiser's keel.

Whatever the case, iron or lead ingots are the most satisfactory form of ballast. Unfortunately they are also very expensive and often a difficult shape to stow beneath floorboards or bolt to a keel. Lead scraps can be picked up somewhat cheaper than ingots and, by melting down and moulding to the required shape, can be turned out economically and of a suitable shape to fit in the vessel.

The method described here is for the moulding of a lead ballast keel for a yacht, but the same procedure can be employed to mould shaped ballast for interior or exterior fitting.

The mould for a large casting such as a keel needs to be well supported and well built to withstand the weight of metal it is to hold.

The actual construction of the mould can be done in any suitable way, providing it is strong enough. If the keel is to be shaped to a definite pattern and size, care will be necessary when making the mould to ensure that the measurements and shape are correct or the finished ballast will not fit the keel.

The exterior of the mould should be in the form of a strong box, reinforced with heavy battens and beams to take the weight of the filled mould. The interior must be carefully shaped to produce an even, smooth, finish to the moulded keel. This can be done by using concrete or copper sheet or even thick fibreglass, if only one keel is to be cast. The interior mould should be well supported by the exterior framework and then the whole mould lowered into a hole in the ground and packed around with earth.

There are two reasons for placing the mould in the ground: the need for additional support in case of weaknesses in the original structure, and the convenience of having the mould at a low level where the lead can be easily poured into it. It would be disastrous, to say the least, if a mould at bench level broke open as it was being filled with molten lead!

A word at this point about the melting down of the lead. A good solid iron pot is required and a firm furnace construction beneath it. Once again, the possibility of upsetting the pot full of molten lead is not one to take lightly.

Molten lead is a dangerous material to handle, mainly by virtue of the impurities which go into the pot with the lead itself. The lead should be as pure as it is possible to obtain, not only for the reason just mentioned but also to reduce the possibility of electrolysis in the finished keel. In this regard, lead piping is not the best, neither is pewter and other alloys of lead. Sheet lead is usually the purest available as scrap.

When melting down, the impurities in the solution may cause minor explosions. Water will also have this effect and care should be taken to eliminate foreign matter and water as far as possible when filling the pot.

Ballast keels of yachts like this can weigh fifty tons or more. Internal ballast is often carried to supplement the keel weight

As the lead begins to melt, dross will form on the surface and this will retard the melting action. It should be removed by tilting a ladle just beneath the surface and allowing the dross —in a powdery form—to run into it. Lead also skimmed off can be returned later. The melting process can also be speeded by the addition of flux. Animal tallow will suffice for this.

Pouring the lead can be tricky and at this stage the handyman must use his own intelligence to adapt the pouring to his surrounding conditions. If possible the lead should be run directly from the pot to the mould either by pipe or pouring direct to prevent any loss of temperature before setting into the mould. For this reason ladles are not fast enough.

The temperature of the lead is quite important and the best test is to insert a small sliver of timber into the molten liquid. If it fires, the lead is too hot. It should just begin to lightly char the wood when it is ready for pouring. It should then be poured quickly and evenly.

Finishing off the ballast can be done with a plane or heavy duty sander. If shaping is necessary an adze is a good instrument, followed by a plane and sander. Lumps and protrusions should be filed off, even if the ballast is to be dropped into the bilges, as these may cause friction against working timbers adjacent to them.

Freeing "frozen" bolts

Probably one of the most frustrating—and one of the most frequent—jobs that confronts a boat owner is the freeing of bolts which have become corroded, or "frozen". No matter how corrosion-free the metal of the bolt, it is a frustrating fact that, somehow or other, a bolt that is drawn up tight and subjected to use for some time always seems to be difficult to undo.

Needless to say, mild steel bolts, galvanised bolts which have lost their galvanising, and bronze bolts which have been subjected to corrosive action are the villains. But even the co-operative monel and stainless steel are not without their moments when they defy even the firmest spanner to shift them from their ensconced position.

The first stage in freeing a "frozen" bolt

is a good application of a freeing oil, or a lubricant spray from a pressure pack. This will work into the thread of the bolt, loosening any corrosion and lubricating the thread. The penetrating fluid should be given some time to work and an ideal approach, if time permits, is to regularly soak the nut end of the bolt in the fluid for twenty-four hours. Modern penetrating oils should almost certainly free the nut when the spanner is applied.

If the spanner is of the incorrect size or has a loose jaw—as is the case with most shifting spanners—it will be virtually impossible to move the nut and, in addition, the spanner will slip, rounding the corners of the nut and making it even more difficult to move. A spanner of the correct size, well fitted to the nut, is essential.

If all efforts with the spanner fail, it will be necessary to resort to more drastic methods, which means the destruction of the nut. At this stage, loss of the nut is not so important if the bolt is retained with its thread in good shape. A wide screwdriver should be placed at an angle to one of the hexagonal sides of the nut and as close as possible to the right hand edge of it. This should then be tapped lightly with a hammer, the taps becoming firmer and harder if the nut fails to move. At this point, particularly with iron bolts, an application of heat may assist.

As the force of the hammering increases, the screwdriver will begin to mark the face of the nut, particularly if it is of soft metal. Further hammering may well cause the corner of the nut to be chipped away. However, if it is still not moving, the nut can be written off in any case and continued hammering, using another face of the nut, should be carried out in an attempt to move it.

The final stage comes when the nut is disfigured on all faces but has still not moved. Then the only solution is to cut it away. The bolt and its thread may still be saved if the cutting is done carefully. A hacksaw, aligned horizontally across the nut and as close to the bolt as possible without damaging the thread,

Badly corroded bolts like these can be dangerous. They will probably need to be cut away before removal and replacement

should be used to cut downwards through the nut.

With the nut cut through, a screwdriver or similar tool can be used to gently ease the nut back from the thread of the bolt the fraction of an inch required to unscrew it or just lift it off. In this way the bolt can be tapped gently out (using a pad of wood to prevent burring of the thread) and a new nut is all that is required to return to the former secure state.

Spiling

Spiling is the term given to making a pattern of an area to be renewed, such as a hole in planking or decking, where it is not possible to mark the shape of the hole directly on the new timber to be used. Paper or cardboard templates can be cut and shaped by trial and error, but spiling is a fairly accurate and traditional method and produces good results, particularly in difficult areas.

When the hole has been shaped ready for repair, a thin piece of timber veneer or cardboard is cut to fit inside it with a gap all round

The exhilaration and thrills of driving a boat to her limit can only come with the knowledge that she is sound in every part

302

of about quarter-inch to half-inch. Using a straight edge a series of vertical lines is drawn across the old planking and on the spiling piece. These should be at fairly frequent intervals, depending on the size of the repair section.

A pair of dividers should be opened to about three-quarters of an inch, or a little more than the widest gap between the spiling piece and the old planking and clamped in that position. One point of the dividers is placed up against the edge of the old planking on one of the vertical lines and the other point allowed to touch the spiling piece, also on the vertical line. A mark is made on the spiling piece at this point. This is repeated right round the area to be repaired, on each of the vertical lines. The spiling piece is then unclamped and placed on the new section of planking and the process reversed. That is, the dividers, clamped at the same width, are first placed with one point on the mark on the spiling piece and the other on the new timber. Where the latter point touches

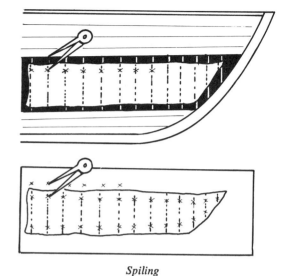

Spiling

the new timber, a mark is made. When this has been repeated for all the vertical lines on the spiling piece, a complete pattern is laid out on the new timber which will coincide exactly with the damaged area of the hull.

Index